The Brazilian Defense Industry

The Brazilian Defense Industry

Patrice Franko-Jones

Westview Press
BOULDER • SAN FRANCISCO • OXFORD

338.43
J78b

Tables 2.1, 3.1, and 3.2 and Figure 6.2 are reproduced by permission of the publishers.

This Westview softcover edition is printed on acid-free paper and bound in library-quality, coated covers that carry the highest rating of the National Association of State Textbook Administrators, in consultation with the Association of American Publishers and the Book Manufacturers' Institute.

Published in 1992 in the United States of America by Westview Press, Inc., 5500 Central Avenue, Boulder, Colorado 80301-2847, and in the United Kingdom by Westview Press, 36 Lonsdale Road, Summertown, Oxford OX2 7EW

A CIP catalog record for this book is available from the Library of Congress.
ISBN 0-8133-7771-4

Printed and bound in the United States of America

The paper used in this publication meets the requirements
of the American National Standard for Permanence of Paper
for Printed Library Materials Z39.48-1984.

10   9   8   7   6   5   4   3   2   1

To my parents, with thanks

Contents

Tables and Figures

Figures

Acknowledgments

The first stage of research for this book was for my doctoral dissertation in economics at the University of Notre Dame. Many thanks to my chair, Kenneth Jameson, and committee members Denis Goulet, Michael Francis and David Ruccio for their insightful comments and support. I owe a special debt to Denis Goulet and his wife, Ana Maria, for introducing me to Brazil and Portuguese.

Colby College has generously financed return trips to Brazil over the past five years. Brazilian colleagues, especially Clovis Brigagão, Renato Dagnino and Domício Proença, Jr., graciously shared time, information and ideas. My research assistant, Margaret H. Peirce, cheerfully processed export data, assistants Katherine A. Smith and Marina Neto Grande helped in the final stages of manuscript preparation. Grace Von Tobel, Colby's manuscript typist, has patiently and carefully moved this project forward; without her assistance it is not clear it would ever have been completed.

As an American Association for the Advancement of Science Fellow from 1990 to 1991, I had the opportunity to work for the assistant secretary of defense for international security affairs in the inter-American region. The glimpse of U.S. policy-making toward Latin America has been invaluable as has been the good humor of the inter-American team in hosting their token professor. Special thanks to Lt. Col. Manuel Vega, country officer for Brazil, for insights on U.S. policy. The opinions (and any errors) in the book are naturally my own.

Finally, I am grateful to my husband, David Jones, for his constant encouragement and to my parents, to whom this book is dedicated, for all they have so selflessly given me.

Patrice Franko-Jones

1

Introduction

By the mid 1980s the Brazilian armaments industry was heralded as a global exporter of conventional weaponry. Despite the difficulty of cracking the international defense market, the three firms forming the backbone of the Brazilian industry, EMBRAER, in aviation, ENGESA, in armored vehicles and AVIBRAS, in missiles, rose from obscurity to make inroads on industrial country market shares. Concentrating sales in the Middle East, Brazilian defense producers aggressively marketed rugged systems which were simple to use and maintain. Ideally suited for Third World environments, they were priced to sell. Brazil rapidly became known not only for its coffee and oranges, but also as a competitor in the technologically advanced arena of armaments.

What was so special about the Brazilian defense industry that it became an internationally recognized armaments producer when other countries with similar aspirations did not? The firms themselves have very different histories. EMBRAER, the Brazilian Aircraft Company, is a mixed economic enterprise with 51% of the voting stock controlled by the Brazilian government. Since its incorporation in 1969, it rapidly grew to become the sixth largest general aviation producer in a market where the first five are U.S. firms. Much of the success of EMBRAER is attributable to its durable, economical products with applications to both civilian and military markets. They were developed in conjunction with the state-run Aeronautics Technology Center, the CTA. Led by its Bandeirante turboprop, in the early 1980s EMBRAER's sales averaged approximately $US 200 million per year. In 1985 EMBRAER aircraft accounted for 40% of the planes flown by the Brazilian Air Force, a percentage which will increase as the new AMX fighter, jointly developed with Italy, and the Tucano trainers are incorporated into the force. The U.S. receives 1/3 of its exports, primarily commuter aircraft, while another third, largely military models, are exported to developing countries including Egypt, Saudi Arabia, Nigeria, Mexico, Chile and Uruguay.

ENGESA claims to be the largest producer of armored vehicles in the world. Unlike EMBRAER, it is a private entity. Its "boomerang" suspension system, developed by the firm for the oil drilling industry, was found to have reliable, high performance applications for military vehicles over tough terrain. Drawing widely upon standard automobile parts and production techniques, ENGESA produced a low cost, sturdy tank enthusiastically received by Third World Armies in the Middle East and Northern Africa. The firm enjoyed a close but informal relationship with the Brazilian Army. In 1983 ENGESA began joint international marketing with IMBEL, the Brazilian government munitions firm, in a collaborative public-private effort to expand military exports. In 1987 defense material was poised to overtake coffee and soya as Brazil's major export.

AVIBRAS completes the producer triumvirate. An intensely private concern, AVIBRAS designs, develops and produces civilian and military rocket systems with 100% national technology. Founded in 1961, in its earliest years the firm benefitted from collaboration in the CTA's SONDA rocket program. More recently, however, its connection with the Brazilian armed forces has been markedly weak. AVIBRAS custom designs equipment for the needs of the foreign customer, as evidenced by the ASTROS II system developed for Iraq. In addition to surface-to-surface and air-to-ground defense systems, AVIBRAS offers civilian products in the areas of space system, electronics, communications, satellites and radar.

The pattern of ownership in the Brazilian defense industry is varied, reflecting a pragmatic philosophy of state intervention only when necessary. This industrial picture was not the result of a tightly sequenced strategy on the part of the Brazilian military. Indeed EMBRAER was formed using state funds only when the private sector failed to respond to incentives for the commercialization of the Bandeirante turboprop prototype. While other Third World nations created state owned firms to attend to perceived needs for indigenous defense industries, a powerful strain in Brazilian strategic thinking argued that the defense industry should, whenever possible, remain in private hands. Security, it was argued, was best achieved by the development of a dynamic private sector.

Rather than a careful industrial plan controlled by the military, the rapid success in international markets by Brazilian firms is better explained by a synergy of economic and political factors. First, unlike most Third World armaments producers, Brazil's defense industry rests on economic foundations. In contrast to the defense industries in India or Argentina, for example, Brazilian firms responded first to market incentives and then attended to the demands of the domestic military. Decisions shaping the level of technology and product designs were made with an eye to economic viability. Holding short run military and political concerns at a distance, economic criteria of efficiency and profitability guided the development of the sector, launching its growth as the largest exporter of weaponry outside the industrialized world.

But simply employing economic standards of efficiency would not have been sufficient for success. The attention to economic criteria was effective due to the particular institutional context in which it was promoted. Activity in the defense sector was characterized by a partnership between the state and the firms. The state intervened in the Brazilian defense industry to supplement but not supplant the workings of the market. This partnership spans a variety of ownership patterns. State activity in the sector was not predicated upon whether the firm is publicly or privately held, but according to whether the firm can accomplish a given task.

Thus, the innovative structure of the Brazilian military industry, based on pragmatic cooperation between the public and private sector and not exclusively state or military ownership, promoted indigenous technological development, international marketing and industrial expansion of suppliers serving the primary defense contractors. Where firms did not have the capital available for the costly development of technological systems, research was performed in the military's technology centers, and passed back to industry. Governmental bargaining power was brought to bear in international technology transfer. As Brazilian firms faced high barriers to entry in the concentrated international armaments markets, they received support from diplomatic posts. But the neither the state nor the military performed functions which could be left in private hands. The growth of the Brazilian armaments industry illustrates a case where the state and the private sector each performed its most suitable activity, cooperatively capturing global markets.

But by 1990 the industry was in a profound crisis. By the late nineteen eighties the political and economic chemistry came apart. Attempting to close the distance between themselves and industrial country producers, the Brazilian industry planned to enter new product markets with the help of the state. Abandoning the rule of simplicity, the new equipment to be produced demanded sophisticated electronic subsystems beyond the capability of the Brazilian industrial sector.

The military, however, saw this as an opportunity to stimulate technological growth in supplier industries. Ambitious programs were embarked upon with the assistance of the military research centers. The defense industry was perceived by military strategists as a locomotive pulling Brazilian industry into more technologically advanced production. After all, it was argued, the military innovations of World War II provided great stimulus to American industry.

However, this costly gamble backfired. Global armaments markets shrunk. The Iran-Iraq war, a critical market for the Brazilians, had ended. Other Third World purchasers of armaments were broke, burdened by debt and slow growth. The post cold war international climate slowed defense acquisition programs. The Brazilian state, beset by its own political and economic crisis, was unable to provide necessary financial support to the industry through this contractionary phase. The Brazilian military's budget was slashed, and ambitious reequipment programs stalled. Defense industrialization has all but ground to a halt in Brazil. The future is highly uncertain.

This book explores the dynamic growth and acute contraction of the Brazilian defense industry. Chapter 2 sketches a framework for understanding the industrial structure of the Brazilian industry. Profiles of the key firms and the broader subsector are presented. The dominance of the top firms is demonstrated as a necessary ingredient for export success.

The economic foundations of the industry are explored from a comparative perspective in chapter 3. The Brazilian industry is distinguished from other Third World armaments producers by the primacy of economic as opposed to military decision making. An investigation of the spectrum of Third World producers of armaments shows that the greater the reliance on economic criteria, the greater the success of the defense industry. Why the Brazilian military encouraged economic decision making is grounded in a history of strategic thought discussed in chapter 4. The roots of the Brazilian strategic concept of *Segurança e Desenvolvimento*, or security and development are developed and shown to explain the relative autonomy the Brazilian defense industry enjoyed.

The pragmatic division between state and private activity is described in chapter 5. This chapter details the institutional relationships between the firms and the state. The link between the structure of the Brazilian defense industry and its success in technology, exports and expansion of the supplier sector is then established in chapters 6 and 7. The system of technological development in the military industrial sector is argued to be a particularly dynamic one. The innovation it encouraged led to products easily marketed internationally. The state encouraged such exports with a policy of minimal interference in export controls, supporting the firms through diplomatic channels only upon request. These two chapters defend the claim that efficacy and not ownership are the appropriate bases for economic decision making to facilitate technological development and export promotion in the defense industry in Brazil.

The crisis of the Brazilian defense industry is then analyzed in chapter 8. While the military and the firms joined forces for a technological leap into new markets, international demand conditions contracted. It remains to be seen whether the industry will be able to recoup the damage of this fall.

The Case Study Approach and Data Limitations

Before delving into the story of armaments production in Brazil, a few words on methodology and data are in order. As little research has been done on the Brazilian armaments industry, the relevant approach is the case study. A case study is appropriate for uncovering the important trends and issues for investigation. Simon, for example, argues:

> In the beginning, there is description. When one does not know anything at all about a problem, one must understand it in a general way before beginning to make specific inquiries about specific aspects of the subject. . . . Descriptive research in the form of case studies is usually the jumping off point for the study of new areas in the social sciences.1

But this case study is not simply descriptive nor it is only a preliminary investigation. The case of the Brazilian armaments industry has important lessons not only for other armaments producers in the Third World, but is relevant to any industry in its infant stages hoping to compete internationally in a high technology industry.

The case study is best able to convey the wealth of economic, political and historical detail necessary to explain the defense industry's behavior in Brazil. Given the strong non-economic influences of national security and foreign policy, the difficulties of quantifying explanatory variables are obvious. The complex interaction of political, economic and social variables conditioning armaments production render quantitative models reductionist, lacking the rich explanatory power of the institutional case study.2

To explain the historical development, current activity and future prospects of the Brazilian defense industry, the locus of inquiry must be the interaction of economic, political and military institutions conditioning its behavior. The institutionalist methodology, which encourages holistic, systemic and evolutionary approaches to the study of economic behavior, is commensurate with the difficult nature of this task.[3] Holism refers to the overarching focus on the pattern of relations among the parts and the whole of the subject. A holistic theorist perceives human systems as dynamic, interactive, and functionally more than a sum of component parts. This calls the researcher to investigate not only economic aspects of production but also to incorporate political and social dimensions. For example, the quantity of resources demanded by the defense sector and its output only illustrate a limited dimension of the story of armaments production. Linkages to other industries and effects on Brazil's foreign and domestic policies must be included. A holistic approach incorporates the critical role of the state in enhancing the availability and lowering the prices of scarce resources as well as the ramifications of armaments production for Brazil's military policies. It is only by understanding these factors traditionally considered exogenous to economic systems that the armaments sector's dynamics can be explained.

Institutionalism contends that not only are component parts of an economic system functionally related to the whole but they are arranged in coherent patterns of historical behavior. A systemic approach, the second characteristic of institutional economics, cautions that the activity of arms production can only be understood in light of larger patterns of industrialization and political-military developments in Brazil. Indeed this book argues the armaments industry is not the result of a singular military threat but of the pattern of Brazilian industrialization promoted throughout the century.

Finally, the evolutionary nature of arms production situates it in the realm of past and future, highlighting historical antecedents and future possibilities. The armaments industry was not created in a vacuum. The historical demand for armaments, unsuccessful private sector attempts, and changing international market conditions shaped the industry. Responses to current short and long run bottlenecks in the system promote adaptation and industrial change. A vision of the future of the market and its constraints informs contemporary decision making and growth in the industry.

In addition to the defining characteristics of holistic, systemic and evolutionary, an emphasis on power permeates the institutional approach employed in this case study of the Brazilian defense industry. As Samuels says:

At a more concrete level, institutional economics has had an appreciation for the centrality of power and conflict in the economic process. . . . Conflict is generated by changes in technology, social institutions, distributions of power and thus is an inherent part of the economic process. . . . At the motivational level, institutional economics has always recognized the importance of nonrational human behavior in economic decision making. A thirst for power and adventure, a sense of independence, altruism, idle curiosity, custom and habit may all be powerful motivations of economic behavior.[4]

Thus, according to Samuels, an institutional approach examines the effects of power, control and the distribution of wealth in a multi-causal model giving primacy to institutional actors over abstract, deterministic economic laws. More than an industry analysis, an institutional case study expands economic decision-making to include political and military participants whose actions have economic consequences. This forms a coherent story of the causes and consequences of arms production in Brazil, focusing on the unique historical and cultural circumstances shaping the industry. Finally, it permits consideration of industry performance against a multi-dimensional set of criteria.

An institutional approach is a useful indicator of the importance of systems analysis, history and the dynamics of economic change. In this study it is complemented by a broad set of concepts derived from industrial organization theory. This sketch of the standard structure-conduct-performance model is enhanced in later chapters by background literature on the role of the State in Brazil, State Owned Enterprises (SOE's), Brazilian national security, technology policy and export promotion schemes. Therefore, this institutional case study is structured according to the theoretical concepts of industrial organization while the nuances of the arguments will be developed by drawing upon a variety of relevant literatures.

This book tells a story of how and why the Brazilian armaments sector achieved rapid domestic and international success. This account is based upon the perspectives of many participants in the industry, various Brazilian State agencies, military personnel and the firms themselves. Material was primarily gathered from written sources within Brazil including newspapers, specialized documents, public opinion journals and extensive interviews.

Data collection was a significant obstacle in this study. Dagnino[5] presents the best methodological critique of data collection in the Brazilian armaments industry. Cataloguing the various national and international sources of information, he convincingly makes the case that because of secrecy and difficulty of verification, all so-called "data" on the industry should be viewed with suspicion.

Ball[6] and Wionczek[7] also discuss the general case of obtaining quantitative data on military production in developing countries.[8] Ball points to the means by which developing countries hide military expenditures, including double bookkeeping, extra-budgetary accounts, highly aggregated budget categories, and manipulation of foreign exchange allocation. She suggests using aggregate data only with appropriate caution. Indeed Brazil is subject to Ball's charges, especially aggregation. According to the trade accounts published by its Export Import Bank, Brazil does not export tanks but "trucks and other vehicles;" in other instances it does not export military aircraft but all the component parts. Thus, a disaggregated microeconomic explanation is more appropriate.

Wionczek, believing qualitative reporting is also good research, argues the lack of aggregate data should not preclude rigorous analysis. Criticizing the scarcity of literature on the economics of the arms race in both the North and South, he attributes the lack of strong economic explanations of the causes and effects of global militarism to:

a) The generally accepted view that the world-wide armaments race is mainly a political and technological phenomenon that exceeds the terms of reference of global, regional and national economic and industrial surveys;

b) The extremely high level of political sensitivity in many countries in respect to so-called national security matters, however defined, and the general belief that the armaments race is both inevitable and uncontrollable;

c) The limited access by international economists to, and the limited understanding of, disaggregated information on armaments production and expenditure;

d) The alleged difficulties of finding reliable quantitative data and the real difficulties of analyzing national and regional policy-making processes with respect to the management of military industries, military technology transfers and the modes of domestic arms procurement and the international arms trade;

e) The limited world-wide supply of highly trained social scientists with reasonably good technological backgrounds capable of treating the political, economic and technological aspects of the armaments race in an inter-disciplinary fashion;

f) The ascendancy in economics of "rococo" econometrics, i.e., superficially impressive quantitative theoretical model-building, divorced from political and institutional economics or, in other worlds, from real life issues.[9]

This project attends to several of Wionczek's concerns, arguing that Brazilian armaments production is firmly rooted in an economic as well as a political rationale and therefore must be analyzed in economic terms. It is limited by the dearth of aggregate data, but makes a significant contribution by presenting information from a variety of sources, distilling pieces of information into a coherent whole.[10] The central story of the project is the distinctive management of the defense sector by both the State and the firms which has permitted smooth transfers of technology from industrial countries, technological recycling to other developing countries, and a strong lucrative program of export promotion. In short, it is an institutional case study of the political economy of arms production in Brazil.

The information for this project was collected from a variety of sources on six trips to Brazil between 1983 and 1991. Instrumental in the collection of this material were several Brazilian analysts of the industry. In addition to these personal sources, many hours spent in the libraries in Rio de Janeiro and the clipping files in the Congressional library in Brasília proved helpful in gathering information. The personal archives of Sr. Clovis Brigagão were indispensable. Library facilities at the Graduate Research Institute (IUPERJ) in Rio de Janeiro as well as seminars and discussions held with the faculty of the Institute de Economia Industrial at the Universidade Federal do Rio de Janeiro were useful. Conversations with Brazilian academics, particularly Renato Dagnino of UNICAMP, Campinas and Domício Proeça, Jr., of COPPE/UFRJ, Rio de Janeiro, profoundly shaped this research.

On-site visits to the firms were of heuristic value. At nearly every level of management, employees strictly confined statistics to those already approved for release to the press. They were extremely kind but conscious of censorship of numbers and sensitive material due to national security. This was expected. Visits to the firms were very important, however, in confirming leads, suspicions and industrial tendencies discovered in already printed sources. They were critical in shaping my sense of the underlying dynamic of the industry. After returning to the U.S. in 1983, the visits were followed up with a questionnaire seeking to obtain further information. EMBRAER returned the questionnaire with approximately 20% of the questions completed, ENGESA returned it with a polite note claiming that national security concerns precluded them from participating, and AVIBRAS did respond at all. On return trips to Brazil in 1987 and 1989 EMBRAER continued to be more cooperative than either ENGESA or AVIBRAS, although in 1989, 1990 and 1991 I was able to speak freely with upper management in ENGESA and with the president of AVIBRAS. This new openness portends well for future studies of the industry.

Oral interviews in Brazil with government and military personnel yielded similar results to those obtained in the private sector. Each interview brought a perspective, and some tidbits of information, contributing to piecing together the story of Brazilian armaments. Information gathering continued upon my return to the United States. Nevertheless, the quality of public data on the Brazilian armaments industry is just as scarce this side of the equator. The U.S. Arms Control and Disarmament Agency (ACDA) and the Pentagon could not release classified numbers. Once again the most beneficial sources were journalists and trade organizations. The staff at *Defense and Foreign Affairs* was helpful in sharing their information on the industry.

This story of the Brazilian armaments industry is then but a puzzle of pieces. However, as Wionczek incisively charges, the lack of a consistent quantitative data base does not excuse exploring the formation and rapid growth of third world military sectors. The case of Brazilian defense industrialization must be explored for what is has to say about the economics of Third World armaments production, innovative relationships between the state and firms and exports of high technology products. Moreover, the scarcity of hard data is arguably a blessing in disguise. It focuses attention upon the political and institutional variables often omitted in more mathematical approaches because of the difficulties of quantification. Yet, it is precisely these slippery, immeasurable factors which best explain the behavior in the Brazilian defense sector. Certainly in the case of the Brazilian defense industry we have been able to reach important conclusions about how this sector behaves and its effects on the broader process of industrialization in Brazil. It is an important story, a story with serious implications for both Brazil and the world.

Notes

1.   Julian L. Simon, *Basic Research Methods in Social Science,* (New York: Random House, 1978), p. 44.

2.   Janne Nolan, *Military Industry in Taiwan and Korea,* (New York: St. Martins, 1986). Nolan argues for the case study as the appropriate methodological tool to investigate production due to political influences. See pp. 15-18, "A Note on Methodology."

3.   See Charles K. Wilber and Robert Harrison, "The Methodological Basis of Institutional Economics: Pattern Model, Storytelling & Holism," *Journal of Economic Issues*, Vol. XII, No. 1, March 1978.

4.   Warren Samuels in Wilber, "The Methodological Basis."

5.   Renato Peixoto Dagnino, "A Indústria de Armamentos Brasileira: Uma Tentativa de Avaliação," Doctoral thesis presented to the Institute of Economics, UNICAMP, Campinas, SP, Brasil, August 1989.

6.   Nicole Ball, "Measuring Third World Security Expenditure: A Research Note," *World Development*, 1984.

7.   Miguel Wionczek, "The Emergence of Military Industries in the South: Longer Term Implications," *Industry and Development*, Vol. 12, 1984, pp. 115-120.

8.   See also Ulrich Albrecht et al., *A Short Research Guide on Arms and Armed Forces*, (London: Croom Helm, 1978), pp. 49-61; and Michael Brzoska, "The Reporting of Military Expenditures," *Journal of Peace Research*, Vol. 18, No. 3., 1981, p. 264.

9.   Wionczek, "The Emergence of Military Industries in the South: Longer Term Implications," pp. 115-120.

10.   Nolan argues for the validity of eclectic data collection from trade journals, private reports and interviews as the best available information for a case study of military industries. See p. 45 and note, and pp. 152-153.

2

The Industrial Structure of the Brazilian Armaments Industry

Introduction

The chapter describes the organization and structure of the Brazilian armaments industry. It draws broadly from the structure-conduct-performance paradigm described in the text of F. M. Scherer as the conceptual framework within which to situate this institutional case study.[1] The chapter shows how basic supply and demand conditions in the international and domestic markets for conventional armaments shaped the structure of the Brazilian industry and influenced its conduct and performance. This chapter sets the stage for the more detailed explorations of particular aspects of the industry in the chapters that follow. Understanding the industrial context within which the aeronautical producer EMBRAER, the motor vehicle firm ENGESA and the missile enterprise AVIBRAS operate, prepares the reader to investigate the dynamic partnership between the state and firms which fostered technological development and rapid export growth in the early part of the 1980s. Finally, this industrial profile will shape an explanation of the current crisis of the Brazilian defense industry and the prospects for the future.

The Industrial Structure of the Brazilian Armaments Industry

This section provides a conceptual foundation for the study of armaments production in Brazil. Following the constructs of industrial organization outlined by Scherer, it forms the theoretical framework for describing the behavior of the defense sector and evaluating the effects of the industry on society.[2] As illustrated by Table 2.1, Scherer defines four categories to explain the workings of a market: (1) basic supply and demand conditions, (2) the structure of the industry, (3) the conduct of the sector and (4) performance for society. The discussion summarizes how these conditions coalesced in specific political and economic arenas in Brazil to form EMBRAER, ENGESA and AVIBRAS.

Supply Conditions

Basic supply and demand conditions in an industry interact to determine market structure. Supply factors include the availability of raw materials, the state of technology, characteristics of the labor force, the degree of product durability, business attitudes and public policies. In the Brazilian armaments industry, supply conditions including a strong resource base, a gap between required and available technology, an expensive product, a relatively skilled labor force, a reticent business community, supportive public policies, and limited international availability favored the creation of a concentrated industrial structure where a small number of firms dominate the market.

Brazil is resource rich, with immense deposits of iron ore and manganese, and substantial quantities of bauxite, copper, lead, zinc, nickel, tungsten, tin, uranium and chrome. This strong resource base provides the armaments industry with primary inputs for production. The abundance of natural resources is complemented by a relatively well articulated industrial sector to transform primary products into manufactured inputs.

The resource most lacking in Brazil was oil. In the early 1980s Brazil was forced to import over 80% of its petroleum needs, pressuring balance of payments. As shown in later chapters, Brazil transformed this dependence upon oil into countertrade agreements with oil exporters. Brazil traded arms for oil, on barter terms, effectively loosening the foreign exchange constraint upon imports of intermediate products. Thus, this resource weakness provided an impetus for industrial development. The ability to negotiate offset agreements is facilitated by a limited number of large firms.

The second supply factor, technology, was more problematic as technological requirements for armaments production were high relative to existing technology in Brazil. The need for technological inputs beyond the scope of existing firms led the state to provide technology through military research and development centers and import subsidies. By selecting lead firms as technology recipients, the state promoted monopolies in the aircraft, armored vehicle and missile sectors. Indeed, the need for sophisticated technology presented one of the strongest forces for the single firm market structure. Chapter 4 takes up the issue of technology policy and military production in Brazil, showing how technological development was concentrated in the military's own installations, which maintained close links with the monopolistic producer firms. A multiple firm production structure would have undermined the collaborative nature of this arrangement.

The primary technological actors were CTA, the Air Force's Technology Center and CTEX, belonging to the Army. CTA was critical to the formation of EMBRAER. The Bandeirante, the project which launched EMBRAER was developed within CTA; the well-connected military engineers also provided the political force necessary for the formation of the firm. As EMBRAER's own in-house technological capabilities matured, CTA dynamically shifted its focus toward the supplier firms in the industry. For example, IFI, CTA's institute for industrial promotion, later mounted a program to nationalize subsystems for the AMX strike fighter plane. CTEX did not play a central role in the development of the armored vehicle sector, principally because the technology embodied in the earliest ENGESA tanks was similar to that in the automobile industry and well within the grasp of the firm. However, as electronics technologies increasingly constrained the industry, CTEX assumed a more important role. Overall, it should be emphasized that the state technology centers supplemented the activities of the firms without supplanting market mechanisms.

Unlike many Third World defense producers, the Brazilian industry had a strong pool of skilled workers to draw upon for the defense labor force. In aircraft and missile production, firms relied upon the cadre of engineers graduated since 1945 from the Aeronautical Engineering Institute (ITA). As explored in Chapter 6, this transfer of human capital brought to the firm trained engineers and technicians with strong ties to ITA, fostering a flow of new technologies. Such a transfer of human capital could not have been sustained with a large number of firms. In addition to the Army Engineering Institute (IME), the armored vehicle sector selected from the pool of labor trained in the automobile sector. The spectrum of international automobile producers represented in Brazil trained assembly workers, technicians and engineers in heavy vehicle production; these skills were easily transferred to the Brazilian tank industry. The fact that the defense firms were large contributed to their ability to attract the most talented labor.

As discussed in Chapter 4, public policy favored military production since the 1930s. The overarching concept of "security and development" institutionalized within the Superior War College, ESG, provided the rationale for public support and investment in the defense sector. When the military took over in 1964, ESG-trained leaders launched a program of military industrialization, providing incentives and outright subsidies to participants in the defense sector. But despite strong political demand for domestic military production, private markets did not spontaneously respond. Initial capital investments were high, technologies uncertain and alternative opportunities more promising for domestic ventures. Foreign capital, strong in high technology manufacturing, was not welcome due to national security concerns. Thus, the promotion of military industries fell to the state. This lack of private initiative is discussed in Chapter 5. With EMBRAER the state was forced to create a new mixed economic enterprise in the aeronautical sector. For ENGESA and AVIBRAS the state interceded with heavily subsidized technologies, enhancing the expected rate of return. Bestowing state favors of technology, human capital, and guaranteed purchases on a selected few firms, overwhelmingly created conditions for concentration in the Brazilian defense sector.

This concentration and resolve to support the industry was reinforced by international supply conditions. With authoritarianism and repression under military governments, international support for Brazil waned in the 1970s. Under the Carter administration in 1976, the U.S. implemented the International Security Assistance and Arms Export Control Act, which prohibited arms transfers to countries in gross violation of international standards of human rights.[3] Although this did not cause the creation of the armaments industry in Brazil (note that the major firms of EMBRAER, ENGESA and AVIBRAS were well in place by 1976), it acted as a catalyst to concentrated expansion. Unable to depend on North American allies, Brazilian authorities renewed their efforts in defense production. Greater resources were dedicated to the industry, and the state facilitated technological transfer agreements with alternative sources in Europe. As with the receipt of technology from domestic state institutions, this reinforced monopolistic tendencies of the market.

Supply conditions in international markets worked to reinforce concentration in another way. As the international arms market became increasingly competitive, only large firms capable of maintaining extensive sales and follow on support networks were likely to survive. Smaller firms find these costs difficult to absorb.

TABLE 2.1
A Model of Industrial Organization

Basic Conditions

SUPPLY	*DEMAND*
Raw materials	Price elasticity
Technology	Substitutes
Unionization	Rate of growth
Production durability	Cyclical and seasonal
Value/weight	character
Business attitudes	Purchase method
Public policies	Marketing type
International availability*	International demand*

Market Structure
Number of sellers and buyers
Product differentiation
Barriers to entry
Cost structures
Vertical integration
Conglomerateness

Conduct
Pricing behavior
Product strategy and advertising
Research and innovation
Plant investment
Legal tactics

Performance
Production and allocative efficiency
Progress
Full employment
Equity
National security*

*Addendum for the case of Brazilian Armaments
Source: F. M. Scherer, *Industrial Market Structure and Economic Performance*
(Boston, MA: Houghton Mifflin Company, 1980); second edition, p. 4.

Demand

But supply conditions alone did not determine the market structure of the Brazilian defense industry. These basic production characteristics interacted with a demand vector composed of the rate of growth of demand, availability of substitutes, price elasticities, the cyclical or seasonal character of defense as a good, purchasing method, and accepted marketing procedures. The salient demand characteristics shaping the Brazilian armaments industry are that the Brazilian military is the single source of domestic demand for defense products, and that there is a dual use of military products to meet civilian and international demand for appropriate military technologies.

The primary purchaser of domestic defense products is the national military. This single purchaser may requisition particular weapons as well as set prices. The Brazilian military, however, often forfeits its natural monopsony power to encourage expression of two additional sources of demand: dual purpose products and foreign military sales. Many Brazilian defense products are dual-use technologies. Some of the same aircraft used in military operations are used in commercial transportation. The armored vehicle industry also produces off-road vehicles and agricultural equipment. The Brazilian military has promoted dual applications for three reasons. First, it legitimizes large subsidies to the sector. It is easier for a citizen frequently riding a Bandeirante commuter aircraft between Rio and São Paulo to rationalize the Aerospace Technology Center (CTA) underwriting such projects. Secondly, these dual-use products strengthen the transportation and agricultural infrastructure of the economy. This is in keeping with the principle of "Security and Development," to use the state to promote economic development. Finally, civilian demand allows manufacturers to lengthen production runs, reduce costs, and enhance intra-firm learning processes, thus strengthening the firms and the stability of the defense sector. This is consistent with the view of the Brazilian military that defense firms must be economically viable to truly add to the nation's security.

But despite dual-use technologies, the Brazilian market alone would not support the defense industry. Thus, from the start, Brazilian defense firms were oriented toward the external market. As shown in Figure 2.1, demand for armaments by other Third World producers was strong and growing in the late 1970s, the early stages of defense industrialization in Brazil. A larger firm was better able to court such demand, providing marketing networks throughout the Third World.

FIGURE 2.1
Third World Armaments Imports 1969-1988

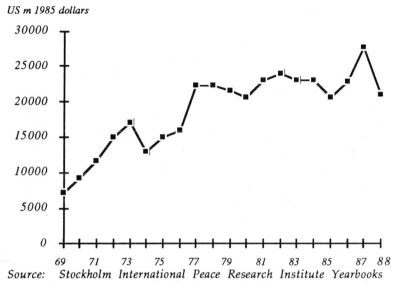

US m 1985 dollars

Source: Stockholm International Peace Research Institute Yearbooks

International marketing also lengthens production runs. Moreover, as will be seen in Chapter 7, the Brazilian military has been most accommodating in allowing firms the flexibility to maximize rewards in the international market, deferring production to foreign customers when international demand is strong, placing back orders during slow periods. Third World armies received Brazilian military products with enthusiasm. Easy to operate and designed for rugged terrain, these intermediate technologies meet the demand for regional wars and counterinsurgency operations. Brazilian armaments producers capitalized upon this need for basic weaponry rather than the elaborate, expensive armaments offered by industrialized states.

Market Structure

The interaction of supply and demand characteristics determines market structure which is defined by the number of buyers and sellers, little or no barriers to entry, costs and vertical integration. A competitive market has a large number of independent buyers and sellers, no barriers to entry and low average costs. In contrast, a concentrated market is characterized by a limited number of participants with interdependent decision-making criteria, high barriers to entry and higher average costs.

Strong domestic demand from a single buyer, the Armed Forces, in conjunction with international military sales practices, reinforced supply characteristics of Brazilian defense production to form a single dominant firm in each of the military sectors. Thus the industry is hierarchically shaped, with EMBRAER in aeronautics, ENGESA in armored vehicles and AVIBRAS in missiles on top. Underneath are subsidiaries producing subsystems and smaller firms; at the bottom are parts suppliers.

EMBRAER accounts for approximately 95–97% of total aircraft production in Brazil. Best known for its range of turboprops aircraft, EMBRAER offers military versions of the Brasília and Bandeirante planes which have found great commercial success in U.S. commuter markets, and the Xingu, an executive aircraft used for liaison and training of military transport pilots. The most successful military aircraft of EMBRAER is the Tucano, a turboprop military trainer. The firm is in the last stages of testing the CBA 123 Vector, a joint project with Argentina, and is at work on the EMB 145, a larger commuter plane. Militarily, EMBRAER's current project is the more technologically advanced AMX ground attack aircraft, which it is coproducing with Aeritalia and Aermacchi[4]

The EMBRAER group is comprised of six firms. Two producers subcontract for EMBRAER. The first is NEIVA, acquired by EMBRAER in 1980. Located in Botucatu, in the interior of the state of São Paulo, NEIVA has a work force of 355 responsible for the Ipanema and all Piper models. Founded in 1953, prior to this acquisition NEIVA produced Regentes and Universals, trainer aircraft for the Brazilian Air Force (FAB), and assumed production of the Paulistinha after the Paulista Aeronautics Company was dissolved; between 1959 and 1975 NEIVA produced 500 aircraft.[5] Already in the red, when it lost a FAB bid to EMBRAER's Xavante, the Ministry of Aeronautics engineered its acquisition by EMBRAER to maintain production potential in the secondary tier. The second firm was the healthier AEROTEC, also producing a basic trainer, the Uirapuru and the Tangará I and II. Created in 1962, today it produces parts and components such as wings for EMBRAER. Like NEIVA, AEROTEC is maintained to augment production capabilities in times of conflict as well as ease bottlenecks at EMBRAER, shortening production time.

AVIBRAS is active in four interrelated areas of production: defense, space research, chemical research and electronic communications.[6] To attend to these different sectors, the rapidly growing firm increased employment from 3,000 late in 1983 to 4,000 people by mid-1985.[7] The first installation, located in São Jose dos Campos (São Paulo), houses administration, research and development, advanced engineering, electronic and mechanical manufacturing and the production of antennas and earth stations for satellite communications. The second plant, in Jacarei (São Paulo), manufactures, assembles and tests defense systems.[8] With the addition of a third facility in Lorena (São Paulo), the firm claims to be the largest producer of rockets in the world, capable of rapidly attending to multiple orders on the magnitude of Iraq's $192 million purchase.[9]

AVIBRAS has three subsidiaries. TECTRAN, located between São Paulo and Rio de Janeiro, was formed to produce the launch vehicle central to the Astros II system and self-propelled porticos for industrial use;[10] TECTRONIC produces power electronics, control panels circuit breakers and trolley buses; while TRANSVIP works in transportation and tourism.[11] However, the crisis affecting the defense industry in the late 1980s has resulted in the consolidation, at least temporarily, of facilities.

The eleven companies comprising ENGESA are described in Table 2.3. The major production unit is ENGESA Viaturas, a modern plant in São Jose dos Campos manufacturing the firm's principal product, armored vehicles. In addition to the rugged and versatile armored cars such as the Urutu and the Cascavel, ENGESA's latest project, the Osório Main Battle Tank, is assembled here. Located nearby is a complete proving ground for testing the vehicles.

To procure parts, components and systems not available in the automobile industry, ENGESA verticalized its production structure, purchasing or forming firms to provide critical components or services.[12] Verticalization also circumvents discontinuities of foreign supplies due to shortages, embargoes, or political difficulties with final use certificates.[13]

The ENGEX plant, constructed in Bahia in 1977, guarantees the availability of guns to be mounted on ENGESA tanks, gears, the boomerang suspension system and oil production equipment. ENGELECTRICA, a second verticalized subsidiary, produces electric motors for industrial application as well as the generators and motors for ENGESA combat cars. ENGESA-FNV, in addition to moving the ENGESA group into railway equipment, supplies the firm with automotive and other steel parts for the Osório tank. A recent acquisition is ENGETRôNICA, a joint venture between ENGESA and

TABLE 2.2
The EMBRAER Group, 1989

EDE-EMBRAER	
Equipment Division	Producing subsystems
NEIVA Aeronautics	A light aircraft subsidiary
EAC-EMBRAER	A wholly owned US subsidiary in Fort Lauderdale, Florida
EAI-EMBRAER	
Aviation International	Branch office in Le Bourget, France
ÓRBITA Aerospacial Systems	40% ownership in this missile producing firm

Source: Compiled from EMBRAER Company Report

Philips do Brasil, owning 60% and 40% respectively. ENGETRôNICA will supply electronic systems, optronics and avionics to ENGESA and other defense producers. Contracts include communications equipment for the army, avionics for EMBRAER and exports. Feasibility studies are being conducted to produce standard control panels for ENGESA trucks, electronic equipment for torpedoes and electronic components for missiles of British Aerospace.[14] Since ENGESA uses components produced by Signaal of Holland, a Philips corporation, this new venture will replicate these domestically, fostering indigenous research and development.[15] ENGETRôNICA also produces the fire control system for the Osório Main Battle Tank.[16]

ENGESA's integrated companies offer products and services to complement ENGESA tanks. ENGEQUIMICA sells ammunition and explosives in addition to the guns sold through ENGEX. Support services are provided through AEROBRASIL, ENGEVIDEO and AXIAL. AEROBRASIL is a transportation company to move ENGESA products rapidly and discreetly between the thirty-five bases ENGESA has abroad. AEROBRASIL, a joint venture between ENGESA and TRANSBRASIL with the participation of several other exporters, was made possible after a 1980 law designed to speed export deliveries eliminated Varig's monopoly on international air exports. ENGEVIDEO

TABLE 2.3
The ENGESA Group, 1988

Firm	Description
ENGEX	Guns, transfer cases, gears, boomerang suspension system pumping units for oil production, sucker rods
ENGEQUIMICA	Heavy ammunition and explosives for military and civil applications; In association with IMBEL, the War Material industry of the Army Ministry
ENGEVIDEO	Video training programs of ENGESA products for civilian and military personnel
AEROBRASIL	Air cargo company of ENGESA companies connecting the 35 ENGESA bases abroad
AXIAL	Insurance to the ENGESA companies covering damage, credit and political risks, and performance
ENGESA VIATURAS	Armored vehicles, utility military vehicles, armored turrets, timber forwarders, agricultural tractors and 4x4, 4x6 and 6x6 conversions for off road usage
ENGEXCO	Trading company
ENGESA FNV	Railway and mining equipment, automotive parts, hoisting and excavating machines, trailers, steel foundry
ENGEPEQ	Research engineering development and testing
ENGETRONICA	Military and civilian electronic systems, optronics, VHF and HF radio systems, avionics, transformers, fire control systems
ENGELETRICA	Electric motors for industrial application and combat cars

Source: Drawn from *ENGESA Military Products*, (ENGESA Catalog), ENGESA , Barueri, São Paulo, Brasil, 1983 and 1988.

supplies training films in a variety of languages, including Arabic, and AXIAL coordinates insurance for ENGESA companies. ENGEPEQ is the research arm while EXGEXCO is the export trading company, handling 90% of all military exports from Brazil from 1974–1985.[17] ENGEXCO is also an agent for EMBRAER, Villares, IMBEL, Companhia Brasileira de Cartuchos and Arco Flex.[18]

ENGESA expanded rapidly. At the end of 1983, for example, the ENGESA group was comprised of only seven enterprises: ENGESA, ENGEX, FAMABRA (munitions, jointly held with IMBEL), the newly formed ENGETRôNICA, ENGEPEQ, ENGESAVIDEO and EXGEXCO. In the late eighties FNV, ENGEQUIMICA, AEROBRASIL and AXIAL were added to attend to exports. FNV was an important acquisition to build the new Osório tank; furthermore, its electrical equipment will be produced by ENGETRONICA while the cannons are manufactured by ENGEX in Bahia.[19] However, as we will see in Chapter 8, this rapid expansion in the face of falling domestic and international demand has contributed to the current crisis of the industry.

ENGESA was able to mobilize production for the Armed Forces rapidly due to ready suppliers within the automobile sector. From the initial order for the Brazilian military through current international marketing strategies, ENGESA complemented its vertical production structure with a policy of horizontal procurement, buying parts and components from other firms. Wherever possible, the firm strove to procure components for the tanks "off the shelves" of Brazilian industry.

Nobody in ENGESA denies that its success is owed to the philosophy of horizontal procurement. Instead of producing its own components it turned to acquire them in the market of other industries, including auto parts. With horizontalization, ENGESA's production costs are lower and can offer light tanks in the international market at a more competitive price. In addition, they have the advantage of easy maintenance in whatever part of the world.[20]

Thus, the armored vehicle did not stimulate growth of new industries but rather became a new source of demand for automobile suppliers.[21] ENGESA draws from 850 of the 1,500 domestic auto parts factories [22] with approximately 400 of the suppliers on permanent contracts.[23] To facilitate rapid deliveries and spread production risks, ENGESA also practices widespread subcontracting. In 1983 an estimated 30% of the production and assembly of ENGESA vehicles was subcontracted.[24] Through the complementary practices of drawing from domestic automotive producers, subcontracting, and acquiring firms to produce key high technology equipment, ENGESA has been able to achieve the high rate of nationalization of production of 98.5%.[25]

Moreover, automotive components became a major selling point of the tanks. Because parts are of a standard variety, there is little backlog in producing spares and often components can be found within the automobile repair sector of the purchasing sector. This is attractive in war when a force is paralyzed due to mechanical breakdown of sophisticated systems. In its product catalog ENGESA emphasizes this feature, stating:

> Standard off-the-shelf automotive components are utilized to manufacture ENGESA military equipment. This enables them to perform highly strategic operations while decreasing maintenance problems and avoiding possibilities of embargoes.[26]

Thus the structure of the armored vehicle sector is composed of ENGESA on top and subcontractors and secondary producers in the second tier, all utilizing automotive suppliers.

As in aircraft, the secondary tier in the armored vehicle sector is comprised of smaller producers supplementing the dominant firm. The army is careful to promote different product lines so as not to duplicate capabilities or incite destructive competition.[27] Up until ENGESA's entry with the Osório, it produced armored cars while tank production and refurbishment was carefully apportioned to other firms so as to avoid predatory competition.[28] Bernardi, formed in 1912 to produce strong boxes and steel office furniture, later turned to tanks.[29] With idle capacity, in the mid-1960s, it began production of bodies for trucks for the Navy and the Army. Building upon this experience it then modernized old M-3A1 tanks in conjunction with the firms Biselli and Novotração.[30] The new design includes different chassis, a motor of national origin, drive chain, tires, the ENGESA/ELETROMETAL cannon and sight finders by D.F. Vasconcellos.[31] During the 1960s, its research and development center brought forth the twenty-ton tank XIAI. After the Brazilian government acquired industrial rights to the M-41 Bulldog from the U.S. for $5,000, it passed them on to Bernardini,[32] which made it more economical and battleworthy, improved gas mileage and put in a new transmission and cannons.[33] With a strong global market for modernization of M41s (6,000 were produced),[34] Bernardini now exports overhaul kits.[35] The firm is currently studying modernization of the M-4 Sherman tank.[36] Because the firm works directly with the Army in refurbishing old equipment to current military specifications, there is a close relationship between engineers in the firm and in the army research and development facilities.[37]

Of three hundred employees, half are involved in military production. The firm draws upon one hundred suppliers;[38] its production line could be easily expanded as most of its equipment is made in Brazil.[39] After consolidating the learning process of tank technology through overhauls, the firm began indigenous design and production. With the assistance of the Army Technology Center (CTEX), it developed a medium weight tank, the Tamoyo. With 20% of its volume destined for the export market, this private firm draws upon thirty suppliers in a horizontalized production structure.[40]

Other military producers include Gurgel, Biselli and Motopeças. Gurgel produces light off-road vehicles which have tested well against French, German and Italian competitors. On average, 10% of annual production is marketed in forty countries including Guatemala,

Panama, Colombia, Peru, Bolivia, Chile and Paraguay.[41] Biselli produces chassis and trailers for military trucks and transporters and an amphibious truck for the marines. Although Biselli already exports its civilian line to Latin America, Africa and the Middle East, it has just begun to probe the international defense market.[42] Motopeças, a highly regarded company in the field of auto components, has expanded its defense line. In 1982, it made a decisive entry into the defense market, offering its kit for modernizing the armored personnel carrier, the M113B.[43] While the bulk of AVIBRAS' production has been oriented toward military exports, the firm is currently looking to its civilian production to counterbalance declining demand in international defense markets.

In January 1987 a new missile firm, ÓRBITA, was created as an association between ENGESA (40%), EMBRAER (40%) and four minority shareholders IMBEL (tied to the army ministry), Eska-Engenharia and Parcom-Participações. According to an EMBRAER press release, ÓRBITA will subcontract manufacturing of parts and components for its parent companies, as well as designing, developing and marketing guided weapons and missile systems, sounding rockets and launchers for civilian space applications.[44] The firm intends to be the industrial arm of military research centers.[45]

The creation of ÓRBITA is a curious anomaly in the Brazilian defense sector. Whereas in the aircraft and armored vehicle industries the state promoted the growth of a primary producer, with ÓRBITA the State encouraged the formation of a firm in direct competition with AVIBRAS. Indeed, AVIBRAS officials publicly challenged the constitutionality of the decree-law that constituted the firm on the grounds that a public enterprise cannot be formed to compete with already existing private firms.[46] Despite this resistance, ÓRBITA continued to receive the favor of the state. Closely affiliated with the Air Force's technology center (CTA), it was involved in the commercialization of the air to missile Piranha, MAA-1 (later named MOL for Aeronautics Minister Octávio Moreira Lima) to be used on EMBRAER's subsonic fighter the AMX. In conjunction with British Aerospace it also offers the surface to air MSA 3.1.[47] With Oto Melara of Italy it is producing the "Leo" MSS 1.2 (to humor Army Minister Leonidas Pires Gonçalves) anti-tank missile to be used with ENGESA's Main Battle Tank, the Osório . While it is rumored that ÓRBITA's favor derives from personal animosity between AVIBRAS director Engineer João Verdi and Brigadier Hugo de Oliveira Piva of the Air Force,[48] it is unclear that the close relationship to the state will carry the firm through the crisis of the industry described in Chapter 8.

Indeed, its operations have in 1987 been scaled down considerably.

Supplier firms demonstrate a wide degree of variability. Novatração, with extensive research capability in rubber and plastics, produces tires and tracks for armored vehicles, exporting to Argentina, Ecuador, the U.S. and Uruguay.[49] D.F. Vasconcellos produces high technology optics for civilian and military use worldwide. With forty years of experience and a staff of 1,000, it is the leading optics center in South America. In recent years the firm rapidly expanded its military line.[50] In the 1970s it provided the Brazilian Armed Forces with fuses, bombs, air to ground rockets, and periscopes for tanks. From 1983 to 1986 under contract with CTA, it worked on the air to air missile Piranha.[51] DFV produces night vision equipment in a joint venture of the British firm Pilkington, and produces a "head up display" for EMBRAER's Tucano using Swiss technology. It is interesting to note that DFV has successfully drawn upon foreign, national, and its own in-house center for technological development. But only 5% of the firm's $28 m in annual sales derives from the military market. Tecnasa, expanding in electronics, has developed radar, air traffic control equipment, radios and antennas.[52] To overcome problems of scale, each of these firms offers a variety of military products for both the armored vehicle and aeronautics industries.

ABC Simuladores e Aviônica is part of a larger conglomerate, the ABC group. The simulator and avionics arm had its genesis within CTA, to commercialize the simulator produced for the Tucano in 1983.[53] While a contract did not materialize for two years, ABC also entered into an international licensing agreement with the US firm GMI to produce simulators for the more advanced EMBRAER plane the Brasília. ABC simulator's history has been rocky, limited by EMBRAER's own inexperience in providing specifications for the production of the simulator, as well as small procurement demands on the part of the Brazilian Armed Forces. For example, while US producers might manufacture 50 simulators annually, ABC normally produces one or two. This severely constrains the firm's ability to invest in research and development, leaving it perennially behind industrial country producers. In addition to simulators, ABC produces avionic equipment. Beginning in 1987 the military made a concerted effort to expand domestic suppliers for the AMX. Called the PIC, the Complementary Industry Program, the project was targeted at stimulating the electronics sector. The state purchased the necessary machines, negotiated the technology transfer with the Italian firm Aeritalia, and sent 15 people to study in Italy to learn to replicate the product for the AMX. In terms of being able to absorb the production technology, the project has been successful—although the "know why" is still lacking. ABC is somewhat pessimistic about significant expansion through new joint ventures. The problem is the fact that in general Brazil's comparative advantage is in its cheaper labor, but much of avionics production processes have been automatized.

In addition to the production of major weapons systems, mention should be made of the small arms industry in Brazil. IMBEL, a company owned by the Brazilian Army, is a holding company which, produces explosives, accessories, war heads for all ammunition types and propellers for missiles and rockets. In addition to its four factories, it has a subsidiary, Prólogo, an electronics firm, and stock participation in: CBC, a small arms firm; ABC XTAL, fiber optics; ENGESA Química, munitions with a caliber greater than 40mm; D.F. Vasconcelos, optical and night vision equipment; and ÔRBITA, the missile firm. Closely aligned with CTEX, IMBEL acts as a source of R &D of indigenous and internationally acquired technological systems.[54] Eighty percent of its sales are destined for the civilian market, with only twenty percent being strictly military.

This profile of the Brazilian defense industry illustrates that there is a wide array of firms producing a fairly broad range of military equipment. However, despite this achievement, the industry in no way approximates the mythical third world giant of a defense structure erroneously portrayed in the literature. Indeed Table 2.4 shows that even in 1987, the last strong year that the industry enjoyed, total receipts for the top three firms do not exceed 1 billion dollars. The other smaller firms in material transport do not even appear on this "who's who" listing of top firms in the vehicle sector. While indeed it is notable that the Brazilian defense industry achieved the recognition that it did in such a short period of time, it in no way is comparable to the industrial power defense sectors. While much is made of the fact that Brazil is one of the top exporters of armaments in the world, it only accounts for .8% of the trade in major conventional weapons. This is not to undercut the fact that Brazil was able to mount a defense industry capable of selling armaments globally. There are indeed important development lessons to be garnered from the achievement of entering the high technology international defense market at all. But an AVIBRAS, the only Brazilian firm to make to SIPRI list of the 100 largest arms producing companies in 1988, is dwarfed in its sales of 370 million dollars by a McDonnell Douglas or Lockheed, each of which made over 8 billion dollars in arms sales in 1988. Given their relatively small size, the Brazilian firms are more likely to have

Table 2.4
Transportation Material Sector, 1987
Gross receipts, 1986 prices

rank 87	rank 86	EMPRESA	receita US$Million
1	1	Massey Perkins	430
2	3	EMBRAER	331
3	4	Caterpillar	281
4	2	AVIBRAS	185
5	6	Ishibras	170
6	7	Valmet	168
7	5	Verolme	166
8	8	Moto Honda	155
9	9	ENGESA	129
10	13	Marchesan	124

Source: Abstracted from Gazeta Mercantil, *Balanco Anual,* 1988

difficulty in weathering the downturn in the international defense market.

Given the modest size of the Brazilian defense industry in international terms, a concentrated domestic industrial sector was critical. Politically, national security demanded a strong military production unit capable of supplying Brazil in war time. Economically, smaller production units would not meet the minimal optimal scale for profitability. In the U.S. for example, the minimal optimal scale for commercial transport and aircraft in 1967 was 10% of total demand.[55] With the smaller Brazilian market, the trend to monopoly is obvious. Furthermore, economies of scale in management and engineering favor concentration. During World War II U.S. aviation labor costs fell by 20% with each doubling of output.[56] Learning by doing and lower overhead contributed to this decline; these same characteristics apply to Brazil.

Concentration in the Brazilian defense industry is reinforced by the international market where power is integral to success. Size brings advantages in advertising, product distribution and service. Mutually reinforcing, monopoly in the home market contributes to global competitive ability; rewards from international marketing in turn solidify the firms' dominant domestic position.

Industry Conduct

The structure of the market delimits the conduct of the industry, particularly in pricing, product strategy, research and innovation, and plant investment. Concentration permits price fixing, larger investments in plant and equipment, research and development, and sophisticated marketing. Competitive firms, forced to accept market prices, generally cannot sustain high levels of plant or product investments from lower profits.

Chapters 5 through 8 provide detailed descriptions of the defense industry's conduct. After establishing in Chapter 5 that the industry's conduct is shaped by its partnership with the state, the following two chapters characterize the activity of the state and the firms in technological development and export promotion. It is argued that the monopolistic structure of the industry advanced by the state fostered technological achievement, export promotion and the expansion of the industrial sector. In Chapter 8, however, we see how this successful strategy begins to break down as the industry confronts declining international demand at the same time that domestic funds dwindle due to the fiscal crisis of the Brazilian state.

Performance:

Conduct conditions the performance of the firm. Scherer measures performance in terms of productive and allocative efficiency, progress, full employment and equity in using the following four standards:

1. Decisions as to what, how much and how to produce should be efficient in two respects: Scarce resources should not be wasted outright, and production decisions should be responsive qualitatively and quantitatively to consumer demands.

2. The operations of producers should be progressive, taking advantage of opportunities opened up by science and technology to increase output per unit of input and to provide consumers with superior new products, in both ways contributing to the long-run growth of real income per capita.

3. The operations of producers should facilitate stable full employment of resources, especially human resources. Or at minimum, they should not make maintenance of full employment through the use of macroeconomic policy instruments excessively difficult.

4. The distribution of income should be equitable. Equity is a notoriously slippery concept, but it implies at least that producers do not secure rewards far in excess of what is needed to call forth the amount of services supplied. A subfacet of this

goal is the desire to achieve reasonable price stability, for rampant inflation distorts the distribution of income in ways widely disapproved.[57]

Sherer's criteria for performance thus encompass how the industry uses society's scarce resources, its contribution to the growth of that society, the social goal of maximum employment and some concept of economic fairness in the distribution of returns.

As will be shown throughout this book, according to Sherer's criteria, the armaments industry (1) efficiently utilizes resources, and is responsive to the Armed Forces and international market demands, (2) takes advantage of new technological opportunities, (3) promotes the development of human capital in advanced engineering capacities and (4) contributes to fiscal stability by delivering appropriate military equipment at reasonable cost as well as earning foreign exchange. It is also contended that Brazil enhanced military security through the promotion and expansion of the defense industry. Nevertheless, it is argued that as the basic supply condition of technology reached more sophisticated levels and as international demand decreases as other developing nations mobilize indigenous defense sectors, the benefits of Brazilian arms production began to outweigh the costs in the late 1980s.

Notes

1. F. M. Scherer, *Industrial Market Structure and Economic Performance*, (Boston: Houghton Mifflin, 1981). See also Gavin C. Reid, *Theories of Industrial Organization*, (New York: Basil Blackwell, 1987). Chapter 2 provides a summary of the structure-conduct-performance paradigm.

2. See Scherer, *Industrial Market Structure*, Chapter 1 for a full discussion of the industrial organization approach.

3. See Andrew J. Pierre, *The Global Politics of Arms Sales*, (Princeton: Princeton University Press, 1982), pp. 31-34 for a discussion of the Carter human rights policy and its effects on arms transactions.

4. The catalog *Brazilian Defense Equipment 1987* (Brasília: Fundação Visconde de Cabo Frio, 1987) is a useful guide to military products offered by the industry.

5. *Planejamento e Desenvolvimento*, Vol 6, No. 68, January 1979, p. 48.

6. Pedro Vidal, technical director of AVIBRAS in *Jornal do Brasil*, "Brasil terá maior fábrica de foquete do mundo em 83," (Milton F. de Rocha Filho) April 25, 1982.

7. *Equipamento Militar*, Ano 1, No. 3, Edição do Exercito.

8. AVIBRAS catalog, 1985.

9.   "Indústria de armas será maior exportadora do Brasil em 85," *Jornal do Brasil*, November 1, 1982.

10.   *Equipamento Militar*,Vol. 1, No. 3, 1983, and "Potyguara: não faltaram fornecedores de armas," *Estado de São Paulo*, March 8,1977.

11.   AVIBRAS catalog, 1985.

12.   Interview with Armando Eliezer, ENGESA, November 1983.

13.   *Jornal do Brasil*, May 27, 1979.

14.   Unpublished document on ENGETRôNICA obtained from EMBRAER.

15.   "Motortec já exporta serviços," *Jornal do Brasil*, January 18,1982.

16.   ENGESA catalog, 1988.

17.   "ENGESA: A Marca do Brasil que Brilha no Mundo," *Equipamento Militar*, Vol. 1, No. 3, December/January 1983/84, p. 65, and ENGESA 1988 (ENGESA Catalog).

18.   "Guerra e paz nos planos da ENGESA," *EXAME*, November 4, 1981.

19.   "Protótipo de tanque de combate da ENGESA custa CR\$ 27 bilhões," *Jornal do Brasil*, July 11, 1983, p. 13.

20.   Ibid. On horizontal production see also "Indústria bélica negocia com os EUA e a China," *Jornal do Brasil*, August 3, 1980; "Indústria de armas será maior exportadora do Brasil em 85," *Jornal do Brasil* (Antonio Augusto Oliveira) November 1, 1982; and "Uma nova trincheira," *VEJA*, October 17, 1979.

21.   Interview with Sr. Paulo Meira, Director of Sales, GM do Brasil, October 24, 1983.

22.   *Brazilian Defense Equipment* published by Brasil Comércio e Indústria, Fundação Visconde de Cabo Frio, 1983.

23.   "Guerra e paz nos planos da ENGESA," *EXAME*, November 4, 1981.

24.   Interview with Sr. Paulo Meira.

25.   "ENGESA: A Marca do Brasil que Brilha no Mundo," *Equipamento Militar*.

26.   "ENGESA Military Products," ENGESA Group, Barueri, São Paulo, Brasil, 1983.

27.   "Material bélico é nova alternativa industrial," *Jornal Brasilese*, April 10,1983, p. 8.

28.   Dagnino, "A Indústria de Armamentos Brasileira: Uma Tentativa de Avaliação."

29.   Ibid.

30.   "Nossas armas ameaçando o mercado russo," *Estado de São Paulo*, April 24, 1981, p. 12.

31.   Ibid.

32.   Ibid.

33.   "Um re-equipamento que exige o melhor," *Jornal do Brasil*, October 5, 1970.

34.   "Indústria bélica negocia com os EUA e a China," *Jornal de Brasil*, August 3, 1980, 1st section.

35.   "Nossas armas ameaçando o mercado russo," *Estado de São Paulo*.

36.   "Exército nacional acelera re-equipamento," *Fohla de São Paulo*, October 17, 1982.

37.   Dagnino, "A Indústria de Armamentos Brasileira: Uma Tentativa de Avaliação."

38.   "Bernardini, cofres e carros de combate," *Tecnologia e Defesa,* No. 3, May 1983, p. 48.

39.   "Indústria bélica negocia com os EUA e a China," *Jornal do Brasil,* August 3, 1980, 1st section.

40.   "Indústria opera mesmo que sua fábrica seja totalmente destruída ou ocupada," *Jornal do Brazil,* 13 June 1984.

41.   "Os Jipes Gurgel," *Tecnologia e Defesa,* No.3, May 1983, p. 23.

42.   "Biselli," *Tecnologia e Defesa,* No.3, May 1983, p. 6.

43.   Brazilian Defense Equipment 1987 (Brasilia: Fundaçào Visconde de Cabo Frio, 1987).

44.   "EMBRAER is Partner in New Aerospace Business," EMBRAER News Press Release No. 003/87, 30 January 1987.

45.   "Órbita anuncia vendas de US$3bi o mais em mísseis," *O Globo,* August 17, 1987.

46.   "AVIBRAS afirma que criação da Órbita é inconstitucional," *Folha de São Paulo* January 11, 1987.

47.   "Missile to be Built with British Aerospace," FBIS-LAT-87-193, October 6, 1987, originally reported in *Estado de São Paulo,* September 29, 1987. Also discussed in a technical data sheet distributed by ENGEXCO.

48.   "AVIBRAS afirma que criação de Órbita é inconstitucional."

49.   "Novatração," *Tecnologia e Defesa,* No. 3, May 1983, p. 13.

50.   "D.F. Vasconcellos," *Defesa,* No. 3, May 1983, p. 42.

51.   D.F. Vasconcelos Company Report "Perfil DFV."

52.   "Tecnasa" Especialistas em Eletrônica," *Tecnologia e Defesa,* p. 58.

53.   Information on ABC was gathered in an interview with Roberto A.R. Almeida, Director of Technology and Marketing, July 25, 1990, São José dos Campos.

54.   "O que é a IMBEL," company publication.

55.   Scherer, *Industrial Market Structure.*

56.   Ibid.

57.   Ibid.

3

The Economic Foundations of Brazil's Armaments Industry

The Brazilian defense sector is successful because it is as responsive to economic realities as it is to military command. This policy evolved from a view of industrialization which held economic growth as a pillar of military security. Economic and military standards grounded decision making, resulting in the choice of technologies and marketing strategies promoting growth.

Presentation of this argument begins by considering comparative experience. Unlike the strong economic influences in Brazil, in the majority of cases defense industries in developing countries have been militarily motivated and controlled. Attention to military exigencies instead of economic sense retards efficiency, paradoxically weakening national defense. Why economic criteria played a significant role in shaping the Brazilian defense sector is then considered in Chapter 4. It is demonstrated that throughout the Brazilian industrialization experience a multidimensional concept of security emphasizing economic strength as a prerequisite to military might informed development policy. Simultaneously, there existed strong sentiment that, wherever possible, economic activity should be left to the private sector. Together, these ideological foundations favoring industrial promotion and private economic activity coalesced to shape an industry responding first to the dictates of the market, and then the military.

Comparative Evidence

Brazil is a global arms merchant. As Table 3.1 illustrates, Brazil vies with Israel as largest Third World exporter of major weapons, capturing one fourth of all military exports from developing nations from 1982-1986. Brazil exports to more Third World nations than any other developing country, and also includes as its clients the highest number of first world states sold to by a third world exporter. Ninety-nine percent of Brazil's weapons exports were produced in the country. This stands in contrast to Israel and Egypt which only produce domestically 91 and 5 percent respectively, with the balance accounted for by re-exports of imported weaponry.[1]

Such success has jettisoned Brazil into the club of global exporters of conventional weaponry. Indeed table 3.2 shows only Brazil and Israel among the top ten armaments exporters. While clearly in a different class from the United States and the Soviet Union, one can see that Brazil and Israel have become competitive with the "second tier" of exporting nations. Table 3.3 demonstrates that with the exception of the U.K. the second tier of arms producers have shown large positive increases in global weapons market shares, while the U.S. and the USSR have shown losses.

If world market shares are considered, it can be shown that the increase in exports of countries in the second tier, including Israel and Brazil, has principally come at the expense of U.S. armaments exports. Of course, while the share of Brazilian exports remains dwarfed by the

TABLE 3.1
Major Weapons, 1982–86

Supplier	% Share in Total TW Exports of Major Weapons 82-86	# Customers TW	Indus-trial-ized	Region	Share	Country	Share
Israel	23.90	15	2	F. East	38.8	Taiwan	38.0
Brazil	23.30	24	4	M. East	48.3	Iraq	36.7
Egypt	14.10	9	0	M. East	89.2	Iraq	89.2
Jordan	7.30	2	1	M. East	91.4	Iraq	88.
Libya	7.30	8	0	M. East	80.8	Syria	47.4
S. Korea	7.20	6	0	F. East	43.4	Malaysia	31.6
N. Korea	5.50	5	0	M. East	95.8	Iran	95.8
Syria	3.30	2	1	M. East	98.9	Iran	88.5
Singapore	2.10	6	0	F. East	50.9	Taiwan	40.7
Indonesia	1.60	3	0	M. East	64.3	Saudi Arabia	64.3
Others	4.40						

Source: SIPRI Yearbook 1987, Stockholm International Peace Research Institute, p. 198

TABLE 3.2

Global Arms Exporters, 1977-1980

Rank	Country	% of Global Exports
1	USA	43.3%
2	USSR	27.4%
3	France	10.8%
4	Italy	4.0%
5	United Kingdom	3.7%
6	FR Germany	3.0%
7	Norway	1.3%
8	Netherlands	.9%
9	Brazil	.7%
10	Israel	.6%
11	Australia	.6%
12	China	.5%
13	Sweden	.4%
14	Switzerland	.4%
15	Canada	.3%
16	South Africa	.2%
17	Finland	.2%
18	Czechoslovakia	.2%
	Others	1.3%
	Total	100.0%

Source: *SIPRI Yearbook 1981*, Stockholm International Peace Research Institute, 1981.

superpower states, that Brazil has been able to enter this market at all is worthy of discussion. Indeed although many developing countries, including Argentina, India, Chile, Mexico, Peru, Nigeria, Egypt, Saudi Arabia, Iran, Indonesia, Pakistan, North and South Korea and Taiwan, have attempted armaments production only two—Brazil and Israel—are internationally competitive.[2]

Why is Brazil a successful exporter? One can point to Brazil's natural and scientific endowments as a partial explanation. It has a stronger industrial base, more resources, and a larger scientific community than most developing nations. Abundantly endowed with mineral resources, it has approximately one-third of the world's reserves of iron ore, large quantities of manganese and other industrial

TABLE 3.3
Value of Major Exports
World Market Shares 1967-76 and 1977-87

Country	%67-76	%77-87	% change between periods
USSR	37.75%	36.53%	-3.23%
USA	38.49%	27.42%	-28.74%
France	7.17%	13.69%	91.00%
UK	7.71%	5.34%	-30.75%
China	2.27%	3.16%	39.22%
FR Germany	1.10%	2.81%	155.04%
Italy	1.19%	3.21%	168.84%
Spain	0.04%	0.88%	1967.22%
Israel	0.28%	1.15%	312.66%
Brazil	0.18%	0.90%	407.17%
Other Third World	0.74%	1.88%	154.08%
Other Ind., West	1.95%	1.47	-24.66%
Other Ind., neutral	0.34%	1.05%	207.80%
Other Ind., East	0.80%	0.52%	-34.86%

Source: Calculated from SIPRI data.

metals.[3] In 1986 it produced 35% of all scientific papers and books in Latin America.[4]

Rich natural sources and a relatively strong scientific base distinguishes Brazil as a country likely to produce armaments. Wulf (1983) ranked countries for potential to produce armaments as shown in column 1 of Table 3.4.[5] Identifying six industries as 'relevant' to military production—iron and steel, non-ferrous metal, metal products, machinery, electrical machinery and transportation equipment—and specifying a human capital component comprised of workers in relevant industries plus the size of scientific community, Brazil ranks second to India. While 25% of Brazil's industrial base is comprised of industries relevant to arms production, India's production structure shows only 16%.[6] The secondary ranking comes from having fewer scientists, engineers and technicians. Wulf notes from the *United Nations Statistical Handbook*, for example, that India has ninety-seven thousand scientists, engineers and technicians involved in research and development while Brazil only has eight thousand.[7] Given these criteria of manufacturing base and research and development, it is

TABLE 3.4
Rank Order of Potential Armament Producers, Actual Industries and the
Export Performance of These Military Industries

Rank	Potential	Size & Diversification	Exports
	(1)	(2)	(3)
1	India	Israel	Brazil
2	Brazil	India	Israel
3	Yugoslavia	Brazil	South Africa
4	South Africa	Yugoslavia	Libya
5	Mexico	South Africa	Egypt
6	Argentina	Argentina	South Korea
7	Taiwan	Taiwan	Argentina
8	South Korea	South Korea	Saudi Arabia
9	Turkey	Philippines	Singapore
10	Greece	Turkey	Indonesia
11	Iran	Indonesia	Cuba
12	Israel	Egypt	India

Sources: Col (1): Wulf, "Developing Countries," in Ball and Leitenberg, *The Structure of the Defense Industry*, p. 326.; Col (2): Ibid, p. 321; Col (3): *SIPRI Yearbook 1980*, Stockholm International Peace Research Institute, 1980. See footnote p.2 for explanation of columns 1 & 2.

interesting to note that Israel only places twelfth on the list of potential arms exporters.

Wulf also ranks military sectors by performance, measured by diversification across defense subsectors and industrial output. The range of weapons, including aircraft, armored vehicles, missiles, ships and small munitions and the capability to design rather than license systems distinguishes technologically sophisticated and industrially mature producers. Column 2 of Table 3.4 shows Brazil third, falling short of India and Israel in the number of weapons systems produced. All three, however, (in conjunction with Yugoslavia) are described as having diversified and sizeable production structures. This is in contrast to countries such as Argentina, which falls in the second category of "production of most of the twelve weapons categories," Egypt or the Philippines, which are described as "production in several weapons categories without substantial capacity for indigenous development" or Mexico, Chile or Libya which only have "isolated projects."[8]

Ayres (1983) also ranks potential defense capacity using share of manufacturing in Gross National Product (GNP) as a crude index. He concludes that only Brazil, Portugal, Argentina, Yugoslavia, Singapore and Israel demonstrate sufficient strength to consider large scale arms production.[9]   Finally, Neuman (1984) categorizes military potential by emphasizing factors which contribute to scale economies including population, land size, size of the military, GNP, GNP per capita, the number of professional and technical workers and the number of industrial workers.[10]   Since it has been widely argued that scale economies are critical to defense production, she suggests that the determinants of economies of scale should identify potential arms producers. Looney and Fredericksen (1986) refine Neuman's work by using discriminate analysis. Both studies name Brazil as having high arms production potential.[11]

But high arms production potential does not necessarily translate into strong performance. Despite the appeal of the argument that the strength of the industrial base will explain armaments export performance, this relationship does not always hold.   India, for example, supersedes Brazil in both arms production potential and actual size, but exports little. While Mexico has industrial potential, domestic armament production is inconsequential. In contrast, Israel overcame low potential to become the largest Third World producer and the second largest exporter. These anomalies point to fact that the industrial base is not the sole determinant of the size or export capability of an armaments industry.

Political motivations, particularly a perceived need for national autonomy, often override weak industrial potential.[12] Sovereign states prefer domestic procurement to dependence on the political and military agendas of seller nations. When a nation's mobilization capacity is contingent upon the supplies of another nation, military capabilities are compromised. Even in cases where ready supplies are available, the perception of dependence weakens the public profile of the armed forces. This desire for autonomy has been reinforced by Third World nonalignment and nationalism. Thus, countries are willing to commit economic resources to armaments production on political grounds of independence where the economic potential might indicate an alternative use.

Furthermore, countries such as Israel, Taiwan, or South Africa began armaments industries not out of a preference for national production but to have access to the supply of any weaponry.   For international pariah states, procurement in international markets was increasingly problematic and supplies insecure.[13] As a result of existing or threatened international embargoes, these countries accelerated arms production programs. For example, Klieman argues Israel faced a "force majeure" with respect to armament production. Klare notes that South Africa expanded its armaments infrastructure after the 1965 United Nations embargo on weapons deliveries. Indeed South Africa transformed a small arms and munitions industry into a sophisticated complex offering missiles, aircraft, and armored vehicles following the mandatory international embargo in 1977. This was achieved with considerable assistance from abroad despite the voluntary embargo on military technology transfers dating back to 1963.[14] India and Pakistan promoted indigenous production after the British and America cut off supplies follow the 1966 war over the Kashmir.[15] Restrictions on supplies from the Soviet Union during a critical period in the 1967 war spurred development in the Egyptian defense sector.[16] These cases show how international ostracization spurred independent production structures despite low industrial potential in Israel and Pakistan.

Beyond autonomous procurement, arms production may confer status upon a nation, signalling membership in the club of the military elite. Aspirants to positions of regional supremacy include arms production capabilities as a key element of the power equation. Said a West European diplomat of the Indian case, "More than anything else, India wants to be taken seriously. It wants to be viewed as a world power. That is an end in itself."[17]

But political motivations do not suffice to create a dynamic and internationally competitive defense sector. State control to achieve political goals can leave the sector subject to decisions made for national glory, not economic viability. Technologies chosen for their resemblance to superpower weaponry are often beyond the capabilities of the indigenous scientific base. Profits from exports are likely to be bypassed as the state focuses on internal needs. What is the correlation between state involvement in the armaments sector and international sales? Does a focus upon political considerations of autonomy or power preclude an economically viable and internationally competitive industry?

Table 3.5 addresses the relationship between political motivations for arms production and export success in international markets. The order of a country's appearance in the table is organized according to defense production potential as defined by Wulf. These might be considered supply side factors in defense industrialization—the natural endowments, industrial structure and human capital that would point to strong economic foundations for export success. The next column captures the demand for weaponry in categorizing countries according to the strength of external threats. The supply factors of ability to

TABLE 3.5
Armaments Industries, State Support and Export Promotion
in Developing Countries

Country	External Threat Assessment	Extent of Government Participation	Export Performance
India	High (Pakistan & China)	Owned and run by Ministry of Defense; not integrated into private sector; undertook high tech projects not capable of sustaining	Very low; only 1% of production
Brazil	Low	Mixed w/ emphasis on private	High
S. Africa	High internal & external	Mixed; 1/4 state through ARMSCOR; licensing agreements w/ROC, France, Israel, W. Germany	High regional exports pariah status
Mexico	Low	Owned and run by "DINA" the state defense firm	Low
Argentina	Medium (post Falkland-Malvinas)	Owned and controlled; 5 year plan to privatize	Very low; regional
ROC (Taiwan)	High	Mixed; strong US ties	Increasing export orientation toward ASEAN countries
S. Korea	High	Mixed public/ tied to US	Medium to high private; in small arms
Israel	Extremely high	State owns major firms with a public/private mix at other levels; high degree transnational participation	High, focus on small arms; other projects restricted by US
Countries not ranked by Wulf			
China	High (Vietnam, India, USSR)	Owned and controlled government ownership consistent with socialized economy	High on political basis; old, poor quality equipment

TABLE 3.5 [Continued]

Country	External Threat Assessment	Extent of Government Participation	Export Performance
Egypt	High (Middle East)	Owned and controlled high multinational	Low- medium; some regional integration; industry run at deficit of 45% of value of production
N. Korea	High	State; tied to Soviet Union	Medium to high in small arms
Pakistan	High	Owned and run by Armed Forces; highly inefficient and bureaucratic	Low to medium within Moslem world
Philippines	High internal; low external	Mixed; state owned plus private sector organized under the Association of Defense Contractors	Low

Sources: Evaluation of threat perception is based on information in the following country studies in J. Katz, *Arms Production in Developing Countries* (MA:D.C. Heath, 1984), "Argentina" by Jacqueline S. Porth; "People's Republic of China" by John Fr; "Egypt" by Mohammad El-Sayed Selim; "India" by Thomas W. Graham; "Israel" by W. Harkavy & S. Neuman; "South Korea" by Edward A. Olsen; "Mexico" by Marvin Alisky; "Pakistan" by Hasan Askari Rizvi; "Philippines" by Andrew L. Ross; "Republic of China" by A. James Gregor; "South Africa" by Ewan W. Anderson.

produce interact with the demand conditions or the desire for independent production to shape the extent of government participation in the industry. Arms production potential conditioned by the demand for security will characterize the extent of government participation. The lower the potential or the higher the threat, the greater the extent of state participation.

But "extent" as a measure of *quantity* of involvement must be seen in conjunction with the *quality* or kind of state intervention. That is, the state might enter the defense industry, assume complete ownership and control of production. Alternatively, the state might choose to intervene in the market selectively, providing incentives for defense production designed to supplement the supply side production capabilities of the market. It is postulated that countries which intervene in markets selectively and allow the market and firms greatest freedom in the determination of production decisions, have greatest success in export markets. Conversely, in those countries where the military assumed nearly complete control of the defense industry without attention to economic factors, the export performance is low.

If this relationship holds, we arrive at the paradox that strong state intervention on political grounds may actually undermine the goals of regional or international power because of the failure to achieve strong export performance. That is to say, blindly pursuing a process of defense industrialization while neglecting the market, most often results in a weak industry which cannot bring about the desired effects of international prestige. Furthermore, as it will be argued later, this industry is unlikely to be economically viable in the long run, and policy makers will be forced with burdensome subsidization of the sector at the expense of alternative development projects. Without massive influx of resources it will not be capable of addressing the defined security needs of the nation, thus failing to achieve its political-military aim.

The majority of countries implemented armaments industries for political reasons, namely an external enemy. Egypt and Israel in the Middle East, North and South Korea, China, Taiwan, India and Pakistan and South Africa are currently involved in long-standing regional tensions cultivating national insecurity. Each perceives itself to be facing a high external threat which motivated the formation of an armaments industry. Of the list of armaments exporters all except Mexico, the Philippines, Argentina, and Brazil face a high external threat. Of these exceptions, during the late 1960s and early 1970s Argentina and Brazil perceived themselves as facing significant internal security challenges and the Philippines continues to assess its security needs in this manner. Given the high degree of external threat, it is not surprising that most Third World arms producers exhibit much government participation in the defense industries.

To achieve the prestige of domestic defense production many developing country armaments industries have relied on international participation. Egypt, Israel and South Africa are tightly integrated into the international defense production network through licensing agreements. While national autonomy is sacrificed, domestic production would not otherwise be possible.

But arms exports appear constrained by both state and foreign participation in defense industries. When analyzed by degree of export performance we can see that the countries with strongest export records—Israel, Taiwan, South Africa and Brazil—all accord a significant role to the private sector in defense production. Of this group, Brazil is distinguished by its low external threat and the absence of pariah status. Despite this difference the argument advanced in this text is that participation of the private sector places a premium on efficiency and propels the firm to seek projects in foreign markets.

Examples abound of economic inefficiency in armaments production. India's Military-Industrial-Research-Complex, MIRC, owned by the Indian government and run by the Ministry of Defense, is a case in point. Although manufacturing between 10–15% of India's industrial output, it has failed to become an indigenous developer of technology, instead relying heavily on licensing agreements. It uses foreign exchange intensively and only exports between one and two percent of total production. While some successes such as the development of a 150 mile ballistic missile that can carry a payload of 2,000 lbs have been noted, India has also been a top importer of armaments to stock its arsenal.[18] Additionally, it regularly operates with excess capacity and has produced a series of inferior quality aircraft unable to be marketed.[19] For example, the government run Defense Research and Development Organization (DRDO) produced six prototype tanks in fourteen years, none to the satisfaction of the Army, which rejected them as not "safe, reliable, or maintainable."[20]

The MIRC's mandate was military and political; this military installation remains dependent upon a continual infusion of funds from the Indian government. In a state troubled by economic stagnation, political divisiveness and social concerns, such dependency makes the defense complex vulnerable to the vagaries of fiscal cycles. Thus, economic inefficiency may lead to military insecurity.

The Egyptian government took over the armaments industry after private sector failure. Despite strong emphasis on privatization in other sectors, the technical requirements of armaments production precluded private control.[21] The capabilities of the Egyptian industry are limited to small arms and assembly, although it is creating a small Middle East export market.[22] The Philippine State is the sole producer and consumer of its armaments. The small domestic market, simultaneously serving as buyer and seller, limits autonomous defense production and has consequently compromised military security.[23] The government-owned South Korean industry has focused on "politically prestigious but militarily inefficient systems."[24] Furthermore, close ties with the U.S. and dependence on American imports severely restrict exports.

Brazil is often compared to Argentina to evaluate economic

performance; similar historic tendencies motivated an armaments industry in the two countries. Figure 3.1 shows the relative defense burdens measured by military expenditures over GNP for Argentina, Brazil and Chile. Yet, despite greater spending, the state owned Argentine industry is grossly inefficient, weighted by military bureaucracy. This is particularly detrimental to Argentine growth as the primary defense producer, Fabricaciones Militares (FAMA), was the country's largest manufacturing firm, accounting for 2% of annual GDP and employing 140,000 people in the mid 1980s.[25] Debt service in foreign currency for the DGFM, the (General Directorate of Ordnance Production) reached 21% of sales in 1985.[26] Despite having the oldest aircraft industry in Latin America, Argentina still shows a low level of nationalization for its indigenously designed, conventional plane, the Pucara.[27]

The weaker progress in the Argentine defense sector as compared to the Brazilian may be attributed to ideological divisions within the Armed Forces. Milenky (1980) describes one group, the statists, as having "supported a national defense industry as one aspect of extensive government involvement in the development of heavy industry and a rejection of reliance on outside powers."[28] The statists stand in contrast to those who argued for greater private control. This ideological division is not particular to the defense sector in Argentina—it underlies that country's broader development debate. However, in defense the question was resolved in favor of nearly complete control by the military. While this generated the institutional mechanism to substitute imported weaponry with domestically manufactured armaments, the incentives for efficient production were absent. That is to say, selection of armaments and technologies were geared toward the demand of the Armed Forces and not international commercial prospects. As both consumer and producer of armaments, the Argentine military did not concern itself with profitability. Rather, its priorities were focused upon prestige and autonomous procurement of arms.

The Argentine defense industry came to be seen as a net economic drain, especially in the external sector where the firm imports far in excess of exports. It was concluded the military enterprises would be better managed along private lines.[29] Plans were announced to strip FAMA of some of its economic power by selling its shareholdings in important petrochemical plants.[30] Civilians are being integrated into the aircraft industry to reorient decision makers to the foreign sector. Critics argue that "military people don't make good marketing people," and that the Argentine military "has no monopoly or even preponderance of trained manpower and professionals."[31] These commentators applaud increased private participation, hoping entrepreneurship will increase the industry's efficiency and enhance national security. Furthermore, it can be argued that divorcing the military from tight control over the defense industry creates another opportunity for the expansion of democratic opening, allowing greater civilian control of the military.[32]

There are signals of increased export activity in the Argentine defense sector. The creation of new firms, many as a result of an association between the government and private capital, have increased export potential.[33] The sale of the TAM, a medium combat car, to Ecuador was an important boost to the international profile of the tank. However, the tank is not of indigenous design, but is licensed and technically supported through the German firm Thyssen Henschel.[34] It is also interesting to note that this contract, reportedly worth more than $100 million dollars, was facilitated by easy finance terms of thirteen years, the first three of which are interest free, at a rate of 5% per year.[35] A project of the DGFM, the TAM is thus benefitting from the close contacts with the Argentine state. The TAM is only one example of strong German influence in expanding the Argentine armaments industry. Germans have reportedly offered the Argentines the "full spectrum of submarine technology," and Dornier is assisting the Argentines with fighter jets.[36] Some suggest that armaments exports will be further amplified under the government of Carlos Ménem.[37]

China has also undergone an interesting transformation of its armaments sector in the 1980s. In an effort to increase hard currency earnings, it restructured its military-industrial structure along commercial lines.[38] Attempting to replicate the more aggressive strategies of successful exporters, China, despite a system of state control, is allowing economic market incentives to direct export policy. Deng Xiaoping, in his capacity as chair of the military affairs committee, created the China North Industries Corporation (Norinco) in the early 1980s with the aim of replacing military grants to allies with sales.[39] The results were marked, with defense equipment accounting for nearly seven percent of total exports in 1984.[40] It is interesting to note that the debate which prompted structural changes in the Chinese armaments industry revolved around the relationship between the defense industry and general economic performance. As in the Brazilian case discussed in the following chapter, the conclusion reached was that a modern defense industry was inextricably linked to a strong industrial structure.[41]

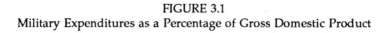

FIGURE 3.1

Military Expenditures as a Percentage of Gross Domestic Product

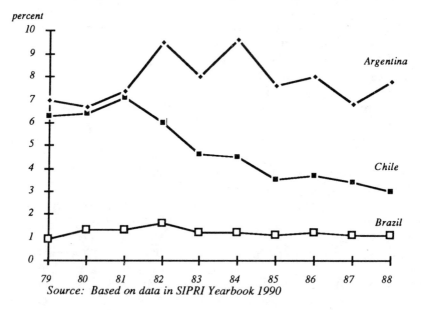

Source: Based on data in SIPRI Yearbook 1990

Two armaments industries demonstrating success in production and exports are the Taiwanese and the Israeli. The Taiwanese armaments industry is increasing private participation. Until recently wholly owned and operated by the government, exports were low and research and development activity weak.[42] As more responsibility is accorded to private institutions, however, it is expected that the performance of the sector will improve.[43]

Israel's successful export record in armaments may also be attributed to both state and private efforts. With one-third of the GNP traceable to military industries, strong emphasis is placed on economic efficiency. Defense production has been perceived by Israeli leaders as part of the industrial base, source of technology, training and foreign exchange.[44] Despite the strong role of government, private participation is also critical to the success of the Israeli industry. Up to one third of sales are accounted for by a complex network of at least one thousand private dealers with Israeli Defense Ministry authorization to market Israeli armaments abroad.[45] The efforts of private dealers are supported by Sibat, the government's Defense Sales Office. Supplementing the

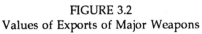

FIGURE 3.2
Values of Exports of Major Weapons

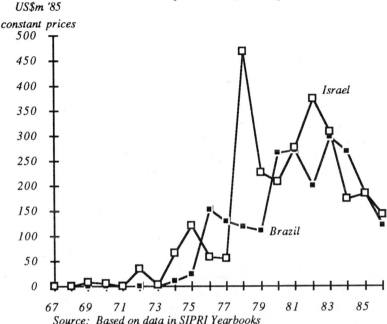

Source: Based on data in SIPRI Yearbooks

efforts of both state forms and the private sector, Sibat engages in market research and promotion and the negotiation of sales and licensing contracts.[46] It is therefore not surprising that Israel shares with Brazil the position of net exporter of military equipment.

But Israeli armaments exports are limited by licensing agreements with the United States. The institutional framework for the exchange of weapons technology is the 1970 Master Defense Development Data Exchange Agreement.[47] The U.S. has participated in a variety of packages providing technical assistance at no cost or a nominal charge.[48] Because of the strong leverage of the United States, some private Israeli firms were restricted in their defense sales in late 1986.[49] Nevertheless, IAI the state-owned aircraft industry and IMI, owned and partly operated by the Ministry of Defense, on average are able to export 50–60% of the total production.[50]

From this survey of Third World arms producers it may be concluded that defense industries controlled by the state are generally inefficient unless, as with Israel, there is a strong commitment on the part of the government to run the sector as an economic, as opposed to military, endeavor. Evidence of increasing privatization in Argentina and Taiwan point to the need for economic criteria in product development and international marketing.

But in no case is complete privatization contemplated. The technical demands of defense production exceed the capacity of private markets in developing countries. Moreover, as defense industries tend toward natural monopolies, the state should share in the windfall profits.[51] What is critical is balance—and prototypical of the brand of state-private partnership necessary is the Brazilian defense sector. The Brazilian emphasis on the economically efficient foundations for the defense sector set the framework for this balance. We now turn to examine why the Brazilian industry has focused on the economic, as opposed to purely military, aspects of armaments production.

Notes

1.   Michael Broska and Thomas Ohlson, "The Trade in Major Conventional Weapons," in *The SIPRI Yearbook 1986*, (Stockholm: The Stockholm International Peace Research Institute, 1987).

2.   Note should be made of the particular position of China. Both SIPRI (Stockholm International Peace Research Institute) and ACDA (US Arms Control and Disarmaments Agency) sources place China in the category of "Other Communist" and not in the "Third World Arms" producer category. SIPRI includes N. Korea in the Third World; ACDA lists it as other (i.e., non-Warsaw pact) communist.

3.   Werner Baer, *The Brazilian Economy: Growth and Development*, Third Edition (New York: Praeger, 1989) p. 6.

4.   *Economic and Social Progress in Latin America*, 1988 Report, Special Section: Science and Technology, (Washington, D.C.: Inter-American Development Bank, 1988) Calculated from Table XI-10, p. 306.

5.   Herbert Wulf, "Developing Countries," in *The Structure of the Defense Industry*, (ed) Nicole Ball and Milton Leitenburg, (New York: St. Martin's Press, 1983), pp. 310-343; H. Wulf et.al, "Transnational Transfer of Arms Production Technology," IFSH Study Group on Armament and Underdevelopment, The 1980 United Nations Study on Disarmaments and Development; Wulf, "The Economic Impact of the Arms Sector in Developing Countries," *Development and Peace*, 5 (1984), pp. 114-125.

6.   Wulf, *Developing Countries*, p. 326, Table 10.4, column 3.

7.   Wulf, *Developing Countries*, p. 326, Table 10.4, column 6.

8.   Wulf, *Developing Countries*, p. 321, Table 10.3.

9.   Ron Ayres, "Arms Production as a Form of Import- Substituting Industrialization: The Turkish Case," in *World Development*, Vol. II, No. 9, pp. 812-823, 1983.

10.   Stephanie Neuman, "Third World Military Industries," *International Organization*, Winter 1984, Vol. 38, No. 1.

11.   R. Looney and P.C. Frederiksen, "Profiles of Current Latin American Arms Producers," *International Organization*, Vol. 40, No. 3, Summer 1986.

12.   Several studies examine motivations of Third World military production and conclude political factors are the primary reason. See Albrecht et. al," Militarization, Arms Transfer and Arms Production in Peripheral Countries," *Journal of Peace Research*, Vol XII, No 3, 1975; Lock and Wulf, "Register of Arms Production in Developing Countries," Study Group on Armaments and Underdevelopment, March 1977, Hamburg; Moodie, "Defense Industries in the Third World," in Harkavy & Neuman, *Arms Transfers in the Third World*, (New York: Praeger, 1980); Oberg, "Third World Armament: Domestic Production in Israel, South Africa, Brazil, Argentina and India," *Instant Research on Peace and Violence*, Vol V, No.4 1975; Neuman, "International Stratification and Third World Military Industries, *Industrial Organization*, Winter 1984, Vol 38, No 1; Katz, "Understanding Arms Production in Developing Countries," *Arms Production in Developing Countries*, (Lexington, MA: Lexington Books, 1984).

13.   See Aaron Klieman, *Israel's Global Reach* (Washington, D.C.: Pergammon-Brassey's International Defense Publishers, 1985), Chapter 8, "Special Military Relationships" for a discussion of pariah states.

14.   Nicole Ball, "The Growth of Arms Production in the Third World," *National Forum*, Vol. 66, Fall 1986, pp. 24-27.

15.   Michael T. Klare, "The Unnoticed arms trade: Exports of conventional arms-making technology," *International Security*, Vol. 8, No.2, Fall 1983, pp. 68-90.

16.   Kenneth Timmerman, "Home Grown Arms Industry is By-Product of Changing Alliances," *International Herald Tribune*, June 29, 1988, p. 12.

17.   Ross Munro, "The Awakening of An Asian Power," *Time*, April 3, 1989, p. 34.

18.   Ross Munro, "The Awakening of An Asian Power," p. 32.

19.   Thomas W. Graham, "India," Katz, 1984, *Arms Production*.

20.   Brahma Cellaney, "India shoots for military self-sufficiency," *Christian Science Monitor*, Monday, March 21, 1989 p. 10.

21.   Mohammad El-Sayed Selim, "Egypt" in Katz, 1984, *Arms Production*.

22.   Michael Dunn, "Egypt: From Domestic Needs to Export Market," in Katz, *The Implications of Third World Military Industrialization*, (Lexington, MA: Lexington Books, 1986) p. 119.

23.   Andrew L. Ross, "The Philippines," in Katz, 1984.

24.   "Taking up arms against the free market" Latin American Weekly Report, WR7905 Nov. 30, 1979.

25.   "Taking up arms against the free market"; Carlos H. Waisman, "Argentina: Economic and Political Implications in Katz, 1986, p. 93 says that this is equivalent to 14 percent of manufacturing GDP.

26.   Guillermo Lassaga, "Fabricaciones Militares crescimiento o desaparación?," *Realidade Econômica* No.6, January 1986, pp. 77-81.

27.   Herbert Wulf, "Arms Production in the Third World," Christian Schmidt (ed) *The Economics of Military Expenditures* (New York: St. Martins, 1987) pp 104-134; quote from p. 374.
28.   Edward S. Milenky, "Arms Production and National Security in Argentina," *Journal of Interamerican Studies and World Affairs*, Vol. 22, No. 3, August 1980, p. 273.
29.   Jacquelyn S. Porth, "Argentina," in Katz, *Arms Production*, 1984, p. 66.
30.   In SIPRI, *1987 Yearbook*, cites Latin American Weekly Report, WR-87-02 (January 15, 1987, p. 8)
31.   Jacquelyn S. Porth, "Argentina;" also "Os militares argentinos testam um novo míssil," *Estado de São Paulo*, July 2, 1989, p. 8.
32.   Paul W. Zayorski, "Civil-Military Relations in Argentina," *Armed Forces and Society*, Vol. 14, No. 3, Spring 1988.
33.   Jorge Félix Neuñez Padín, "Argentina expande exportações," *Segurança e Defesa*, No. 21, Ano 1988, p. 30.
34.   Maurício Dorrêa, "Indústria bélica da Argentina preocupa militares brasileiros," *Jornal do Brasil*, September 26, 1988.
35.   Roberto Godoy, "Equador dá preferência a tanque da Argentina," *Estado de São Paulo*, May 26, 1988.
36.   Ulrich Albrecht, "The Federal Republic of Germany and Italy: New Strategies of Mid-sized Weapons Exporters? *Journal of International Affairs*, Vol. 40, Summer 1986, p. 140.
37.   Jorge Félix Neuñez Padín, "Argentina expande exportações," *Segurança e Defesa*, No. 21, Ano 1988, p. 30.
38.   SIPRI, 1987.
39.   "China's Arms Industry Finds a World Market," *Defense and Foreign Affairs*, June 1985.
40.   Ibid.
41.   David L. Shambaugh, "China's Defense Industries," Indigenous and Foreign Procurement," Chapter 3 in Paul H. B. Godwin, *The Chinese Defense Establishment: Continuity and Change in the 1980s* (Boulder, CO: Westview Press, 1983).
42.   Nolan, *Military Industry in Taiwan and South Korea*, pp. 49-51.
43.   Ibid.
44.   G. Steinman, "Israel," in N. Ball and M. Leitenburg, *The Structure of the Defense Industry*, (New York: St. Martin's Press, 1983) p. 286. Also see A. S. Klieman's *Israel's Global Reach: Arms Sales as Diplomacy*.
45.   Bishoara A. Bahbah, "Israel's Private Arms Network," *Middle East Report*, February 17, 1987, pp. 9-10.
46.   Christian Catrina, *Arms Transfers and Dependence* (New York: Taylor and Francis, 1988).
47.   Sheila Ryan, "U.S. Military Contractors in Israel," *Middle East Report*, January-February 1987, pp. 17-22.
48.   Ibid.
49.   SIPRI Yearbook 1987, p. 199.
50.   Thomas Ohlson, "Third World Arms Exporters—A New Facet of the Global Arms Race," *Bulletin of Peace Proposals*, 13, No. 3, 1982.

51. T. Riddell makes this argument in "Concentration and Inefficiency in the Defense Sector," *Journal of Economic Issues*, Volume 19, June 1985, pp. 451-461.

4

Historical Development of the
Defense Industry's
Economic Rationale

The late 1960s were opportune to mobilize the Brazilian armaments industry. The military coup of 1964 and an era of unprecedented growth created a supportive political climate for defense industrialization. But the Brazilian armaments industry was not created solely by the military elite. Rather, it is the result of the interaction of political, military and economic forces underlying Brazilian modernization.

Brazilian military strategists have long appreciated the potential economic benefits of indigenous production, clearly articulating a political and military ideology to support defense industrialization. "Segurança Nacional," the vision of national security embracing economic, political and military dimensions which provided the conceptual justification for initiating an armaments sector was first articulated at the turn of the 20th century. Following this blueprint, the industrialization policies of the Vargas Administration (1930-1954) were oriented toward developing a military industrial sector. As Hilton argues:

> The creation of a "military-industrial complex," one of the striking offshoots of Brazil's remarkable economic development in recent times, was not accidental . . . the drive for general self-sufficiency has been a major component of Brazilian national strategy for fifty years, but that drive, along with its complementary campaign for arms autonomy, has deep roots in elite perceptions of national needs and in Brazil's experiences with arms dependence during the turbulent first half of the century.[1]

The Brazilian armaments industry did not simply spring up as a result of military governance, but has been part of the Brazilian economic model of development over time. The industry is therefore not an enclave, but is integrated with Brazil's industrial structure.

This section discusses the ideological antecedents of the armaments industry in Brazil, analyzing the concept of "segurança nacional" and the role of the Superior War College (ESG) in institutionalizing it. It shows how the broad definition of national security to include economic security shaped a military industry strongly tied to civilian industrial production. Chapter 5 later argues that this emphasis on economic political and military determinants predisposed the armaments sector toward state support, yet permitted independent microeconomic decisions. This strong economic component in national security differentiated the Brazilian experience from other nations.

The multidimensional definition of national security began with Alberto Torres' two books of 1914, *O Problema Nacional Brasileiro* and *Organização Nacional* where he argued that true political sovereignty was preceded by economic development.[2]   But such development necessitated the formation of strong state leadership.[3] Domestic political energies needed to be channeled toward well structured economic ends to achieve the industrial prowess for international political recognition. Fragmented domestic political systems had to be transformed into effective agents of economic change. Torres called for the creation of an institution transcending political parties with the strength and legitimacy to implement a broad national development program. Economic progress would in turn enhance domestic security by encouraging cohesion and stability and by fostering international perceptions of Brazil as a world power.

The military strategist, General Pedro A. de Goes Monteiro, elaborated on this call for a comprehensive national strategy, charging the army with responsibility for economic production, moral development, education and the formation of a national consciousness. He says:

> The politics of the army and the preparation for war interests involves all levels of national activity; in the material sphere – that which refers to the economy, to the production of goods and resources of all kinds – and in the moral sphere, above all that which concerns the education of the people and the formation of a consciousness that puts before everything the interests of the nation.[4]

The army was thus placed at the center of the development process. Its mandate was to be the guiding hand of the moral economy — to foster a sense of nationhood leading to wealth and greatness. Because the armed forces was the only strong national organization, Monteiro argued that its sole objective must be the "greatness of the common homeland" where greatness was broadly defined to include economic social as well as military objectives. He says:

> What is necessary is to construct the perfect country, in order that afterwards the perfect army may be organized. They [the armed forces] do not appear before the fact of development; they arise as a result of the material and cultural development of the country. An efficient army does not exist in a poor country.[5]

The seeming contradiction between the huge burden Monteiro places on the armed forces as an agent of development and the prerequisite of development for efficient force organization can be resolved by perceiving the army as a changing entity. They are the group capable of organizing the political will critical to industrial growth. As the economy matures, however, the function of political mobilization is to be superseded by more professional military concerns. A well equipped, modern army could only be supported by a healthy industrial structure. Thus, the development of the nation's political economy enhanced the Army's potential. A powerful army in an economically weak and underdeveloped nation seemed impossible to Monteiro. The task to achieve true national security was economic development.

Experience in the first World War reinforced the arguments for economic development as a prong in national security. Vulnerability in arms supplies made obvious the need for domestic procurement. But national production hinged upon the creation of basic industries such a steel.[6] Broadly viewing arms production as part of a larger industrialization strategy, the state was called upon "whatever the sacrifices required" to organize production in the military sector.[7]

Brazil's participation in World War II was in good measure precipitated not by dislike for the Nazis but by pursuit of national development and international prestige. Indeed, prior to the outbreak of the war, Brazil maintained strong ties with Germany through weapons purchases. In 1939, for example, Brazil signed a $55 million agreement with Krupp for artillery and accessories as part of a 5-year rearmament effort.[8] Although Brazil received several shipments, the war left Brazil with little choice but to turn to the United States. The U.S. desperately needed a long list of natural resources and air and naval bases in the South Atlantic. Brazilian President Vargas resourcefully exchanged these for American assistance in constructing the largest steel mill in South America at Volta Redonda.[9] This agreement proved critical to prepare the Brazilian industrial base for armaments production two decades later.

The war made obvious Brazil's dependence on foreign arms suppliers. With priority given to American and European forces, Brazilians rarely received requested armaments. Insulted, the military felt national security was gravely compromised by this subservient, second-rate position. Said President Vargas:

> Our first lesson from the present war was that only the countries which can really be considered military powers are those sufficiently industrialized and able to produce within their own frontiers the war materials they need.[10]

Participation in the war confirmed the belief that true national power was vested in indigenous industrial capacity to produce armaments. However, economic growth and technological change transformed the art of war, making it as dependent upon industrial inputs as military strategy. Reflecting upon his experiences in World War II, President Castello Branco stated:

> The industrial revolution made war much more technical, and highlighted the importance of economic development as an element of security. This importance of development for security is a result of modern industrial abilities.[11]

Thus, industrialization was a prerequisite to military power. This argument that economic and political development was integral to national security found an institutional home in the Superior War College, ESG. Created by federal law on August 20, 1949, ESG was conceived as an "Institute of Higher Studies" for planning and directing national security.[12] The ideas of Goes Monteiro finally assumed concrete form.[13]

The dominant concern of ESG was to bring civilian and military personnel together to achieve national security through rapid industrialization. Four precepts were established. The first expanded defense to include economic and political security. As ESG became the articulator of development policy for Brazil, this broad concept of national security often legitimized painful economic and political programs in the name of defense. This influence also mobilized financial and political support for the development of a military industrial complex in Brazil.

Secondly, ESG underscored the natural wealth of Brazil, arguing that it possessed resources and geopolitical endowments to be a world power. Military strategists such as Meira Mattos adhered to the geopolitical school of Haufshofer's "lebenstraum" or "vital space" and Ratzel's "Space is power,"[14] believing Brazil's strategic geographic location and vast resources destined the country to dominate Latin America and Western Africa. Not coincidentally, these areas later became a natural market for Brazil's armaments industry.

To explain Brazil's lack of international prestige, the third belief ESG supported was that the nation was retarded by the incapacity of the federal government to formulate and execute a national development strategy. Weakened by internal divisions among political groups and minus effective power, civilian governments were not able to mobilize resources to achieve Brazil's potential.

This necessitated the fourth change, elaboration of a process to formulate national policy within a rigorous scientific establishment able to order and implement national priorities. Proponents perceived that the military, particularly ESG, could best specify a development · policy consistent with the precepts of national security, greatness and efficient governance. This succinctly defined ESG's agenda for the following 25 years and became branded "developmental nationalism."

Although developmental nationalism enjoyed favor from 1949 through 1964, ESG as an institution exerted little direct influence in government. Rather, it continued to train civilian and military elites in the doctrine of security and development, to prepare them to become the major institutional actors in Brazil:

> Rarely if ever has one educational institution, in less than two decades of existence, had so profound an impact upon the course of a nation's development...By 1955, nearly half the new general officers had been through it, and by 1962 the proportion had risen to nearly 80%. At the time of the 1964 coup, nearly two- thirds of the active duty generals were ESG graduates.[15]

With the 1964 military coup, the ESG program was put into practice by the new chief, Castello Branco and his principal counselors:

> When the Revolution of 1964 arrived, the doctrine of the Superior War College was already formulated and exercised in laboratory or academic terms. It was easy for the Chief of the Revolution, President Castello Branco and his principal accessories Golberry, Ernesto Geisel, Juarez Tavora, Cordeiro Farias, all ex-military men, active participants in the formulation of this doctrine [of national security] as they had participated in the framework of ESG, to transform into governmental practice the doctrine formulated during the fourteen years in the large house at Fort São João.[16]

"Segurança Nacional" was the motto of the military administration. As President Castello Branco emphasized in his inaugural lecture to ESG in 1967, ". . .'Segurança Nacional' is the doctrine of our program, in its essence, it is the new Brazilian constitution and modern law."[17] Article 7 of Decree No.200, the Law of Administrative Reform, consecrated "development and security" as the government's official slogan. It stated:

> Governmental action will obey the plan destined to promote the economic and social development of the country and national security.[18]

In tandem with the goal of industrial promotion was the perceived threat of internal subversion by leftist guerilla forces.[19] The law presented a development strategy to become a powerful industrial nation, enhance military capabilities and international prestige. In practice the military modified the law to attend to what it defined as violations of national security, subversive forces undermining the nation. Says Castello Branco:

> . . . the concept of national security is far-reaching. We understand it as the global defense of institutions, incorporating by this psycho-social aspects, the preservation of development and of internal political stability. In addition to this, the concept of security is much more than strictly defense, taking into account the internal aggression embodied in infiltration and subversive ideology, of the guerrilla movements motivated most probably by external forces.[20]

Thus, in addition to development, the military defined its mission as safeguarding Brazil from the so-called subversive influences of communism. According to the military, Brazil faced a dual crisis. Internationally, Washington's declaration of Cold War called it to guard against Soviet infiltration. The Soviet presence in Castro's Cuba was regionally unsettling. Domestically, the military waged war against those it perceived as subversive, leftist rebels seeking to undermine the glory and good of Brazil.

Addressing ESG in 1976, the Brazilian Joint Chief of Staff General Antonio Jorge Correa emphasized the military's unconditional acceptance of segurança nacional.[21] Categorically stating "the binomium 'Development and Security' is the essence of the Revolutionary doctrine," he qualified national security as more than military security. Development was the key to Brazilian security—development defined to include economic social, political and military dimensions. Nevertheless, exception to the "undeniable dominance" of development over security was justified during crisis —the condition the military believed dominated the epoch.

Increasing repression of the population under the military regime threatened to destabilize the balance between military and economic components of national security. While in one breath the military government was preaching the miracle of economic development, in the next it was looking to drain the treasury to re-equip the armed forces. As repressive tactics escalated, the demand for counterinsurgency weapons increased. The classic tradeoff between guns and butter was felt in Brazil. The national mobilization plan to re-equip the armed forces attempted to resolve this contradiction between economic development and national security:

> A powerful instrument at the disposal of the government, national mobilization may be used in situations of emergency to assemble a set of activities organized by the State, aiming, compulsorily and rapidly, to transfer existing resources and to promote the opportune production of additional means, to attend to the serious situations related to National Security.[22]

National mobilization sought to achieve two goals simultaneously: industrial development through defense production and rapid equipment of the armed forces. State intervention in the name of military preparedness would serve to promote industrial growth. Industrial development would permit a permanent stream of defense supplies. Thus, both elements of the revered security doctrine could simultaneously be upheld.

In the 1970s the strategic mission of the Brazilian military changed its focus to include the technological revolution in warfare.[23] In addition to an increasingly external orientation directed at relations with Argentina and the Soviet presence in the South Atlantic, the military high command became preoccupied with technological advance and the control of industrialized nations over key military applications. Indeed, we will see in Chapter 8 that this initial preoccupation with technology has assumed increasing importance for the Brazilian military. Rejecting the possibility of an external enemy in the short run, strategists now point to technological development as a principle goal for enhancing national security and the *raison d'être* of the Brazilian defense industry.

Focus on the economic elements of national security indeed promoted the formulation of an industrial base as well as prompted the expansion of the defense sector. As demonstrated in the last chapter, this stands in contrast to the experience of other third world producers who highlighted the military and strategic components of national security without incorporating the economic element. The next chapter characterizes the specific form of the Brazilian industry took under the ideology of security and development.

Notes

1.   Hilton, Stanley, in "The Armed Forces and Industrialists in Modern Brazil: The Drive for Military Autonomy (1889-1954)," *Hispanic American Historical Review*, Vol.62, No. 4, 1982, pp. 629-673.

2   "Origens Nacionais da Doutrina da ESG," *Convivium*, Ano XVII, Vol. 22, 1979, pp. 514-518.

3.   Frank D. McCann, Jr.,"The Formative Period of Twentieth Century Brazilian Army Thought, 1900-1922," *Hispanic American Historical Review*, Vol. 64, No. 4, 1984, p. 762.

4.   Monteiro, Goes, "A Revolução de 30 e a Finalidade Política do Exército," in Edmundo Campos Coelho, *Em Busca da Identidade: O Exército e a Política na Sociedade Brasiliera*, (Rio de Janeiro: Forense Universitária, 1976.)

5.   See Frank D. McCann, Jr., "Origins of the New Professionalism of the Brazilian Military," *Journal of Interamerican Studies & World Affairs*, Vol. 21, No. 4, Nov 1979.

6.   McCann, "Brazilian Army Thought," p. 760.

7.   Brazilian president Delfin Moreira de Costa Ribeiro in 1919 Message to Congress, as quoted in McCann, "Brazilian Army Thought," p. 761.

8.   See McCann, "The Brazilian Army and the Problem of Mission 1939-1964," *Journal of Latin American Studies* Vol. 12, No. I, 1980 for an excellent discussion of this period.

9.   In McCann, "The Brazilian Army and the Problem of Mission 1939-1964."

10.   In McCann, "A Influência Estrangeira no Exército Brasileiro, 1905-1945," *A Revolução de 30*, Seminário realizado pelo Centro de Pesquisa e Documentacão de História Contemporânea do Brasil (CPDOC) da Fundacão Getulio Vargas, Rio de Janeiro, September 1980, (Editora Universidade de Brasília, 1983).

11.   Quoted in Gen. Meira Mattos, *Brasil: Geopolítica e Destino*, (Rio de Janeiro: Livraria José Olympio Editora, 1979).

12.   General de Exército Antonio Jorge Correa, Ministro Chefe do EMFA, in the inaugural lecture of ESG for 1976; reprinted in *Segurança e Desenvolvimento*, No. 163, 1976.

13.   Edmundo Campos Coelho, *Em Busca da Identidade: O Exército e a Política na Sociedade Brasiliera*, (Rio de Janeiro: Forense Universitária, 1976) makes this argument.

14.   General Meira Mattos, *Brasil: Geopolítica e Destino* and "Origens Nacionais da Doutrina da ESG."

15.   Ronald M. Schneider, *The Political System of Brazil: Emergence of a "Modernizing Authoritarian Regime," 1964-1970*, New York, 1971.

16.   Mattos, *Brasil: Geopolitica e Destino.*

17.   Ibid.

18.   General Antonio Jorge Correa, Ministro Chefe do EMFA, "A Influência da ESG no Pensamento Político e Estratégico das Elites Brasileiras," inaugural lecture at ESG, reprinted in *Segurança e Desenvolvimento*, No 163, 1976.

19.   See Stanley Hilton, "The Brazilian Military: Changing Strategic Perceptions and the Question of Mission," *Armed Forces and Society 1987*, Vol. 13, No. 3, Spring, pp. 329-351, for a discussion of the period.

20.   Meira Mattos, *Brasil: Geopolítica e Destino.*

21.   Correa, "A Influência da ESG."

22.   Ibid.

23.   Hilton, "*The Brazilian Military.*"

5

The State in
Defense Industrialization

While the Brazilian defense industry is differentiated from other Third World arms producers by minimal political and military control, the state does play an economic role in armaments production. The behavior of the state in the Brazilian defense sector may be described as entrepreneurial. Freeman and Duvall distinguish the entrepreneurial state as one where "there is direct state control of commercial noninfrastructure enterprise and agents of the state substitute for private entrepreneurs in operating such enterprises in substantial part according to standard business criteria."[1]

This chapter investigates the economic basis for entrepreneurial state intervention in the Brazilian arms industry and describes the dynamic partnership between government organs and the leading firms to promote technology, exports and industrial expansion. It is argued that the Brazilian state supplements and does not supplant the activities of the firm. The state and the firm each perform the economic tasks in which they have a comparative advantage. Activity in the sector, then, is not divided on the basis of public or private ownership but rather by asking how best to get the job done. Thus, at times state firms behave "as if private" and private firms rely upon the state. By not focusing upon patterns of ownership but upon the most efficacious manner of completing a task, the state has enhanced its ability to act as an entrepreneur. That is, it is best able to create opportunities for economic returns for both public and private enterprise by assuming those tasks which complement the efforts of the firm.

The Rationale for State Intervention

Why do states assume entrepreneurial roles? Jones suggests four reasons for establishing public enterprises: ideology, acquisition or consolidation of political or economic power, a pragmatic response to economic problems and historical inertia.[2]   Ideologically, state intervention in the Brazilian economy is legitimized by developmental nationalism. Stepan describes the state as having a moral obligation to supplement the workings of the market with all available means.[3] While according a significant role to the private sector, the developmental nationalists argued that the state must promote growth through (1) intervention in large-scale projects, (2) nationalization or control of industries such as oil and steel and (3) fiscal and monetary mediation.   As demonstrated in chapter 4, which discussed the historical foundations of the industry's development, the power to implement the ideology of nationalism was consolidated in the Superior War College and implemented nationally after the 1964 coup. Developmental nationalism is a radical departure from economic liberalism in its emphasis on intervention, control and planning. Although some contend that the free market generates lower prices, higher output, minimum costs and a fairer distribution of economic returns than a system characterized by state intervention, these benefits were not part of the Brazilian experience. While ideally free markets were preferable, nationalists perceived state intervention as a pragmatic response to the failures of the laissez-faire model. As Glade suggests, the basis for state participation in Brazil was grounded in a fundamental "dissatisfaction with the decisions that automatically result from the free play of market forces."[4]   Indeed Dye and Souza write, "one of the most salient features of the Brazilian political model is precisely the rationalization of the state apparatus for the purpose of stimulating the growth of the private economy."[5] Thus ideology, consolidation and pragmatism help explain the development of the armaments industry in Brazil.[6]

Trebat's conceptualization of the role of the state in Brazil further expands our understanding of the development of the industry. He considers six hypotheses which explain state activity:

- Weak private sector hypothesis
- Economies of scale hypothesis
- External economies hypothesis
- Dynamic public managers hypothesis
- Natural resource rents hypothesis
- Public-historical hypothesis [7]

In steel, electrical energy and telecommunications, public enterprises were inaugurated only after the private sector failure. Large investments in industries where economies of scale determined viability provided further grounds for state participation. In railroads, electrical energy, port facilities, shipping and heavy construction, industries of significant public importance, external economies came into play. In tourism, engineering and data processing, it was argued that public firms were more dynamic and commercially successful. The natural resource rents hypothesis was invoked in mining iron and bauxite and in petroleum to allow state appropriation of profits.

Intervention in the armaments industry follows the general pattern of state activity hypothesized by Trebat. A weak private sector, defense as a public good, economies of scale, dynamic public managers and political factors shaped state involvement. These factors are now discussed in turn for their relevance in explaining state intervention in the Brazilian defense sector.

Until the 1960s, arms production in Brazil was characterized by *private market failure.* In the beginning of the century there were three inefficient munitions plants, one producing cartridges and two for gunpowder. The military tried to expand the sector with imports of German machinery; however, this expensive endeavor was hindered by a scarcity of technicians. In ensuing decades leaders urged domestic production after suffering from shortages during crises. World War I made apparent Brazil's dependent position in armaments markets. As an Army spokesman argued in 1917:

> We need to manufacture our explosives and powders, our rifles and machine guns; cast our cannon and battleships; build our vessels, our airplanes and dirigibles, our submarines and minesweepers, make our canned goods and fodder; weave our cloth, [and produce] our gear and utensils, from the raw material to the delicate finishing touch.[8]

In 1919 President Delfim Moreira ordered military industries organized "whatever the sacrifices required."[9] Despite these declarations, it was argued that whenever possible production is best left to the private sector. Finance Minister João P. Calogeras, an outspoken advocate of autonomy, cautioned that "the only thing that we can and should do is stimulate production by guaranteeing a market."[10] Many Brazilians believed that as in the U.S., private initiative could meet the security needs of the nation. But experience proved that a wholly private organization was not possible for Brazil. Domestic industries delivered shoes, dishes, building materials and paper to the armed forces, but production of weapons remained extremely weak.[11] The private sector was unable to muster the finances or master the technology for full-scale production.

Notwithstanding poor performance, private procurement was adhered to. Further deficiencies resulted, including the disastrous São Paulo revolt of 1932. To wage this civil war over constitutional issues, Brazil placed orders for armaments in eight countries. When the material was not received until after the fighting ended, Vargas and military elites renewed their pledge to expand domestic capabilities, marking a turning point against private control. New machinery was ordered from Germany to equip federal plants to make ammunition, rifle barrels, and artillery shells. Vargas established three state war plants, arguing that a "military industrial complex would serve as a stimulus to steel production and to subsidiary civilian industries."[12] Achievements of the period included the formation of the National Steel Commission (CSN), a civilian-military body under the Ministry of War to examine industrial possibilities for Brazil's iron ore. Plans for an aircraft factory matured and a contract was awarded to the French-Brazilian firm of Construções Aeronauticas in 1939 for an aircraft plant in Minais Gerais.

Despite Vargas' achievements, some continued to argue for private production. Minister of Finance Oswaldo Aranha said

> he was radically opposed to federal production of aircraft, artillery, machine guns and the like. Private industry, having guaranteed consumption, and with small initial favors, can and should manufacture all this and with great advantages.[13]

Yet ironically these "small initial favors" were substantial, including technical information, machines, engineers, tax exemptions and federal loans. The statutes of the Bank of Brazil were rewritten in 1939 to establish private factories for national defense.[14] Both the army, through its technical school and the newly created Army Technical and Production Department (DPTE), and the Air Force through the Aeronautical Technical Center (CTA), trained technicians. The CTA installed an aeronautical park in São Jose dos Campos providing "great laboratories for the development of industries in general."[15]

But success was limited; a comprehensive program was necessary, particularly in the aviation sector where private endeavors had repeatedly failed. By 1966, a Ministry of Aeronautics study concluded that only the public sector could support a viable aviation industry in Brazil.[16] Indeed, that the CTA's tender in 1968 of a completed prototype and an initial order of eighty units for commercialization went unanswered by the private market confirmed the Ministry's position. Therefore, despite lingering opposition to public ownership, EMBRAER was created as a mixed economic enterprise in August 1969 and IMBEL, the state corporation coordinating and producing munitions and armored vehicles, was formed in 1975. Cross-country evidence reinforces this conclusion; British Aerospace, French SNIAS and all Italian producers with the exception of Piaggio and Aermacchi are state owned.[17] Bluestone contends that

> without the Federal government, there would simply be no aircraft industry . . . No aspect of the industry, including the commercial sector, could exist without the research and development funds provided by the state or the state's purchases of military equipment.[18]

Weak private markets were not the sole cause of state intervention. The second of Trebat's criteria applied to state activity in arms production is the nature of *defense as a public good.* Two components of the public good argument compel intervention: the product is indivisible and the state must ensure its delivery in the event of private market failure. Defense is the classic public good, not divisible into shares paid for according to individual preference.[19] The demand for defense is therefore articulated politically. In *The Wealth of Nations* Adam Smith points to defense as the first duty of government.[20] If, as demonstrated above, the private sector cannot transform financial and physical resources into the weapons perceived to be necessary for defense, it falls within the purview of the state to take an active economic role in the provision of this public good.

Economies of scale in the defense industry also dispose it to state intervention. Economies of scale exist when, by definition, all input quantities are doubled and output increases by more than twofold. The greater fixed costs, the higher the level of output at which increasing returns occur. Thus, if the market size is less than twice the minimum necessary for increasing returns, monopolization is efficient. Where costs exceed potential returns or strict regulation is required, nationalization is suggested. Do armaments industries indicate economies of scale? Olvey argues scale economies exist in defense firms due to sophisticated machinery and research and development.[21] Kennedy says:

> Defense contractors are large corporations because it is only in this size of organization that defense contracting in major weapon systems is possible. A large aircraft company developing a new combat fighter can

have several design teams operating in parallel on specific aspects of the project which would be beyond the means of a small company.[22]

While the scale for defense production is large, the demand for arms in Brazil is small. Brazil's 1982 military expenditure of US$ 2,576 million (.9% of GNP) is substantially lower than U.S. outlays of US$ 196,390 million (6.1% of GNP) or Italy's budget of US$ 10,167 million (2.7% of GNP).[23] Said the Estado de São Paulo:

> . . . it is an old idea to implement in Brazil a program of import substitution of military equipment. Nevertheless, the existence of a small limited cyclical market, as well as the limited size of our Armed Forces was always the impediment to the concretization of this dream. [24]

Given increasing returns, the scale for arms production in Brazil is the entire national market. High fixed costs and expensive research and development means losses in the sector in the absence subsidies. Thus, economies of scale have predisposed the Brazilian sector toward active state participation.

Trebat points to the benefits of *public management* of state firms. Without Ozires Silva's leadership it is doubtful whether EMBRAER would have attained such success. The driving force behind the creation of the company, he mobilized political support in the CTA, the Air Force Ministry and Brasília. Singled out as one of Brazil's most capable entrepreneurs, he later held the post of president of Petrobras, the state-owned Brazilian oil firm. Subsequently he assumed the position of Minister of Infrastructure in the Collor government. The magazine *Veja* said Silva

> differentiated himself from all other directors of government firms by his definitively "privatist" approach to management and his conviction that a state firm is not a public welfare agency. . . . Brazil needs a competent team to administer a giant the size of Petrobras. There aren't many Ozires in the plaza. The choice of his name is a good bet. [25]

Trebat's hypotheses go far in explaining why the Brazilian state intervened in the defense industry. Intervention took place only after private sector failure and was targeted to take advantage of economies of scale and the talents of public managers. But state control was not imposed on all defense firms—just where it was necessary. The philosophy that private initiative was the preferred structure prevailed. Where that failed, given the politico-military demand for autonomous procurement, state intervention in the defense sector was pursued as a second best alternative.

Patterns of State Intervention
in the Defense Sector

Having established the reasons why the state intervened in the armaments industry, we now turn to examine the institutional pattern of intervention.

Specifically, this chapter refers to four types of state activity in the defense sector: outright state ownership; joint ventures with private firms; the operation of technology centers; and fiscal promotion. Ownership broadly refers to that group of firms called public enterprises. A public enterprise is an organization in which 50% ownership is held by state authorities, the top management is appointed or controlled by public authorities, is established for a public purpose, is engaged in a business activity in which it markets goods and services and earns financial returns.[26]

In this study of defense production in Brazil, both EMBRAER and IMBEL are categorized as public enterprises. State intervention, however, extends beyond the scope of these two public firms. In particular, we consider the relationship between ENGESA and IMBEL as a joint venture between the public IMBEL and the private ENGESA for the purpose of international marketing. The third category of state intervention is through the research and technical centers. The structure of the air force and army technical center is differentiated from that of a public enterprise in that its purpose is not to produce a commodity for sale in a market but rather to support the activities of other firms and promote industrial development. This third form of state intervention, unlike the first two, is not directed at securing a financial return for itself but toward improving the position of other public or private firms. Finally, the fourth form, financial intervention, is distinguished by the absence of direct productive activity—making a plane or designing a missile—as well as the lack of sector-specific institutes of administration. That is to say, financial intervention in the defense sector has largely been part of a broad package of incentives administered to public and private firms or research institutes through multi-purpose funding agencies.

A central argument of this book is that despite the ownership characteristics of the defense firm—public EMBRAER or private ENGESA and AVIBRAS—the state has consistently promoted the strengths of the firms and worked to supplement the weaknesses in the sector. Whether through joint ventures, research and technical centers or through financial intervention, the cases presented illustrate the varying combinations of public and private efforts to promote the defense industry.

The following sections discuss three patterns of state entrepreneurship. First we consider the case of the state aerospace technical center, CTA, and the public enterprise EMBRAER. CTA is considered the "father" of the firm, but has dynamically adapted as the firm has matured and its needs have changed. The second case involves the partnership during the early 1980s between the private ENGESA and the public enterprise IMBEL. To compete more effectively in international markets in the early 1980s, IMBEL was placed temporarily under ENGESA's management, bringing with it the political advantages of a public concern. By the beginning of the nineties, the position was reversed, with state owned IMBEL likely to oversee ENGESA's operations. In both cases we note the complementary, cooperative behavior between state institutions and the firms and a relationship that changed over time. Irrespective of the ownership status of the firms, the state has promoted industrial expansion. This evenhandedness is also noted in the allocation of fiscal incentives to the firms, the third pattern examined. In all cases, the state allowed the firm to perform the duties to which it was best suited and supplemented these efforts with public support where appropriate.

The Aerospace Technical Center: Parenting an Industry

The relationship between EMBRAER and the CTA is prototypical of an efficient, harmonious division of labor between a firm and a governmental institution. Indeed the President of EMBRAER, Ozires Silva, describes the CTA as a father to the firm.[27] That the CTA and EMBRAER, a mixed economic enterprise, both fall under the Ministry of Aeronautics certainly facilitates interaction. The institutional goals of the CTA are to train aeronautical engineers, to perform aviation research and to foster the growth of supplier firms by transferring new products and processes to the private sector. This triad of education, research and industrial promotion reflects an institutional philosophy that the CTA should only perform those tasks outside the capabilities of private industry.

The training function is fulfilled by the ITA, the Aerospace Technical Institute. A respected intellectual force since 1950, it has graduated over 72,200 engineers and given 300 postgraduate degrees.[28] Indeed, most captains of the Brazilian aerospace industry are ITA graduates.

AVIBRAS, for example, was formed by ITA alumni; the management of EMBRAER is likewise trained.

The IPD, the Institute of Research and Development, holds up the research end of the CTA triangle, upgrading design capabilities and developing aeronautical processes and products. Divisions within IPD include Aeronautics (PAR), Electronics (PEA), Materials (PMD), and Mechanics (PMO). Current research is diverse, ranging from a helicopter design to the viability of using balloons to transport heavy cargo. The IAE, the Institute of Space Activities, is responsible for R&D in the space sector. The IAE has six divisions: Launching (EDL), Weaponry (ESB), Atmosphere Sciences (ECA), Chemistry (EDQ), and Advanced Studies (EAV), working in pure and applied science. AVIBRAS has benefitted from the activities of the IAE.[29] Together they developed a solid rocket propellent with two key uses: to fuel the early stages of the CTA's SONDA rocket program and to motor the commercially successful AVIBRAS rockets. Expertise garnered in partnership with CTA refined the engineering capabilities of AVIBRAS, promoting innovative techniques later applied to private market activities.

The Institute of Industrial Coordination and Promotion (IFI) acts as a liaison between the CTA and the private sector to detect opportunities and deficiencies in the aeronautics industry, analyze them, propose solutions and facilitate development. It is also concerned with quality control and certification, developing standards, norms and measurements.

These CTA institutes supplement the activities of the firm. Particularly during the earliest years of EMBRAER's history, it was necessary to provide support in training, research, testing and development while the firm mastered production and marketing techniques. With the successful creation of EMBRAER and the launching of the two pilot projects, the Bandeirante and the Ipanema, CTA's role in aerospace was questioned in the late 1970s. With EMBRAER ready to begin in-house R&D, some argued the CTA should specialize in pure science. In addition, however, the "Basic Planning Directives" of the third National Development Plan (PNDIII) designated two new roles for CTA: setting national aviation standards, testing, and promoting aviation supplier firms.[30] The specific form of technology transfer is considered in the following chapter. What is highlighted here is the changed role of CTA in promoting defense industrialization in Brazil. We now turn to analyze this problem of expanding aeronautical suppliers as the lack of domestically produced parts and subsystems currently represents the greatest challenge to Brazilian aviation. The joint action of the CTA and EMBRAER to promote industrial expansion illustrates the changing relationship, from paternalism to partnership, between the state agency and the firm.

EMBRAER's operations presented the opportunity to create an aeronautical complex in Brazil. Says CTA engineer Damiani:

> In the wake of the development of the Bandeirante and Embraer arose opportunities for the amplification of the national aerospace park, motivated in the form of backward linkages.[31]

But the simple existence of EMBRAER did not automatically generate industrial growth. Impeded by the need for sophisticated technologies, limited domestic demand and barriers to international marketing, market expansion has been slow, with 356 firms producing 3,395 products, mostly parts with low unit values.[32] Only 188 of the 356 are certified to produce items directly entering EMBRAER's production line such as electrical and steel cables, metal plates and molds, instruments, tires, special dyes, plastics for the windows, antennae, and brakes.[33] Just ten sell complex equipment, including AEROMOT's alarm system and D. F Vasconcellos' sight finder for the EMB-Tucano.[34] As presented in Table 5.1, in a confidential questionnaire from the municipality of São José dos Campos, EMBRAER reported only six of seventeen critical inputs are produced in Brazil.

With few domestic suppliers, EMBRAER, exempt from duties, must import aircraft engines, landing gear, and avionics. Imported equipment and components exceeded $100 million in 1977, accounting for 41% of the Xavante, 27% of the Ipanema and between 47% and 71% of the various Piper models.[35] U.S. firms had the largest share, supplying over $50 million of parts and avionics equipment.[36] Foreign inputs as a percentage of EMBRAER's costs are particularly high in the last stages of production.[37] Using the Bandeirante as an example, the first stage, the production of parts and assembly of the basic structure, requires 20,000 parts bought outside the firm equal to only 6% ($50,000) of the value of the aircraft. EMBRAER's greatest profits are accrued here; for every one dollar of parts purchases, it creates sixteen dollars' worth of merchandise. In the second production stage, construction after parts purchases until the aircraft is prepared for avionics, outside purchases increase by $110,000 or 14%, including 4,000 items from 150 firms, 70 domestic. Suppliers to the first and second stages thus divide $160,000 per aircraft, with less than half to national firms. Assembly is completed with sophisticated avionics accounting for 80% or $640,000 of EMBRAER's purchases. Approximately 20 companies sell these

TABLE 5.1
Suppliers to EMBRAER

Item	Supplier	National	Foreign
Assembly kits			
light aircraft	Piper	na*	USA
jet aircraft	Macchi	na	Italy
Aluminum plates	divers	na	USA
Connectors	diverse	na	USA
Molds	AISA	São Paulo	na
Steel bars	Villares	São Paulo	na
Precision tubes	Mannesman	Minais Gerais	na
INOX plates	diverse	na	USA
Bolts	diverse	São Paulo	USA
Nuts	diverse	na	USA
Plates	diverse	na	USA
Copper cable	Pizelli	São Paulo	na
Electronic relays	diverse	na	USA
Acrylic sheets	Naufal	São Paulo	na
Connectors	diverse	na	USA
Incision valves	Air Brake	na	USA
Rotaries to fasten aircraft	L'Hotelier	na	France

*na signifies not applicable
Source: Confidential report to Municipality of São José dos Campos.

systems and accompanying maintenance contracts; almost all are foreign. The U.S. alone exports 54% of the cost of materials for the Bandeirante.[38] The Brasília will be sold in the international market at a base price of $4.5 million; 40% of this price is for imports. The outer surface of the plane, for example, is an aluminum by ALCOA; pressurization is supplied by GARRET industries. COLLINS will produce radar equipment and the French ERAN the landing gear.[39]

Intensive reliance on imported components compromises the autonomy and procurement ability of Brazilian defense. The private market failed to meet the needs of EMBRAER. This threat to national security as well as the drain of hard currency for imports prompted a campaign for import substitution in the aeronautical park orchestrated by CTA. Its Institute for Industrial Promotion, IFI, is tasked with establishing a range of industries including engines, electronics, instruments, materials, communications, hydraulic systems, rocketry, and armaments. Support includes technical know-how, testing facilities, and development of industrial prototypes for private industry. The research arm, IPD, is developing motors and components, boarding systems, and other avionic parts and materials.[40] An initial project taken up by IFI was the indigenous development of a piston engine, the Lycoming 0-235 and the Pratt & Whitney PT-6 to gain the technical capacity to produce Brazilian motors for the Bandeirante. Although Project Motors successfully nationalized 46% of the value of the motor, it underscored the difficulty of quality control in aviation:

> . . . the level of quality control in the Brazilian industrial park may be characterized as sufficient to attend to the demands of the automobile industry. The production of the 0-235 and the PT-6 brought with them requirements for which the firms were unprepared, and forced IFI to strongly emphasize Quality Engineering, training personnel in the industry and supporting it in the implementation of systems of quality guarantees.[41]

EMBRAER and IFI's recent campaign to promote aviation suppliers is fraught with such difficulties. First is the problem of economies of scale in the small domestic market. For example, the firm made numerous appeals to domestic industry to develop a technologically simple product, lightweight carpeting for the Bandeirante. The request went unanswered due to the low quantity demanded. Even then President of EMBRAER Silva admitted it is a losing proposition as the firm rarely demands more than 60 sq.m. per month.[42]

To attain economies of scale, suppliers must market globally. But international aviation marketing is problematic. This strategy is viable for low technology items like carpeting but becomes difficult for precision parts or complex avionics which must be certified by the recipient country's aviation board. For example, to sell landing gear to the U.S., the Brazilian product must meet U.S. Federal Aviation Administration (FAA) approval. This is time-consuming and often thwarted by protectionism.

Furthermore, many potential suppliers are unfamiliar with international marketing strategies. At a November 1983 meeting titled "Industrial Opportunities in the Aerospace Sector" convened by EMBRAER and the CTA in conjunction with Caterpillar, AVIBRAS and ENGESA, smaller firms were alerted to opportunities in defense production. It was suggested that with leads from EMBRAER and technology and marketing support from CTA, firms could develop aviation products. Said Engineer Wanderley:

We believe very much in the spontaneous process, provoked by motivation, arriving in the right moment, coming to stay. In our opinion this is the only road to competency. . . . we decided some time back that we would not use the process of procuring national industry with a specimen in the hand, looking later to receive a prototype to verify that it served us.[43]

The ultimate responsibility would reside with the supplier to develop, produce, certify, commercialize and guarantee the product, including customary ten year maintenance and spare parts on location within seventy-two hours. EMBRAER would provide information on its needs and global demand for a given product, CTA would assist in development and marketing and the supplier would control production. To give further incentive to the exports of components, the Brazilian government required that foreign companies selling aircraft to Brazil must spend at least 10% of the purchase price on buying locally produced components over the payment period of the purchase.[44]

The proposal for private expansion in the supplier sector met some opposition. Representatives from small firms feared overseas marketing and the difficulties of securing trade agreements with aerospace conglomerates or foreign governments. They wanted assurances that investments in product development would pay off. EMBRAER and CTA could not make such promises. In contrast, arguments were made that EMBRAER should be used as a state vehicle to pump up the sagging industrial sector. Some considered defense production a cure, saying

EMBRAER could send part of its orders to the capital goods industry to reduce the idle capacity of that sector in light of the fabrication of military equipment.[45]

EMBRAER president Silva's response to this challenge was guarded, agreeing the conversion of the capital goods industry to military production is a "valid option" to reduce idle capacity "that no entrepreneur could throw out."[46] He was cautious, however, in using EMBRAER as an engine for the aeronautical sector. Promoting domestic suppliers is constrained by systems already in place in EMBRAER aircraft. Substitution of suppliers is difficult and must be taken on a case by case basis to maintain consistency. Military production demands a high level of quality control and it is a tightly staged process. Once a supplier is selected, the part is a piece in a complex electronic system. "It is not possible to easily change a supplier for another; It is marriage without divorce."[47] EMBRAER's engineer Wanderley says:

> Practically, complex systems such as the motor, the landing gear,
> pressurization, etc. will be difficult to be substituted in the short run
> without great penalties in costs. . . . It is a one shot decision.[48]

A new supplier should be introduced with a new product. The choice of
suppliers is also restricted by clients' specifications for foreign
components.[49] EMBRAER's continued use of foreign suppliers aroused
criticism from Brazilian firms. José Diniz de Souza, the president of
ELETROMETAL, a prominent supplier to ENGESA, charges that
EMBRAER acts contrary to the strategy of nationalization espoused by
the CTA. Diniz says ELETROMETAL supplies components for foreign
aircraft such as the Tristar, the Hercules and the Skyhawk, but has no
part in the Bandeirante.[50]

Silva countered that "the only manner of making the idea possible
would be through orders from the Armed Forces or for export."[51] That
is, the firm would not change suppliers in midstream on existing projects
without new orders from the Air Force or new foreign contracts. State
intervention was necessary to lower the transitional costs to new,
unproven supplier. Indeed this option was later pursued in the AMX
strike fighter program.

EMBRAER's reticence to respond rapidly to calls for nationalization
of the aviation industry is well placed caution. While in its own
interest to augment domestic suppliers, it is cognizant of difficulties in
international marketing. The parts and subsystems the firm uses must
be internationally certified or EMBRAER's planes will not fly abroad.
Brazilian suppliers must build a reputation, as EMBRAER has, for
quality at low cost. This cannot be done overnight and it is not likely to
be accomplished without the resolute assistance of the CTA. Just as the
market needed state support to create a viable aircraft producer,
assistance is necessary to expand industrial capacity. The next chapter
discusses how CTA supported technology acquisition in the supplier
sector. EMBRAER and CTA's program to substitute imports with
domestic inputs gradually is well conceived. Furthermore, the
partnership between EMBRAER and CTA is the appropriate vehicle to
accomplish this task. EMBRAER can facilitate the flow of information
from domestic and international markets to potential suppliers while
CTA assists in technological development, allowing the firm to increase
responsibility gradually. The relationship between CTA and EMBRAER
in these efforts shows how the state can dynamically respond to
evolving market conditions.

IMBEL: Coordination and Promotion

Like CTA, the Industry for War Material (IMBEL), shifted focus with changes in the Brazilian defense industry. After establishing that this state agency was created to streamline Army defense production, the symbiotic affiliation of IMBEL with the private firm ENGESA is shown to have evolved in response to the perception that an infusion of private decision making was a necessary ingredient to meet national security objectives.

IMBEL was created in July 1975 by President Geisel as a state holding company to organize and vitalize the embryonic armaments industry.[52] The army owned seven munitions facilities which inefficiently duplicated efforts. Table 5.2 lists the plants at this time. It was argued that IMBEL would exhibit more entrepreneurship, attending to "the necessity of a profound reorganization of the military factories, giving them the character and dynamism of private industry . . ."[53] Greater coordination and planning between state and private ventures was also targeted:

> The necessity to give incentive to the private defense industry through a system of global planning, that would permit the division of labor among all through programs such as the leasing of facilities, machines and equipment, financial participation and technology sharing. . . . There is a need for coordination with civilian industry, concentrating on areas where private initiative confronts difficulties, such as in the area of high precision instruments.[54]

This division of labor designated research and development, financial investment and provision of equipment at reduced costs as activities in which the state has a competitive advantage over the private sector. Nevertheless, it did not seek to take over tasks where the private sector was capable. Thus, the articles continue "it is government policy to transfer to private initiative that which is not necessary or obligatory to be maintained in the hand of the state."[55] Coordination, planning and support of private firms would, it was argued, coalesce to increase armaments exports.[56]

As a state entity, IMBEL benefitted from federal money, allowing it to produce weapons not economical for private firms. Its initial funding was assigned at CR$25 million,[57] and it was exempt from all tariffs and taxes.[58] All federal agencies were ordered to give priority to IMBEL's products and IMBEL employees, including engineers, were on the army payroll.[59] Yet IMBEL was also admonished to resort to

TABLE 5.2
IMBEL Plants, 1975

Plant	State	Description & Comments
Andarai	RJ	components for munitions
Realango	RJ	munitions for revolvers, pistols, rifles, machine guns and anti-air cannons
Estrela	RJ	black gunpowder, other explosives
Pres. Vargas	SP	gunpowder, dynamite, explosives
Juiz de Fora	MG	"Famabra plant;" Heavy artillery
Itajuba	MG	Light arms; Belgian licensing agreement with FN-Herstal; Offers new modernized automatic rifle using standard NATO dimensions
CPDET	RJ	Electronic and telecommunications Research Center

Source: Drawn from IMBEL publication "O que é a IMBEL"

independent funding and private enterprise whenever possible. It was a warning it did not heed. Products were arguably of a poor quality, the work force was poorly trained, capital was antiquated, and the firm was loosing money. By 1983 the organization's management was placed in private hands.

For the first six years of its existence, IMBEL was run by a general. When the first director, General Augusto de Olveira Pereira left in 1978, he was replaced by General Arnaldo Calderari, president until 1982. In that year the directorship of IMBEL was handed to a civilian: Jose Luiz Whitaker Ribeiro, the president of ENGESA.

IMBEL was brought under the management of ENGESA to enhance economic efficiency and export promotion. Whitaker Ribeiro was considered the shining star of Brazilian arms exports. His leadership was perceived as critical to turning the firm's losses in profits, augmenting the production of arms, and opening export markets.[60] The appointment of a civilian was politically costly, underscoring the importance of increasing international sales to the Brazilian government.[61] Critics also assailed handing the presidency of IMBEL to Whitaker as an implicit subsidy to ENGESA.[62] But the goal of global marketing outweighed domestic ramifications. IMBEL was not well equipped to sell abroad. The organization had not, Barros charged, changed its old patrimonial military style to become an efficient capitalist corporation.[63] Its products were not distinguished by innovative technology or low price. Most importantly, it lacked an effective international marketing network and the sales appeal of other Brazilian armaments: apolitical export terms.[64] By placing IMBEL in the hands of ENGESA's aggressive president, IMBEL's products could be marketed with ENGESA's as a package, taking advantage of ENGESA's established markets and strong international sales and maintenance staff. Furthermore, IMBEL could now sell to pariah states and countries engaged in war without the sale being directly traceable to a state agency, thus minimizing diplomatic tensions, particularly with the United States.[65]

Whitaker consolidated IMBEL's operations with ENGESA. He sold the CR$700 million building in Brasília, moving IMBEL to an ENGESA facility in São Paulo. The telephones were answered "ENGESA" and employees served both firms. IMBEL dissociated itself from its trading company, CODECE, comprised of three firms, Mayrink Veiga and Paembra with 35% each and IMBEL with the remaining 30%.[66] Whittaker charged that these automotive firms were extraneous to defense and placed IMBEL's export programs in the hands of ENGEXCO saying:

> We are going to take advantage of the organization that we already have in various countries in order to export IMBEL's products and the products of other firms in the sector.[67]

The Army maintained involvement in IMBEL through an administrative council. The Ministry had to be informed of all IMBEL activities, and retained veto power.[68]

IMBEL and ENGESA were complementary organizations. IMBEL was capable of producing, on its own or through licensing agreements, most of the national requirements for small arms and ammunitions, machine guns and light artillery. Its status as a state firm benefitted ENGESA with formal military connections.[69] When Whitaker took over, exports soared. Within three months of his tenure, he secured US$50 million in contracts. Thus the partnership between IMBEL and ENGESA was dynamic, each organization drawing upon its strengths for improved international performance.

After reorganization under the Whitaker administration, a streamlined IMBEL was passed back to its own administrative board. The Realango plant was deactivated, with its equipment incorporated into CBC, a private producer of small arms, in exchange for a 23.7% shareholding in the firm. The Andarai plant was also closed. The Juiz da Fora installation was passed to ENGESA QUIMICA, giving IMBEL

TABLE 5.3
IMBEL'S Products

WEAPONS
  Light Automatic Rifles 7,62 mm NATO (.308IN), 5,56 mm (.223In) and .22
    LR calibres.
    (Fixed and Foldable Butts)
  Semi Automatic Rifles 7,62 mm NATO (.308 IN), 5,56 (.223 IN) and .22 LR
    calibres.
    (Fixed and Foldable Butts)
  Pistols 9 mm and .45 calibres
  Pistols TP .45 (Practical Shooting)
  Sports Carbine .22 LR calibre

MILITARY EXPLOSIVES
  Chemical powders (Simple and double Bases)
  Trotyle -TNT
  Cyclonite - RDX
  Penthrite
  Explosives compositions
  Detonador capsules for instantaneously setting of explosive charges

CIVIL EXPLOSIVES
  Dynamites
  Explosives for seismogrfics reading
  Detonador capsules for instantaneously setting of explosive charges

ELECTRONIC
  Special Communication Equipment (Field telephone apparatus for
    vessels, mines, etc.)
  Military Communication Equipment (having electronic counter-
    measurements)
  Special Electronic Equipment (Optical barrier-chronometers, etc.

OTHERS
  Nitrocelulose and Collodium
  Purified Linter
  Special chemical and metallurgical products, on request

Source: Drawn from IMBEL Company literature 1989.

49% of its stock. After closing the most inefficient installations, IMBEL
has embarked on a modernization program. It also acts to stimulate
activity in related sectors. Prológo, producer of microcomputers and
crytographers is a wholly owned subsidiary. In addition to the stock
holdings above, it also has interests in ABC IXTAL, maker of crystals
and fiber optics, and D.F. Vasconcellos, which produces optical

equipment. Quite interestingly, in a reversal of roles, it is possible that IMBEL will take over the failing ENGESA.

In both the EMBRAER - CTA and the IMBEL - ENGESA cases, the state institutions dynamically responded to changes in the market. In both the aircraft and the armored vehicle sector, the state and the firms have joined together to cooperatively achieve a common goal. While we might have expected such smooth communication in the aircraft sector since CTA and EMBRAER both come under the jurisdiction of the Ministry of Aeronautics, the decision for ENGESA and IMBEL to join forces can only be explained by the anticipation of increasing rewards for both. Despite differing ownership patterns, there was strong incentive in both sectors for coordination.

The second important aspect in comparing the two sectors is the emphasis, despite ownership patterns, to behave "as if" private. In the aviation sector this mandate given to EMBRAER at its inception is currently being handed to the supplier firms. Although the state is willing to support the activity, it is not willing to assume the position of being the sole economic actor. Likewise with IMBEL, its purpose was to invigorate the state-run munitions plants by subjecting them to the criteria of "as if" private. When it was failing in this objective as indicated by poor international marketing performance, further steps to privatize the behavior--as opposed to the ownership—of the firm were taken in appointing Mr. Whitaker director. This supports the argument that partnership and behavior as if the firm were a private, profit maximizing concern have been the dominant and appropriate criteria for performance in the Brazilian defense sector. This has encouraged flexibility as underlying conditions in the sector changed.

The State as Financier: Fiscal Subsidization

The next section considers state activities not lodged in industry-specific institutions. It highlights how tax incentives, export promotion schemes and import relief facilitated growth. It is argued that the state employed fiscal incentives for both the private and public defense firms. Furthermore, these incentives are part of the broad, outward looking industrialization strategies Brazil used to increase exports of manufactured goods.

To make private investment in the infant aeronautical sector more attractive, the state subsidized the initial capitalization of EMBRAER. A risk free scheme permitted Brazilian corporations to earmark 1% of Federal income taxes to purchase shares in EMBRAER.

TABLE 5.4
Private Shareholders and Government Ownership Patterns,
EMBRAER, 1972-1982

Year	#of share- holders	Fiscal Incentive Receipts	Average holding (US $)	Private share (%)	Govt share (US mil)	Govt share vote stock (%)
1972	73029	7.7	105.44	68.83	1.2	51
1973	95462	10.3	107.9	78.3	21.7	51
1974	117932	15.9	134.82	83.7	16.3	51
1975	117504	21.1	179.57	84	16	51
1976	126156	21.4	169.63	86	1.4	51
1977	160146	33.4	179.21	87.3	12.7	54.4
1978	176758	29.4	166.33	89.2	10.8	54.4
1979	183997	26.3	142.94	90.8	9.2	54.4
1980	222481	24.8	111.47	92	8	54.4
1981	226506	29.8	131.56	92.9	7.1	54.6
1982	223687	31	138.57	92.9	7.1	54.4

Source: EMBRAER company report, "Informaçoes de Caracter Geral . . .," and R. Ramamurti, "High Technology Exports by SOEs in LDCs: A Brazilian Case Study," paper presented at The Conference on Latin American Public Enterprises, IESA, Caracas, Venezuela, 10–13 November 1985 (columns 3 and 8).

Since investment with potential return is preferable to paying taxes, the capitalization program quickly directed private funds into the coffers of EMBRAER.   Table 5.4 shows that over 1972-1982, the number of shareholders in EMBRAER more than tripled from 73,029 to 223,687, with total receipts growing from US$ 7.7 million to US$ 31 million. This brought private participation from 68.8% in 1972 to 92.9% in 1982, with a parallel decline in government ownership from 31.2% to 7.1%. However, the government maintains control over voting stock to reserve for itself the last word in national defense.   Nevertheless, this control is not exercised on a regular basis and does not interfere with the microeconomic decisions of the firm.

EMBRAER management believes the capitalization scheme served the interests of the firm and the state, arguing:

> The method used to capitalize EMBRAER has proven to be effective, fair and profitable for the country and for the individual investors. Because national interests are at stake, both in terms of industrial development and the need to maintain efficiency in military procurements, governmental control of EMBRAER is reasonable and beneficial.[70]

Ramamurti contends money invested in EMBRAER should be considered government equity as the funds would have been retained in government coffers without the tax credit scheme.[71] While in fact this is true—companies would not have invested in the firm absent the incentive—the purpose of any investment tax credit (ITC) is to use government policy to redirect resources. In the U.S. few call the billions of dollars taken in ITCs "government ownership" in the private sector. Although the Brazilian government changed the parameters of investment decisions to allocate money to the aeronautical sector, the capital remains private. This is important because it is precisely this private element in the firm that encourages EMBRAER's dynamic production and marketing decisions.

The Brazilian Government also supplied land, labor and technology to EMBRAER. Given land adjacent to the CTA, proximity has proven especially valuable for access to expensive aerodynamic testing equipment and Brazilian Air Force pilots for the long hours of air time necessary for certification. EMBRAER was also permitted to recruit workers from the Aircraft Division of the Institute for Research and Development at CTA. Although they were legally required to retire from the Armed Forces prior to employment with EMBRAER, strong personal ties with the Air Force and the Research Center eased the firm's access to the military market and enhanced its ability to absorb technology transferred from the CTA, further blurring the distinction between EMBRAER and public military institutions.

EMBRAER and suppliers are exempt from all levies and taxes on imports of raw materials, complimentary equipment, and components if the savings from these duties are channeled to investments within the firm. In particular, EMBRAER was exempt from paying the Industrial Products Tax (IPI) and the Merchandise Circulation Tax (ICM) on its exports. This exemption permitted EMBRAER to accelerate investment in plant, equipment, and R&D. As a result EMBRAER had minimal long term debt and did not have to be allocated funds from the government budget on an annual basis. Thus, by granting fiscal incentives the state has made it possible for the firm to become self-sufficient.

ENGESA benefits from both industry specific and generalized programs to promote production and export. In 1980, as a means to free funds for heavy capital investments, ENGESA's request to suspend income taxes was approved for 3 years.[72] For products acquired directly by the Brazilian Armed Forces, the firm is exempt from the industrialized products tax, IPI.[73] ENGESA does not pay tariffs on imported raw materials, complementary pieces, components and equipment, machines and other inputs without national competitors used in domestic defense production.[74] Exemptions for military products destined for international markets were covered under general export promotion programs. ENGESA made significant commitments to the Special Program of Fiscal Incentives for Exports (BEFIEX) which, in exchange for a promise to achieve export and domestic content targets, the firm was granted a 70-90% duty and tax reduction on imports of machinery and equipment and a reduction of 50% on raw material and intermediate imports, with 100% exemptions granted in special cases.[75] For example, through this program ENGESA was able to purchase GM motors at the same price as U.S. manufacturers.[76] ENGESA and ENGEX together committed the firm to exports of $240 million from July 1977 through December 1981 in exchange for the export concessions.[77] Table 5.5 shows ENGESA's export commitment compared with other BIFIEX recipients. Other export subsidies open to ENGESA included the CIEX program, with shorter target commitments, the Fund for Export Financing (FINEX) export shipment finance and Resolution 674 program which supplies working capital to the firms producing manufactured exports.

Conclusion:
The State in the Defense Sector

It has been argued in this chapter that the Brazilian state has behaved as an effective, pragmatic entrepreneur. If an entrepreneur is one who organizes, manages and assumes the risks of a business or enterprise, the Brazilian state has provided a strong organizational framework with clear objectives, has directly (through appointment) or indirectly (through incentives) managed the activity of defense firms and has incurred business risk. The defense sector was organized according to economic principles. With a clear articulation of goals predicated upon the ideology of developmental nationalism, the state sought to establish a sector which both attended to the needs of the armed forces and also contributed to economic growth. It was reasoned that where viable, private ownership of defense firms should be promoted with state incentives and technological support. This, indeed was the case with ENGESA and AVIBRAS. Where, however, the private market failed, the state assumed ownership. Nevertheless, even in the case of these public enterprises, the criteria of profit maximizing "as if" private behavior was enforced.

The Brazilian state directly and indirectly manages the defense sector. Direct management in public enterprises is maintained through public appointment of the top officers of state firms. More important,

TABLE 5.5
Befiex Program Approvals Through 1977

Firm	period			total commitment US$ mil
Volkswagen	1/73	-	12/82	1028
Ford & PHILC0	7/72	-	12/82	1000
General Motors	7/76	-	7/86	1009.5
Jari	1/76	-	12/85	616
ENGESA & ENGEX	6/77	-	12/88	240
Fiat	6/76	-	12/85	550
Mercedes Benz	1/75	-	12/84	500
Saab-Scania	1/76	-	12/85	415.4
Fiat	1/75	-	12/84	400.
Chrysler	1/73	-	12/82	314.
Volvo	11/76	-	12/84	351.8
Matarazzo	12/74	-	11/84	159
Frutesp	1/76	-	12/80	75.4
Kanebo Textile	7/73	-	12/83	150
J.I. Case	1/76	-	12/85	125
Serido Textile	11/75	-	11/85	133
Kaiowa Refrigerators	12/76	-	12/82	81.8
Ajinomoto	6/74	-	12/86	115.5
Kanebo	3/74	-	3/84	65
COPATE	5/76	-	12/85	40.7
Matsubara	1/76	-	12/85	40.7
Duratex	5/76	-	12/85	36
Hoepke	6/77	-	12/88	43
BRASIPLAN	8/77	-	12/83	22
Orchard	2/77	-	12/85	26
ITABRAS Machines	12/76	-	12/86	28.3
Gunsan Fiação	6/77	-	12/86	22.9
Sew	1/77	-	12/83	12
STAEDLER Design	11/77	-	12/82	4
INGO Machines	9/77	-	12/87	6.7

Source: Extracted from Table 11.8, "Befiex Programs Approved Through 1977," in World Bank Country Study, *Brazil: Industrial Policies and Manufactured Exports*, p. 257.

however, has been the indirect management through a carefully planned set of incentives which have worked to encourage product development and strong expansion domestically and overseas. This system of indirect management and control has been particularly effective since the programs have primarily been directed at reducing the risk in product development and marketing. Assuming that firms avoid risk when possible, measures to promote technology and foreign sales, high risk activities, have been especially successful in spurring growth in the defense sector.

In addition to being entrepreneurial, state activity in the defense sector has also been pragmatic. Indeed it reflects the pragmatic blend of state and private activity described by Mamalakis:

> . . . the private vs. state ownership dilemma is basically a false one. The real choice must be between efficient and inefficient enterprise, regardless of ownership, whether private, public, or a mixture of the two. What matters is the presence of market-dictated rules of the game, which reward inputs and enterprises on the basis of their contribution to output, rather than on the basis of their ownership, political influence, sectorial coalitions, and so on. [78]

The Brazilian defense sector followed neither the market model nor complete state control. Rather, it pursued a pragmatic program, allowing private markets to work where possible, supplementing with public means where necessary. The sector demonstrates an eclectic pattern of ownership: Private ENGESA is in partnership with public IMBEL and mixed enterprise EMBRAER and private AVIBRAS work with the state CTA. Fiscal incentives are applied across the sector without regard to ownership status but on the basis of economic necessity. Differentiating according to the criteria suggested by Trebat, particularly the history of market failure, public enterprises were formed only where private firms had not been able to provide products.

This pragmatic blend of public and private ownership has proven effective for the firms. For example, EMBRAER contends

> In its approach to the regulation of competition in the Brazilian market between EMBRAER and others, Brazil is fortunate to be able to benefit from the experience of other countries, and it is attempting to steer clear of the pitfalls of either the U.S. style *laissez faire* system or the European pattern of nationalization. Either can lead to unhealthy combinations of over- capacity, social hardship and inefficiency. The Brazilian objective is to maintain a healthy industry through a sensible regulation of competition and of capacity from the outset. The existence of a close coordination of government and industrial interests in Brazil is of tremendous importance in the field of aeronautics and an asset which most countries do not enjoy to the same degree. [79]

As Mamalakis suggests, irrespective of ownership, the state has consistently imposed market rules on the defense sector. Admonitions to behave as if private were given to EMBRAER and IMBEL when they were formed. As a result EMBRAER is distinguished as "one of the 425 state firms in the Brazilian economy which performs as well or better than the most energetic private companies."[80] This is attributed to the fact that "Ozires Silva always fought for EMBRAER to act as though it were a private organization in its internal production and its relations with the market."[81] When IMBEL did not respond to international market signals, the state responded by placing the organization under private management. The new formula worked to increase international sales.

But the market is not deified in the Brazilian defense sector. Brazil would not have become a global arms merchant without significant state support. As demonstrated using Trebat's hypotheses, public intervention was necessary to overcome significant economic obstacles. The success of the industry, therefore, may be attributed to a dynamic blend of state promotion and private entrepreneurship, drawing upon the best of both forms of economic organization.

Notes

1.   John R. Freeman and Raymond D. Duvall, "International Economic Relations and the Entrepreneurial State," *Economic Development and Cultural Change*, Vol. 32, No. 2, January 1984, p. 374. See also Duval and Freeman, "The State and Dependent Capitalism," *International Studies Quarterly*, Vol. 25, March 1981, 99-118.

2.   Leroy P. Jones, *Public Enterprise in Less Developed Countries*, (New York: Cambridge University Press, 1982). For a comprehensive discussion of the origins of public enterprise in Latin America see Alfred H. Saulniers, "Public Enterprise in Latin America: Their Origins and Importance," *International Review of Administrative Sciences* 13, No. 4, 1985, 329-349.

3.   Thomas Trebat, *Brazil's State-Owned Enterprises: A Case Study of the State as Entrepreneur* (New York: Cambridge University Press, 1983), p. 2.

4.   In Trebat, *State Owned Enterprises*, 1983, p. 2.

5.   David R. Dye and Carlos Eduardo de Souza e Silva, "A Perspective on the Brazilian State," *Latin American Research Review*, XIV, No. 1, 1979.

6.   Because of the infancy of this industry, Jones' criteria of historical inertia did not play a role.

7.   Trebat, *State Owned Enterprises*, pp. 30-35. See also Paulo Roberto Motta, "Control of Public Enterprises in Brazil," in Praxy Fernandes, *Control Systems for Public Enterprise in Developing Countries* (Ljubljana, Yugoslavia: International Center for Public Enterprises in Developing Countries, 1979), pp. 189-193. Trebat is the acknowledged authority on the economic behavior of Brazilian State Enterprises. However, as Jones and Wortzel point out, the available literature on public enterprises in Brazil, particularly those

enterprises engaged in export promotion, is slim. Note their entire citation: "Thomas J. Trebat, "An Evaluation of the Economic Performance of Public Enterprises in Brazil," (Ph.D. dissertation, Vanderbilt University, 1978); Werner Baer, Issac Kerstenetsky, and Annibal Villela, "The Changing Role of the State in the Brazilian Economy," *World Development*, Vol. 1, No. 11, November 1973, pp. 23-24; Thomas J. Trebat, "The Role of Public Enterprise in the Brazilian Economy: An Evaluation," mimeo (University of Texas, Houston, 1977); Werner Baer, Richard Newfarmer and Thomas J. Trebat, "On State Capitalism in Brazil: Some New Ideas and Questions," *Inter-American Economic Affairs*, Vol. 30, No.3, Winter 1976, pp. 69-91. Indeed, conversations with scholars involved in the study of public enterprises (notably Silvia Raw and Richard Newfarmer) pointed in one direction: read Trebat.

8.   Stanley Hilton, "The Armed Forces and Industrialists in Modern Brazil: The Drive for Military Autonomy," in *HAHR*, Vol. 6, No.4, 1982, pp. 629-673.

9.   Ibid.

10.   Ibid.

11.   Ibid.

12.   Ibid, pp. 646 and 654.

13.   Ibid.

14.   Ibid.

15.   Ibid.

16.   "A Report on Science and Technology of the Ministry of Aeronautics" cited in Clovis Brigagão, "The Case of Brazil: Fortress or Paper Curtain," *Impact of Science on Society*, Vol. 31, No. 1, January/March 1981, and José Ellis Ripper, "A EMBRAER e o CTA," *Segurança e Desenvolvimento*, Vol. 28, No. 174, 1979, pp. 44-50.

17.   Helen Tuomi and Raimo Vavrynen, *Transnational Corporations, Armaments and Development*, (New York: St. Martins Press, 1982).

18.   B. Bluestone, P. Jordan, and M. Sullivan, *Aircraft Industry Dynamics*, (MA: Auburn House Publishing Co., 1981), p 170.

19.   Gavin Kennedy, *Defense Economics*, (New York: St. Martin's Press, 1983), Chapter 2, "Defense and the Theory of the Public Good."

20.   Adam Smith, *The Wealth of Nations*, Book V.

21.   Olvey et.al, *The Economics of National Security*, (Wayne, New Jersey: Avery Publishing, 1984).

22.   Gavin Kennedy, *Defense Economics* (New York: St. Martin's Press, 1983), Chapter 2, "Defense and the Theory of the Public Good."

23.   Ruth Leger Sivard, *World Military and Social Expenditures 1985*, (Washington, D.C.: World Priorities, 1985).

24.   "Multinacionais querem fabricar armas no Brasil," *O Estado de São Paulo*, August 24, 1975.

25.   *Veja*, May 21, 1986, pp. 20–23, 24-25.

26.   P. Fernanades and P. Sicherl, eds., *Seeking the Personality of Public Enterprise Yugoslavia*, (Ljubljana, Yugoslavia: International Center for Public Enterprises in Developing Countries, 1979), p. 24. This definition is the consensus of an Expert Group Meeting to classify public enterprises sponsored

by the International Center for Public Enterprises in Developing Countries, Yugoslavia. In an appendix 29 definitions of public enterprises are presented. (p. 206). However, it should be noted that the term public enterprise has a more specific legal meaning in Brazil. According to Federal Law No. 200/1367 a public enterprise is one whose social capital has been fully covered by the government, while a Sociedade de Economia Mista (Mixed Economic Enterprise) is shared by both government and private enterprise. Nevertheless, most works on state or public enterprise in Brazil use the broader criteria of control through appointment of management plus some degree of equity participation as the relevant criteria to label the firm as "public." See Paulo Roberto Motta, "Control of Public Enterprises in Brazil," in P. Fernandes, *Control Systems for Public Enterprises in Developing Countries*, (Ljubljana, Yugoslavia: International Center for Public Enterprises in Developing Countries, 1979), p. 189.

27.　　Silvia Helena, "A decologem segura de EMBRAER," *Dados e Idéias*, 2, October/November 1977, pp. 13-21.

28.　　Ozires Silva, "O Vôo da EMBRAER," *Revista Brasileira Tecnológica*, Vol. 13, No. 1, January/March 1982.

29.　　*Equipamento Militar*, August 1983.

30.　　*Equipamento Militar*, Ano 1, Numero 2, Edição Aeronáutica, Rio de Janiero: August/September 1982.

31.　　José Henrique de Sousa Damiani, "O EMB-110 Bandeirante e o Processo de Inovação Tecnológica," VIII Simpósio Nacional de Pequisa em Administração de Ciência e Tecnologia, São Paulo, Promoção e Realização por FINEP/USP.

32.　　Ibid.

33.　　*Jornal da Tarde*, April 12, 1973.

34.　　From the text of the presentation made by Engineer Wanderley, of EMBRAER, on November 11, 1983 in the Institute of Engineering, University of São Paulo convened at the invitation of Ozires Silva, the president of EMBRAER.

35.　　See appendix for a description of EMBRAER's products.

36.　　R. Ramamurti, "EMBRAER," Harvard Business School Case Study # 0-383-090, 1982, p.12.

37.　　All figures not otherwise footnoted from Wanderley.

38.　　Ozires Silva, "Manufacturing Aircraft in Brazil—Some Fair Trade Issues," presentation at the Aviation/Space Writers Association Conference, Fort Lauderdale, May 4,1982.

39.　　"Brasília: O Vôo Inaugural," *Tecnologia e Defesa*, No. 6, 1983.

40.　　"Um Debate: Quem Deve Desenvolver a Tecnologia?" *Indústria e Desenvolvimento*, Vol. IX, No. 6, July 1976, p. 9 (FIESP).

41.　　Damiani, "O Emb-110."

42.　　*Folha de São Paulo*, 13 November 1983

43.　　Wanderley, November 11, 1983.

44.　　"EMBRAER has High Hopes for New Turboprop," *Latin American Regional Reports*: Brazil (London) July 3, 1982, p. 14.

45. "Equipamento Militar Pode Ser Saída Para Indústria Nacional," *Journal do Brasil,* September 6, 1983.
46. Ibid.
47. Wanderley, November 11, 1983.
48. Ozires Silva in *Notícias Econômicas* No. 292, Semana de 8 a 14 de abril 1973, pp. 483-486.
49. Wanderley, November 11, 1983.
50. "Eletrometal recebe prêmio por tecnologia estratégica," *O Globo,* July 8, 1982.
51. *Estado de São Paulo,* "Embraer Promete Encomendas," September 6, 1983.
52. IMBEL, Ministério do Exército, September 1975, p. 1. See also *The Folha de São Paulo,* "Defesa Nacional," July 15, 1975 and *Correio Brasiliense,* "IMBEL é a lição de nacionalismo," August 20, 1981 and *Jornal do Brasil* "Brasil exporta este ano US$500 mh em armamento," May 25, 1979 for a summary of the goals, objectives and structure of the state firm.
53. IMBEL, Ministério do Exército.
54. Ibid, emphasis mine.
55. IMBEL, Ministério do Exército.
56. General Antonio Jorge Correa, Chief of the High Command of the Armed Services in *O Globo,* "Chefe do EMFA: Uma das metas da IMBEL é exportar armamentos," December 7, 1976
57. "Brasil exporta este ano US$500 mh em armamento."
58. "'Trading' de material bélico quer negociar venda de tecnologia," *Jornal do Brasil,* August 24, 1981.
59. "Geisel cria empresa para produzir material bélico" *Estado de São Paulo,* April 25, 1975, p. 17.
60 José Drumond Saraiva, "Brasil no Século XXI: Ciência e Tecnologia como Variável Estratégica no Pensamento Brasileiro," unpublished working paper, Rio de Janeiro, July 1989.
61. Whitaker was the second civilian to occupy a military post in Brazil's history. Moreover, President Figueiredo was personally indebted to Calderari. To receive his fourth star needed to be president, in 1978 Calderari, a four-star general, retired to direct IMBEL. To override both precedent and personal ties strong cause must have existed. See *VEJA,* "Uma boa estrela," October 27, 1982, p. 37; Fernandes, op. cit. and *Tribuna da Impresa,* September 4, 1983.
62. Helo Fernandes, "A ENGESA (falida) quer Engolir a IMBEL (Prosperíssima)," *Tribuna da Impresa,* May 14, 1983, p. 4.
63. In J. Katz, *Arms Production in Developing Countries,* (Lexington, Mass.: D. C. Heath & Co., 1984), p. 81. Barros says, the change was "an attempt to shift IMBEL from a patrimonial corporation into a capitalist one, and points toward the adoption of a military industrial complex model in which civilian corporations (or civilian run ones) control the production administration while the military sets the operations requirements." Others disagree. See *Estado de São Paulo,* "Exercito define IMBEL: Rentavel e eficiente,'" August 15, 1981; this is contested in *Visão,* January 31, 1983, "Mudando de areas," p. 25.

64.   The characteristic of Brazilian exports as apolitical is discussed in Chapter 6.

65.   This is an extremely sensitive issue. Interview with Lt. Colonel Loyal G. Bassett, USAF, Office of the Secretary of Defense, Country Director, Latin American Region, July 24, 1985.

66.   "Uma administração nos moldes da empresa privada," *O Globo,* October 28, 1982. It adds to the intrigue of this story to know General Calderari continued to head CODECE. He was quick to defend the group as not "extraneous to the sector" but construed "to avoid disagreeable situations for IMBEL and avoid various problems." *Jornal do Brasil,* "Material bélico," October 29, 1982.

67.   "'Trading' de material bélico quer negociar venda de tecnologia," *Jornal do Brasil,* August 24, 1981.

68.   "Mudando de areas," *Visão,* January 31, 1983, p. 25, Table 4.2.

69.   W. Perry, "Military Policy & Conventional Capabilities of an Emerging Power," *Military Review,* October 24, 1978.

70   *EMBRAER Company Report,* General Information: Brazilian Aeronautical Industry, 1983 English edition.

71.   R. Ramamurti, "High Technology Exports by SOEs in LDCs: A Brazilian Case Study." Paper presented at the Conference on Latin American Public Enterprises, IESA, Caracas, Venezuela, November 10–13, 1985, p. 17.

72   *Jornal do Brasil,* "Engesa não pagará IR por 3 anos," January 24, 1981.

73.   "Isentos de IPI 74 produtos de uso das Forças Armadas," *Estado de São Paulo,* January 6,1979.

74.   "Indústria de armas tem isenção," *Estado de São Paulo,* June 26, 1982, p. 6.

75.   World Bank Country Study, *Brazil: Industrial Policies and Manufactured Exports,* (Washington, D.C.: World Bank Publications), 1983.

76.   Interview with Paulo Meira, director of sales, GM do Brasil, October 24, 1983.

77.   World Bank Country Study, *Brazil: Industrial Policies and Manufactured Exports,* 1983, Table 11.8, p. 257.

78.   Markos Mamalakis, "Introduction: Interamerican Economic Relations, The New Development View," *Journal of Interamerican Studies and World Affairs,* Vol. 27, No.4, Winter 1986-87, pp. 1–8.

79.   EMBRAER Company Report, General Information: Brazilian Aeronautical Industry, 1983, English edition.

80.   "O estilo do piloto," *VEJA,* May 21, 1986, p. 24.

81.   Ibid.

6

Technology Policy for
the Defense Sector

As economic growth is intertwined with technological capability, a critical arena for state intervention is the promotion of technology.[1] A technology may be defined as "a collection of physical processes which transforms inputs into outputs, together with the social arrangements (i.e., organizational modes and procedural methods) which structure the activities involved in carrying out these transformations."[2] A costly, coveted input, technology exacts an expensive commitment of physical and human resources. A nation modernizing in the late twentieth century must not only appropriate a sizable surplus to become an industrial power, it must also command scientific and institutional resources to control technology. Brazil's first science and technology development plan states:

> Economic growth tends to be more and more conditioned by a technological progress which gives rise, to a growing extent, to new industries, new products, new materials (including substitutes for natural raw materials), altering the structures of demand and costs.[3]

But technology is more than a means of production; it is an end in itself. The profusion of computers, electronic gadgetry and nuclear bombs stridently announces international standards for sophistication, power and modernization. To be considered truly "modern" a country displays technological armor. And, in the view of many in the civilian and military elites, defense production is the mechanism best suited to generating technological growth.

But the achievement of this strategic goal is limited by the underdevelopment of technological systems in Brazil. This constraint is imposed by the unique historical circumstances of newly industrializing countries caught between the demand for technology and the handicap of late entry in the global technological race. The country must assimilate products and master technological processes. Without the luxury of an economic adolescence for scientific and technological institutions to take hold, the late industrializer must simultaneously, almost magically, develop products and scientific infrastructure to guide industrial growth in the technological age. This is a difficult if not quixotic task.

In light of these constraints, what political, scientific and economic institutions would best facilitate development of technological products and processes in Brazil? The armaments industry is illustrative of such an institutional mix encouraging indigenous development. To demonstrate that the armaments sector is indeed an ideal model, the historical deficiencies of the technological system in Brazil are first examined. This discussion is not intended to be comprehensive but to highlight systematic trends. Drawing upon the literature critiquing the underdevelopment of technological institutions in Brazil, an ideal technological system is then constructed. That is, the problems specific to the flow of information and know-how between the supplier of the technology and its user are hypothetically reversed to create a technological system that functions smoothly. In particular, the role of the state is highlighted in its ability to promote technological development in an industrializing country. Finally, it is shown that the armaments industry meets the specifications of this ideal technological system and it is argued that the technological success of the Brazilian industry rests on the cooperative relationship between the state and the firms.

Historical Deficiencies

Brazil's contemporary technological weaknesses can be traced to a slow historical start. In the late 1800s, while technology and industry developed in Western Europe, Brazil remained a slave economy. With forced labor and semi-autonomous production units, technical progress was hindered. Moreover, plantation production and political feuds inhibited the development of a unified national market for science and industry. After independence from Portugal, the task of centralizing economic and political power fell to the state. With this goal, in 1916 the Brazilian Academy of Sciences was founded, and through its journal it promoted a scientific community. Laboratories geared toward industry, particularly mineral production, were begun and old military schools were transformed into educational centers for mineralogy.[4] Yet the government was not organized to support scientific and technological developments on a sustained basis. The state floundered in financing private technological institutions and provided no complementary public structure to facilitate research and development. Thus, many institutions started during this period had a short life-span.[5]

Consistent with the Vargas drive for industrialization, the period of the 1930s through the mid-1950s marked a progressive expansion of the Brazilian industrial sector as well as institutions for science and technology policy. It is important to situate science and technology policy in Brazil in the broader context of Brazilian industry.[6] State support was facilitated by economic and political centralization, the modification of the tax structure for inter-regional commerce and the creation of national economic organs including the Federal Council of Foreign Commerce, the Technical Council on Economics and Finance, the National Council on Industrial and Commercial Policy, and diverse sectorial commissions.[7] In education, the state created the National Chemistry Institute, the National Institute of Technology of Rio de Janeiro and the Technological Research Institute of São Paulo to train engineers. National humiliation over the perceived "backwardness" of Brazil after World War II precipitated new demands upon the state, and calls for technological growth found a sympathetic hearing in the sweeping nationalism of the period. Direct state funding of research was institutionalized in 1951 with the creation of the National Science Council (CNPq), which was charged with developing scientific and technological activity.[8]

Despite this surge of institutional infrastructure in science and technology, the mid-'50s to the end of the '60s were characterized by the divergence between technological and economic growth. Because economic growth was dominated by international capital, domestic research and development suffered. Since multinationals performed research and development in their home countries, there was little indigenous demand for Brazilian research and development. Additionally, massive technology imports during the Kubitschek era resulted in the deceleration of state support to institutes of science and technology. The Triennial Plan for Economic and Social Development 1963-1965 lacked an explicit technology policy. The meager attention given to human capital, research and development and the nuclear sector was especially ineffective under restrictive economic conditions.

Furthermore, the Government Plan for Economic Action (PAEG) after the 1964 coup was not substantially different.

Thus, despite the growing sophistication of multinational technology in the industrial park, domestic institutions of research and development declined from a lack of finance and a deficient demand for Brazilian technology by both foreign and domestic firms.[9] Not until 1968 was a coherent plan for technology, the PED or Strategic Development Plan, articulated.[10] Nevertheless, it focused on technical training to the detriment of research. However, in creating the National Fund for Science and Technology (FNDCT) through the National Development Bank (BNDES), and in restructuring the CNPq, the PED paved the way for more systematic planning efforts.[11] Today CNPq oversees eleven scientific research institutes.

In the 1970s Brazil started to plan for systematic technological development. The Basic First Development Plan for Science and Technology (PBDCT I, 1973-1974) began an active commitment to research and development aimed at accelerating technology flows from abroad while simultaneously improving domestic capacity for absorption and innovation. Priority areas included nuclear energy, space research, oceanography, and new technology-intensive industries such as aviation, chemicals, electronics, and computers. The government instituted a system of preferences for the purchase of domestic capital goods, set up research laboratories in government agencies, and gave incentives to private firms for research and development. A major thrust of the plan included integrative measures linking the system of science and technology with the industrial sector. It stated:

> Priority will be given to tying in the system of science and technology with the productive sector, with government planning and, generally speaking, with the contemporary features of Brazilian society. Integration between the system and the various parameters of a changing society, will result in fertile interaction.[12]

On a theoretical level, at least, the need for linkages between science and technology and the productive sector was recognized. Technological development must be perceived as a holistic system, and not take place in isolated sectors.

The special role of the armed forces must be noted. To consolidate the technological infrastructure, the PBDCT targeted "institutional and financial enhancement of the research agencies considered to be of outstanding interest to the priority sectors," including the Board of Research and Technical Education of the Army and its affiliated institutes, the Navy Research Institute, and the Aerospace Technical

Center.[13] The plan funded new technologies as well as improvements in existing systems under the auspices of each branch of the armed forces. The Air Force program included probe rockets, basic R&D in aircraft and aeronautical equipment, especially electronics, an institute to coordinate public and private efforts in aerospace, an engine project, an operational analysis of the Bandeirante, development of teleguided missiles, establishment of a solid propellents laboratory and a testing system for tactical missiles. Indeed this move into missile development formed the base for AVIBRAS and funded the technological expansion of EMBRAER. The Army priority projects included armored vehicles and electronic equipment, portable bridges, a Materials and a Mechanical Research Center, a R&D institute, and a pilot plant to produce heavy water.[14] In retrospect, the broader goals of industrial integration and technological deepening were less successful than these specific defense industry projects. Military institutions showed greater cohesion and coordination to see a project through. Thus, even at the earliest stages the defense sector was seen as an effective vehicle for promoting technological development.

PBDCT II (1975-1980) advocated a dual industrial strategy: increase technology imports while simultaneously promoting manufactured exports. The plan recognized the difficulty of autonomous technological development without the stimulus of imported technology. However, it also shows an appreciation for the high cost of technology. In this way imports of technology were tied to the production of goods for export. It recognized state enterprises as primary sources of science and technology while also supporting private national enterprises with finance and technology. Priority sectors included capital goods, basic electronics and manufacturing inputs. The second plan states:

> The basic orientation of the second PBDCT is to transform science and technology into a motor for national development and modernization of industry, in the economy and the society. It should be considered not as the expansion of a sector but as the impetus for a new source of dynamism and transformation in the service of the society's goals.[15]

Approved in 1980, the goals of the PBDCT III included increasing living standards and enhancing Brazil's bargaining power in international negotiations. Once more it focused on strengthening relationships between science and technology and economic growth to overcome internal and international bottlenecks to development. In particular it emphasized energy and capital goods sectors. However, with the debts and the fiscal problems of the Brazilian State, little was accomplished in the 1980s. President Collor is attempting to reverse the effects of the last decade with a science and technology plan for 91-95 that forecasts a steady increase of funds of 20% a year. Financing will be targeted at private industry, with incentives for joint projects with the universities.

Despite this comprehensive planning role of the state, implementation of science and technology policy has been of limited success. Overall, emphasis on foreign investment encouraged wholesale technology imports without providing for domestic absorption. This reflected Delfim Neto's position,[16] who argued that a country need not become permanently dependent on massive technology imports. Instead, he argued, imports of technology could promote the growth of a scientific center critical to autonomous economic development and domestic development would naturally follow. Furthermore unrealistic estimates of growth in the face of the oil crisis, global recession and accelerating balance of payments problems also thwarted the plans.[17]

More systematic and far-reaching measures are needed to promote domestic technology. Despite the rhetoric of linking research centers with industry, the reality is a system beset by institutional rigidity. The Brazilian technological system is defined by fissures preventing the smooth flow of information between actors. Called *fossozinhos subdesenvolvidos* or the "little underdeveloped gaps," scientific, technological, economic, financial, industrial and political institutions are isolated from each other. This separation of various parts prevents the effective functioning of the technological system. The Organization of American States reported that "the linkage between the government, the industry, the scientific and technological system and the financing sector is missing almost completely in Brazil."[18] The Director of the Brazilian Institute for Technological Research, Pereira de Castro, reported that

> the most disconcerting aspect in the current Brazilian panorama of science and technology policy is the flagrant fault of coordination between the institutes of technology and the different organs of the national productive system, especially large industry firms, the organs of finance of industry, the organs of infrastructure expansion and the central economic planning organs.[19]

These problems are apparent within firms, between major research centers and industrial actors and in the state research and development structure. Brazilian firms pursue little in-house research nor do they solicit research from domestic institutions. Indigenous R&D is limited because investments are high, returns are slow, and foreign technology is readily available.[20] Thus, demand from the final user of the technology to private research and development institutions is weak.

It should be noted that this is not a problem particular to Brazil. The OECD wrote that this "relative isolation of scientific communities from those more directly involved in economic activities has been found to be a common disease of practically all the developing countries..."[21] What is necessary is a technology policy designed to overcome these systemic weaknesses.

Given the weaknesses of firms, analysts agree that the responsibility for domestic research then falls upon public institutions. Says Erber:

> There is a consensus in the literature [on science and technology policy in Brazil] that the intervention of the state is necessary for the development of science and technology. That is, the present dynamic of economic and social forces generate insufficient development of internal scientific and technological capacity, making state intervention necessary to modify these forces.[22]

In addition to the institutional structure described above, one vehicle for mobilizing technological development by the state has been the arm of public enterprises. But state firms, like the private sector, weigh the efficacy of assured imported technology against the uncertainties of indigenous development. Moreover, when state firms do acquire domestic technology they tend to create their own divisions rather than buy in private markets.[23] Central to this bottleneck therefore is the lack of intermediary organs between the public and the private sectors.[24] Thus, as currently designed, state intervention has not been enormously successful in technology promotion.

The domestic system of science and technology exacerbates the problem of foreign control. Biato argues that technological dependence in Brazil is both cause and consequence of the lack of articulation between the productive system and the scientific-technological complex.[25] Caused by characteristic foreign dependence of Brazilian growth, it is also a consequence since the risks then make external sources of technology a logical choice. Biato contends that this vicious circle impedes industrial development. Furthermore, Pirro points out that restrictions on imported technology prohibit or limit the export and sale of products and technology, necessitate the use of foreign trademarks, equipment, or personnel and impose technology assistance on a permanent, paid basis.[26] Thus, foreign control restricts possibilities for domestic firms to take advantage of economies of scale by exploiting international markets.

Institutional constraints, particularly financial, also beset the

Brazilian system. As Erber argues, limitations of long run credit markets and scarce risk capital are critical problems. Investors tend to have a short-term horizon while research and development is a long-term endeavor. Thus the financial system favors the security of foreign licensing over domestic development. Finally, the technological network lacks support services such as consultants, industrial extensions, a coherent system of patents and industrial standards and incentives for quality control.[27]

Indeed, technology policy in Brazil is between a rock and a hard place. Foreign technology overshadows indigenous development of R&D capabilities and constrains long-run development. Correcting for these negative aspects of the Brazilian technology system, a prototype of a smoothly functioning network is now sketched. This conceptualization is then used to characterize the strengths of technology policy in the armaments sector.

A Prototypical Technological System

Several key elements may be distilled from the foregoing discussion of science and technology policy and practice in Brazil. First, it is generally agreed that the state has a pivotal role in the technological development process, although the structure of intervention to date has not been particularly effective. Second, bottlenecks in communication between research institutions and the industrial structure must be addressed. Third, in addition to this problematic relationship between researcher and producer, one must also situate the final user of the product. Without the final user in the feedback loop one looses an important informational component about the efficacy of the product and process. Fourth, the disincentives for indigenous technological development created by multinational presence should be taken into account and finally, adequate financial support must be given.

Jorge Sabato incorporates a number of these elements into what has become commonly known in the literature on technology policy in Latin America as the Sabato Triangle, shown in Figure 6.1.[28] To avoid rigidities in the system Sabato highlights three essential elements: the Scientific and Technological Infrastructure, the Productive Structure and the Government.[29] The shape of the triangle is meant to emphasize the need for linkages and smooth flows of information between the component elements. Thus, firms or the productive structure freely interact with research and development institutions and state

FIGURE 6.1
Sabato Triangle

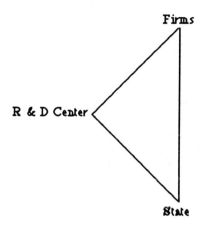

organs. Furthermore the state funding of research and development is critical to their autonomous development.

Adler conceives of the technological system in a slightly different manner. Reflecting the consensus in the literature for a strong role for the state, he places it at the center of his technological triangle. In describing the state as the central arbiter of the technological process he suggests that the state in Brazil has provided the following six functions with respect to technology:

1. Control multinational corporations through guidelines for technology transfer and payments
2. Reinforce the science and technology infrastructure
3. Create the mechanisms to promote national industry, both private and state-owned, identifying priority sectors directly connected with science and technology autonomy, such as capital goods, and providing financial assistance for firms for R&D and technical, consulting and engineering services
4. Guide the relationship between the multinational corporations and national industry by encouraging joint ventures
5. Guide the relationship between science and technology infrastructure and national industry by creating mechanisms, mainly through FINEP, STI, and BNDE, to link domestic supply and demand for science and technology and by centralizing science and technology information services; and
6. Promote multinational investment in local R&D operations.[30]

As pictured below in Figure 6.2, Adler also accords a pivotal role to multinationals. Again, using a triangular form he calls our attention to the need for linkages between individual actors in the technological system.

While the Adler view is particularly instructive with respect to the role of the state, several amendments are in order. As noted above, to bridge the gaps in the technological system users must be seen as part of the flow of information. If they are kept in isolation, innovation in product development is impeded. Secondly, while Adler notes the need for adequate finance, it may be instructive to highlight financial institutions as separate actors. In the context of financial constraints in developing countries it is important to analyze the financial mechanisms supporting the technological endeavors. Finally, rather than merge all of the functions of the multinational corporation into one point on the triangle, it may be more useful to think of a foreign presence in all aspects of the technological system: as donors of technology, producers, financiers and users of the final product. Thus, combining the Sabato Triangle and the Adler conceptualization with these modifications the ideal technological system is represented in Figure 6.3.

To characterize multinational presence, the four institutional actors are then further broken down to reflect ownership patterns and

FIGURE 6.2
Adler's Science and Technology Triangle

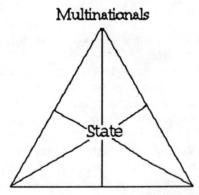

Multinationals

State

Science and Technology
Infrastructure

National Industry
(public and private)

Source: Emanuel Adler, *The Power of Ideology: The Quest for Technological Autonomy in Argentina and Brazil* (Berkeley, Los Angeles and London: University of California Press, 1987), p. 191.

modifying conditions. Ownership may be national of either private or public (state) origin or it may be foreign. This more complex scheme of the actors in the technological system might be represented as a matrix of our four institutional actors cut across by ownership status. Note the dual role of the state. Above, the state mediates interactions between the four institutional actors. However, as illustrated below, any one of these institutional actors may itself be state owned.

This prototypical smoothly functioning technological system integrates institutional actors into a dynamic network of feedback and response. Classified as private national, state or foreign concerns, participants include the technology suppliers, the producer, the final user and financial organizations. The behavior of the firm is conditioned by whether the technology is controlled by private entrepreneurs, the government or multinationals, with particular importance placed on whether the firm may improve the product or sell abroad. Likewise, the final user—domestic private, state or foreign—shapes the choice of technology. Without a robust internal market and subsidies to bridge the early stages of development, domestic suppliers stand little chance of success.

Finance weighs heavily in the technological system. Access to capital markets is problematic in developing countries where well articulated veins of finance seldom exist. The supply of technology depends on external funding. Intermediate producers demand venture capital to bring a product to market and final users respond to easy credit for purchases. The origin of finance—private domestic, state or foreign—determines the terms of lending.

FIGURE 6.3

Technology Flow Diagram

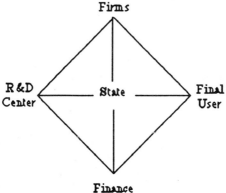

FIGURE 6.4
The Technology Acquisition Process

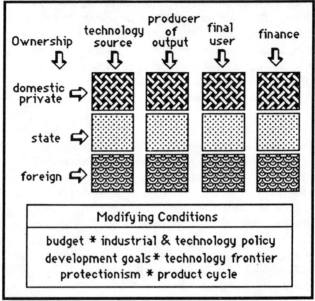

A calculus of technological systems includes political and economic factors at home and abroad. Domestically, political will, a well articulated technology policy and a coherent industrial structure facilitate progress. Foreign participation is sensitive to international economic tides. Protectionist measures of global recession curtail technology imports. In contrast, a growing economy, free trade or a mature product facilitates the transfer of technology at a relatively low cost.

The effectiveness of a technological system is determined by the maturity of each actor in the system and interaction among all participants. Thus, not only is the type and relative strength of the firm important, but also how it interacts with its technology donor, financial institutions, and the buyer of the product is critical to success.

A network of formal and informal feedback and response is integral to the smooth functioning of the system. Information about industrial needs and potential markets must be exchanged between final users, scientists, engineers and industrialists. R&D institutes cannot afford the luxury of isolated experimentation. This exchange must be supported by the financial community; technology flows may also be facilitated by state policy to manage the effects of domestic and international political economy.

The technological system in the Brazilian defense sector exhibits smooth flows of information between suppliers of the technology, producers, the final user and financial systems. Specifically, technologies were developed which were appropriate to the needs of the final user but were also within the industrial capability of the producer. Final demand was defined to include the domestic as well as the international sector, paving the way for export promotion. Finance was available through the defense ministries for funding research and development, as well as through commercial credit sources. Furthermore, broad political conditions, defined by the ideology of "segurança e desenvolvimento," contributed to efficiency in the sector.

Indeed indigenous technological development in the Brazilian arms industry contradicts arguments presented by other studies. Deger and Sen, for example, demonstrate the dependence of the Indian military complex on foreign technology.[31] They contend:

> the lack of any viable control has been the main reason why technology has not been adopted to suit local conditions and its spread has been restricted to enclaves of technical progress without interconnections with the rest of the industrial structure.[32]

In contrast, the Brazilian defense industry has, with effective intervention from state technological centers, developed indigenous armaments and assumed control over foreign technologies. Three specific cases within the defense industry are now examined to illustrate the prototypical technology policy: (1) the development of a technology in CTA, an Air Force research institution, and its transfer to EMBRAER; (2) the international exchange of technology from a multinational aircraft producer, Piper to EMBRAER; (3) the development of a unique technology within a private firm, ENGESA and the subsequent development of the army research and development institute. Discussion centers upon the conditions which made for successful technological development. Specifically, it is suggested that the supportive role of the state in each sector contributed to success. In addition to specifying clearly its needs as final user of defense material, in each case the state directly or indirectly promoted technological development. However, private profit motives were given sufficient play. It is concluded that shared political goals and realistic programming are critical ingredients to facilitate the smooth flow of technology. Finally, by asserting control over technology in the defense sector, Brazil has been able to increase the spin-offs to other

FIGURE 6.5
Aeronautical Sector Technology Flow

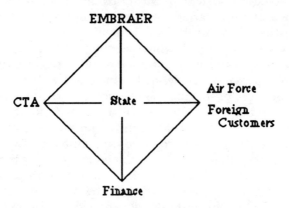

industries. Where Deger and Sen charged that the value of military production to other industries was far too low for India because multinationals controlled the spread of the technologies, for Brazil the spread of newly-acquired techniques was actively promoted by the state-firm partnership.

Case 1:
Domestic Technology Transfer: CTA and EMBRAER

The technological system in the aeronautical sector clearly demonstrates the benefits of a smooth flow of information between the producing firm, the research and development center, the final user and the financial sector. After describing the structure of this sector and its positive effects, this case further demonstrates the dynamism of the model in the Brazilian case. As the firm has matured and its needs have changed the relationship between the actors has also been transformed.

The primary actors in the aeronautical technological system as shown in Figure 6.5 include the firm, EMBRAER; the research and development institute, CTA; the final users comprised of the Brazilian Air Force and as well as foreign buyers; and the financial institutions supporting the process such as the National Development Bank (BNDE) and the Studies and Projects Financing Agency (FINEP). The striking characteristic of this sector is that all of the actors are state owned. Furthermore, EMBRAER, CTA and the Air Force all report to the

Ministry of Aeronautics. Thus, with the key players under one institutional roof, communication and feedback is facilitated.

However, this institutional closeness does not fully explain the success of this technological model. Indeed, as described in the earlier chapter on comparative armaments industries, cases such as Argentina where the state exerts almost incestuous control have weakened rather than strengthened the sector. What are the features which distinguish the Brazilian case as successful? It is important to analyze the historic evolution of the Brazilian case to understand the positive elements of the system.

The Initial Stage

The CTA was particularly critical in the initial stage of technology acquisition at EMBRAER. Figure 6.6 shows the respective roles of CTA and EMBRAER throughout the development of the first product at EMBRAER, the Bandeirante, a nineteen-passenger twin turboprop. The foundation of EMBRAER (as well as nearly all other firms in the aeronautical sector) rests on the core of engineers trained at ITA, the aerospace training institute. A group of ITA trained engineers working in the IPD, the Institute for Research and Development, conceived of the Bandeirante in 1965 after extensive work studying the development of aircraft systems. The design of this plane benefitted from the specifications of the Air Force Ministry which defined a need for a transport aircraft capable of performing under rugged forest conditions as well as linking long distances from north to south. With funding directly through the Ministry of Aeronautics, the IPD transformed the blueprints of this aircraft into a prototype which flew in 1968.

However, CTA did not perceive commercialization of the aircraft as part of its broader mission. That is, CTA strictly adhered to its definition as a research and training institute and not a production center. Philosophically, the preference was for the plane to be produced by private industry. Yet despite the public offering of the technological prototype to the private sector, no qualified candidates appeared. The group of engineers working on the project then appealed to the Ministry of Aeronautics to create a firm to commercialize the Bandeirante. In a very dramatic display the prototype was flown to Brasília by Ozires Silva, soon to become the first president of EMBRAER. In addition to a crowd of journalists and cabinet ministers, the indigenously designed plane was greeted by the Brazilian President Costa e Silva and the Aeronautics Minister Souza Mello. Costa e Silva is reported to have demanded a ride in the plane and

FIGURE 6.6
Contributions of CTA to the RD&E Process in EMBRAER, Initial Phase

CTA DIVISION	STEP IN RD&E CHAIN	CONTRIBUTION TO EMBRAER
ITA (1950)	Basic & Applied Research	Formed Core of Engineers
▼	▼	▼
IPD (1954)	Development of Aircraft & System	Conceived of Bandeirante 1965
▼	▼	▼
IPD	Engineering	First Prototype Flies in 1968
▼	▼	▼

PERSONNEL AND BANDEIRANTE PROTOTYPE TRANSFERRED TO FIRM IN 1969; IPANEMA IN 1970

IPD	Testing	Structural and Flight Testing
▼	▼	▼

PRODUCTION AND MARKETING BY EMBRAER

IPD/IFI (1971)	Improve Supplier Network	Develop & Market Intermediate Inputs

Source: Adapted from José Henrique de Sousa Damiani, "0 EMB-110 e o Processo de Innovação Tecnológica," Paper given at the VII Simpósio Nacional de Pesquisa em Administração de Ciência e Tecnologia, São Paulo, 1983 under the auspices of FINEP/PRTAP, PACTO-IA/FEA/USP. Damiani is a researcher with IFI.

despite its only being a prototype, the nation's vice president, the chief of the security council SNI and the Air Force and Army Ministers all went along for the historic flight. The President of the Republic was so enthusiastic about the project that he signed the law creating EMBRAER that month.[33]

Thus, the first stage of product development including human capital investment, project design and engineering all took place within CTA, with the firm entering after the craft was already airborne. Given this late appearance, feedback between firm and research and development institute certainly should have been problematic. This, however, was quickly solved by the form of technology transfer: in addition to the product, the entire team of engineers was transferred over to EMBRAER. This massive transfer of human capital-embodied technology is perhaps unique. No time was lost in learning the conceptual and scientific framework behind the prototype. The team could focus on production and marketing. Former President of EMBRAER Ozires Silva argues that this was essential:

> We developed the Bandeirante in a research institute—the IPD of the CTA. When it was necessary to produce the plane in an industrial scale, we had to utilize the same people that had designed it and we transferred these people from CTA to EMBRAER. It was the only manner of transferring "know-how" from the IPD to the firm. Clearly this process cannot be generalized as it would result in an emptying of the universities, reducing their capacity.[34]

After turning the product over to the firm CTA continued to play a supportive role. The IPD facilities were used for structural and flight testing, a function that CTA continues to perform for EMBRAER today. Work on the light agricultural aircraft, the Ipanema, continued. CTA, through its industrial promotion institute IFI then began to focus on improving the network of domestic suppliers to EMBRAER, thus shifting its focus to the input market for aviation products. In addition to the Bandeirante, the projects transferred to private industry include the alcohol motor, aircraft engine components, air traffic control system, avionics, flight simulators, meteorological and defensive radar systems, rocket boosters, and missiles.[35] Some of the secondary suppliers have been able to refine these technologies and have become competitive in the international market. An example of this is the case of the firm ELETROMETAL which received from CTA a new process for preparing industrial steel; the firm now produces landing gear for the Boeing Corporation.[36]

With respect to these technology transfer arrangements, military officials often emphasize the benefits to civilian industries, estimating that as much as 96% of the funds dedicated to research and development benefit the private, civilian sector.[37] Nevertheless most of these technologies have dual applications for military and civilian use; thus the percentage is overstated. While it can be said that military research benefits civilian technologies, the primary impetus remains the military sector.

Thus CTA institutes provided the groundwork for the initial stages of education, product development and engineering; they continue to support EMBRAER in testing as well as promotion of the supplier

FIGURE 6.7
Division of Labor Between Firm and Technology Donor

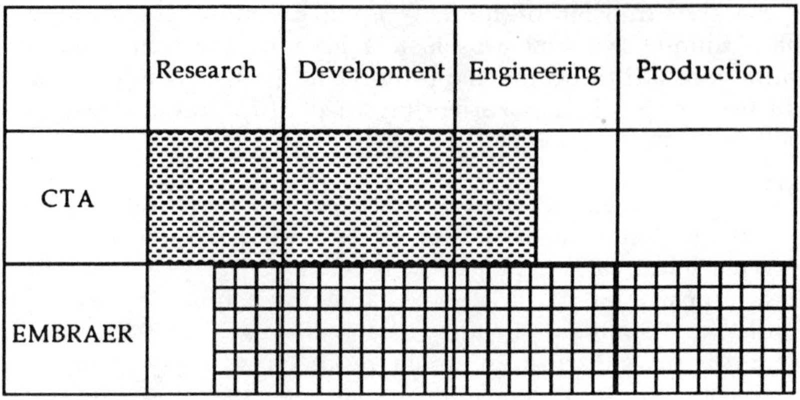

	Research	Development	Engineering	Production
CTA	▓▓▓▓▓	▓▓▓▓▓▓	▓▓▓	
EMBRAER		▦▦▦▦	▦▦▦▦	▦▦▦▦

Source: Adapted from Damiani, op. cit.

park. Changing the recipient from EMBRAER to the supplier park reflects the clearly defined role of CTA as a research institution; commercialization was left to the firms. Director Brigadier Lauro Ney Menezes said of the orientation of the CTA:

> The constant preoccupation and job of the technicians and systems analysts is to introduce, into the industrial process, technologies as yet unused, exercising as such, a pragmatic and central role in the industrial park.[38]

The pragmatism of direct links to industry without usurping industry's role has certainly been an effective model. Because of its ability to adjust its role to the needs of the firm, CTA may be perceived a complementary actor in the research and development process. As illustrated in Figure 6.7 while there is a large degree of overlap and collaboration in the research, development and engineering activities, production is solely the purview of the firm. Furthermore, as engineering moves out of the product stage and into process specific aspects, the firm assumes increasing control.

As the capabilities of the firm matured, the research activity was increasingly performed in-house. With the strong foundation provided by the CTA, EMBRAER now characterizes itself as a firm dedicated to applied aviation research. Indeed Silva argues for firm-specific research:

Research must be, whenever possible, conducted in the firm, where it is applied to the product. There is no vitality when it is produced away from the firm except when it is treated as imported know-how. In this case it does not arrive as research, but as a finished product to be implemented into another assembly line and later reproduced here in the country. But if there is not prior experience [in the importing firm] in the industry, the transfer is practically impossible.[39]

This emphasis on in-house research is evident in the research and development expenditures of the firm. As seen in Table 6.1, from 1973 to 1982 it invested $163.78 million in research and development, an average rate of 11.87% of sales. One-quarter of the firm's work force consists of engineers, technicians and scientists. To put these numbers in the Brazilian context, a ranking of Brazilian firms in 1983 by investment in R&D places EMBRAER fourth in the nation.[40]

Advanced Technologies: The AMX Program

Despite its strong research and development program EMBRAER still benefits from its connection with the state in pushing its technological frontier forward. The AMX strike fighter program underscores this point. The Brazilian Air Force, in its re-equipment plan, needed a dedicated, single seat attack aircraft. With the production of the AMX strike fighter EMBRAER entered a new technological market. Said the Aeronautics Minister Moreira Lima:

In sum, we are dealing with a project very important technologically with various developments for other sectors of the industry such as electronics, for example. This project will also transform EMBRAER, today a firm of the third level, into a firm on the level of the most important European and American producers.[41]

But the technological jump from EMBRAER's existing production line to this system was too demanding. Both international participation and state support were necessary. Back in 1979 then-chief of the Aeronautical high command (Emaer) Clovis Pavan began looking for international partners.[42] Thus EMBRAER entered into a joint production agreement with the Italian companies Aermacchi and Aeritalia to produce the AMX. The initial contract called for a block of thirty aircraft, nine for Brazil and twenty-one for Italy. A second contract has been signed for eighty-four units, twenty-three destined for Brazil and fifty-seven for the Italian Air Force. E M B R A E R is

TABLE 6.1

EMBRAER's Research and Development Expenditures, 1973-1982

Year	R&D Cr$mh	R&D US$mh	R&D/Total Sales (%)
1973	21.1	3.4	9.35%
1974	39.4	5.8	9.28%
1975	74.2	9.1	10.6 %
1976	138.0	12.9	10.34%
1977	177.7	14.6	11.35%
1978	370.4	20.5	16.60%
1979	627.4	23.3	13.57%
1980	1240.5	23.5	13.63%
1981	2229.7	23.9	10.08%
1982	4772.5	26.6	12.9 %
Total (all years)	9690.9		11.87 (avg.)

Source: Adapted from EMBRAER Company Report, *Informações,..*1983; converted at exchange rates in appendix.

responsible for producing 30% of each unit, including the wings, air intake, weapons pylons, jettisonable fuel tanks, landing gears and reconnaissance pallets.[43]

The state provided the necessary capital to construct a new military hanger at EMBRAER and supplemented development costs. In 1981 the government approved a budget of US$300 million to support EMBRAER technically, although the total investment is reported to have surpassed US$1.8 billion by 1987.[44] The financing of the AMX project has proven quite controversial. Funding was announced through the National Development Fund (FND) which was created to finance projects of infrastructure and social programs and is financed by compulsory savings on cars and gasoline.[45] When it was publicized that state funds for social welfare were being applied to a military jet "equipped with cannons, missiles, bombs and rockets"[46] there was substantial public opposition.[47]

This decision is part of the broader Government Action Plan (PAG) originated in the Planning Ministry and submitted to President Sarney. Minister Anibal Teixeira was pressured to make cuts in the plan's budget for macroeconomic reasons, but held fast in his decision that the FND should finance the development of the AMX. The AMX was included in the PAG because it was one of the priorities of the Aeronautics Ministry. It had been under development since 1980 under a rigid international schedule and to fall behind would cause tension with the Italian coproducers.

According to Moreira Lima, the disputed decision was made exclusively by SEPLAN, the National Planning Agency and not by the Air Force.

> The Air Force has been requesting funds to invest in the development of the project. Throughout the years, these funds were always obtained from the national budget, and then assigned to the Air Force Ministry. This year, however, as a result of technical studies it carried out, the SEPLAN decided to assign FND funds to the AMX project. It has been an entirely technical decision made by the SEPLAN.[48]

In Minister Moreira Lima's opinion, the criticism aimed at funding the AMX project through the FND was groundless because it has three exceptional advantages: (1) it helps to develop the Brazilian war materiel industry; (2) it prevents Brazil from spending currency in purchasing this type of plane; and (3) it will bring currency to Brazil through its sale abroad.[49] Thus the AMX would theoretically benefit Brazilian society in achieving dual objectives of national security and balance of international payments.

Furthermore, the project would benefit other firms in the industrial sector. Described as a flying computer, the AMX demands a sophisticated level of electronic components largely unavailable in the Brazilian industrial park. The Ministry of Aeronautics decided to use this project as a lead car for the development of more sophisticated suppliers. The argument given in the press for spending state money from the social fund on a military project was the strong spin-off effects the program was predicted to have. The program initiated is called the PIC or the complementary industrial program. With support from the Ministry of Aeronautics (ultimately the final user), IFI (the department of industrial promotion at CTA) was to promote technological development in selected critical areas. With the Ministry of Aeronautics providing the broad structure of information, legislation, funding and orders, the CTA was to advance development in electronics, electrical equipment and mechanical/ hydraulic systems.[50] In total 49 components or subsystems for the AMX with a targeted total dollar value of US$ 2.2 million were to be produced in seven firms: ABC, ELEBRA, AEROMOT, MICROLAB, ENGETRONICA, PIRELLI and EDE Systems. These firms were carefully screened by IFI and judged capable in the areas of production technology, quality

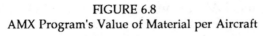

FIGURE 6.8
AMX Program's Value of Material per Aircraft

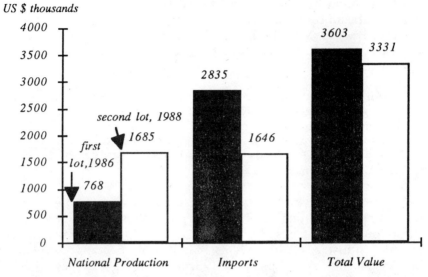

Source: Based on data in "O Esforço de Nacionalizaçao da EMBRAER e do Ministério da Aeronáutica," Internal CTA document.

control, physical capital and financial stability. It is interesting to note that EDE is a subsidiary of EMBRAER created to produce aeronautical equipment and that ENGETRONICA is a subsidiary of ENGESA. Acting as an umbrella for the technological transfer, the CTA and the Ministry of Aeronautics negotiated technology transfer agreements with the Italian firms supplying the AMX production line in Italy. Although the technology contracts were initially more expensive than the outright purchase of components, it was predicted that there would be a long run payoff to the program.

As can be see from Figure 6.8, within a two year time period the program has shown significant results. The proportion of national material incorporated into the AMX has increased 119%. It estimated that as the project reaches its goal of 40% imported equipment for the AMX, the savings in imports will total approximately $116.6 million.

Nevertheless, this has not been an inexpensive program. The investment of the Ministry of Aeronautics in assisting in the purchase of the technology packages under the PIC program is estimated at US$ 47 million. However, it is argued that in the absence of purchasing the technology, testing equipment, technical assistance, training and spare parts in order to incorporate imported components would have totaled US$ 51.95 million, with a net saving of almost US$ 5 million.

Those within IFI at the CTA look at this program as an example of the potential benefits of investment in the military area.[51] With experience in technological acquisition, firms can apply the techniques learned to other areas of production. Indeed, given problems of quality control and the weakness of in-firm research in Brazil, these military contracts are perceived as a means of promoting technological development in the industrial park. Researchers at IFI feel that such technological growth cannot take place in isolation of concrete Air Force projects for a simple reason: the CTA doesn't have buying power. An attempt to promote industrial development without a product with a guaranteed market is, in IFI experience, too risky. Thus, in terms of our technological flow diagram once more we can see the importance of the final user in the feedback system.

Lessons

Several lessons from the technology exchange between CTA and EMBRAER merit attention: consistent objectives, communication, human resource development, technology planning, industrial targeting and a supportive political economy. The technology donor, CTA, the intermediate producer, EMBRAER, and the source of final demand, the Brazilian Air Force, were all institutionally linked under the Ministry of Aeronautics. They shared common goals and were spared interministerial rivalries. Because the industry is of high priority to national security, finance was available through private capital markets, the CTA and Defense Ministry funding. Commercial credit was not necessary for the Brazilian Air Force; later the government facilitated the civilian sales with subsidies to firms to purchase the Bandeirante.

Since EMBRAER physically adjoins CTA, Air Force pilots flight-test EMBRAER aircraft, eat in the company dining room and fraternize freely with EMBRAER employees. Feedback and communication is thus immediate, informal and highly effective. Both middle and top management have access to the practical information necessary to promote innovation and development. In training a core of world-class engineers, ITA has been, according to EMBRAER's president Silva, an innovative source of technological development.[52] By first attending to education, CTA accelerated technology absorption.[53] Indeed, it may be argued that the knowledge acquired, equipment developed, technology assimilated and competency generated has already multiplied far in excess of initial educational investments.[54] The political and economic environment supported aviation development. An aeronautics industry was justified as necessary to facilitate the continued growth and expansion of the nation. An aerospace complex was a sign of industrialization and international prestige. The state was willing to implement protectionist measures to give the new industry time to consolidate operations.

Thus, the relationship between the CTA and EMBRAER demonstrates complementarity in the tasks each assumes, dynamism in responding to the changing abilities of the firm, clear communication of information surrounding potential technologies and strong support in supplying infrastructure and intermediate inputs. By supplementing the capacity of the firm to select, develop and implement new technologies without stifling research activity within EMBRAER, the CTA has set in motion a viable long-run strategy for the sector.

Case 2:
International Technology Transfer: Piper and EMBRAER

In addition to the technology transferred from the CTA, international purchases of technology enabled EMBRAER to acquire a sophisticated manufacturing technology to meet the needs of the Brazilian Air Force within a short period of time. This section examines a key licensing agreement between EMBRAER and an external technology donor, Piper Aircraft, to produce twin and single motor aircraft. This transfer was successful as measured by the ability of EMBRAER to absorb the technology and service the domestic market. The discussion analyzes the conditions facilitating the technology transfer, including demand, the goals and policies of the state, and the positive sum nature of the agreement. The section concludes by extracting key elements of this technology transfer agreement with potential applications to other international technology exchanges.

With rapid economic growth and the need for better integration between geographically distant markets, the Brazilian demand for single and twin engine planes was large and growing. Table 6.2 shows a sixfold increase in imports of 4-8 seater aircraft from 1964 through 1974 for a total of 2,485 aircraft. With 93% of these imports from Beechcraft, Cessna and Piper, Brazil was the largest market outside the U.S. for American-made aircraft of that type.[55] The vigor of this domestic market strengthened EMBRAER's hand in attracting technology donors.[56]

At the end of 1974, Cessna's market share was 59%; Piper and Cessna

TABLE 6.2

Single and Twin Engine Imports—Brazilian Civilian Market 1964-74

Producer	64	65	66	67	68	69	70	71	77	73	74	Total
Beechcraft												
Single	5	2	5	8	16	6	10	19	11	31	32	145
Twin	10	4	11	11	14	9	12	10	14	9	0	106
Market												
Share	16%	10%	6%	11%	16%	9%	17%	14%	10%	8%	6%	10%
Cessna												
Single	54	28	72	94	85	75	53	103	132	297	343	1336
Twin	4	3	5	12	11	11	2	11	13	35	30	137
Market												
Share	64%	53%	47%	60%	51%	51%	44%	55%	57%	65%	69%	59%
Piper												
Single	10	25	27	36	33	25	33	31	7	64	360	651
Twin	45	34	16	18	23	14	20	26	33	41	234	504
Market												
Share	4%	26%	36%	24%	28%	33%	31%	25%	22%	21%	19%	24%
Other												
Single	12	4	7	6	3	6	3	8	14	21	22	106
Twin	1	2	4	2	7	7	7	4	15	6	6	61
Market												
Share	14%	10%	4%	5%	5%	8%	8%	6%	11%	5%	5%	7%

Source: Calculated from EMBRAER company report "Informações de Caráter Geral Sobre a Indústria Aeronáutica Brasileira," 1983.

held 24 and 10% respectively. In 1978, unit prices varied from $20,000 to $30,000 for 2-4 seater recreational planes to over $1 million for 18-20 seater turboprops and a half a million for business jets.[57] Essential to agricultural output and business infrastructure, by 1973 importing planes cost Brazil over $10 million per year. The government was insistent upon import replacement.[58]

After deciding to build single and twin engine aircraft, EMBRAER considered product design and technological capability. Should it be developed by EMBRAER and CTA or purchased abroad? Indigenous development engendered investment risks without assured results. With no guarantee the firm could develop a product meeting market demand within a short period of time, EMBRAER turned abroad. But since the firm's mandate was to develop internal technical, managerial, manufacturing and marketing capabilities, EMBRAER sought an agreement incrementally allowing the firm independent control over advancing production stages. Decreasing multinational participation until the aircraft was 100% nationally made could also conserve foreign exchange.

The stipulation of Brazilian control met with resistance from transnational aircraft producers. To enhance EMBRAER's bargaining position the Brazilian government announced a prohibitive tariff would be placed on imports of foreign aircraft after domestic production began. Thus, only EMBRAER's partner would have access to the huge Brazilian market, albeit through licensing in lieu of finished aircraft. Joint production has become common in newly industrializing countries to increase domestic content, conserve foreign exchange, and/or to uphold security concerns. Says Baranson:

> As a practical matter, opportunities to export finished aircraft are decreasing rapidly. The government of the purchasing party is generally directly or indirectly involved in such decisions—whether they concern civilian or military aircraft—and it usually has political and military, as well as economic reasons, for insisting on national production.[59]

Two important factors influencing the ability of a state to change the terms of the technology agreement are the possible exclusion from a lucrative market and competitive behavior among potential technology suppliers. If the threat of exclusion is credible and predicted losses substantial, the transnational may find the benefits of cooperation outweigh losses. The degree of competition and collusion in the transnational market weighs heavily in the decision to share technology abroad; if monopolistic or characterized by collusive behavior, it is likely to covet the technology. However, if the market is competitive, a firm may prefer to gain an exclusive share through licensing rather than maintain a smaller export share. The potential for the learning partner to surpass the donor in production capabilities in international markets and the rate of obsolescence of the technology transferred also affect the decision to sell technology. Benefits of transnational participation are limited if the learning firm masters the technology rapidly enough to challenge the donor in international markets. On the other hand, if the product is subject to rapid obsolescence, licensing may help amortize the original research and development costs for the transnational without large future losses.

Since exclusion from the Brazilian market would be a significant loss, Cessna and Piper were willing to negotiate with EMBRAER. Since it stood to lose least, Beech declined, maintaining the Brazilians should import its aircraft. Initially the Brazilians favored Cessna, perceiving it of higher quality. However, Cessna did not want to forfeit production control to allow modifications, believing quality would suffer. The Brazilians were piqued at the insinuation that EMBRAER had inadequate quality control and became less enthusiastic. When Cessna demanded royalties for technological know-how acquired, the Brazilians turned to Piper.

Piper stood to benefit, holding only one quarter of the market against Cessna's one half.[60] Furthermore, the opportunity came at a time when Piper's share in Brazil was shrinking. As Piper's president said:

> We chose Brazil for Piper's investment because the country has a pressing need for the planes, a stable economy, accelerated economic growth and both government and private industry are interested the creation of a modern, competitive technology.[61]

Thus, a strong domestic market and demonstrated government support of EMBRAER signaled Piper that joint production would be profitable. But the agreement was so favorable to EMBRAER that an official commented:

> It was a good agreement for us. Frankly, some of us were surprised that Piper accepted all our demands and more. But it was also a good agreement for Piper. Their business in Brazil increased tremendously.[62]

After signing the Piper contract, Brazil increased the tariff on aircraft from 7% to 50% and required importers to make a one year interest free deposit covering the price of manufactured goods. Cessna, which sold 373 aircraft to Brazil in 1974, marketed 5 two years later.[63] Beech was likewise closed out, giving Piper, through parts and technology, effective domain.

The 1974 Piper-EMBRAER agreement provided for the progressive expansion of production through three broad stages: final assembly, subassembly and component production and assembly.[64] In the final phase, EMBRAER estimated the Brazilian content of the planes would approach 70% which indeed was attained in 1978.[65] But even at this high rate of nationalization, Piper continued to profit. Due to economies of scale and technological sophistication, roughly one-third of parts and subsystems were bought from Piper. If EMBRAER achieved 100% nationalization, Piper would be paid a service fee. However, EMBRAER and Piper officials concur that 100% nationalization is unlikely.

The threat that EMBRAER might compete with Piper internationally was limited by restricting EMBRAER's export of Piper models to a case by case review. Thus, Piper could use EMBRAER as a vehicle to penetrate markets in Latin America and Africa with whom Brazilians have a competitive marketing advantage, but restrict competition in existent markets. Nevertheless, nearly all Piper models sold by EMBRAER are in domestic use.[66]

By 1980 EMBRAER advanced beyond the technological level of the Piper line and relocated its production to its subsidiary Indústria Aeronáutica NEIVA, S.A. Piper models were brought to São José dos Campos to be painted, flight tested and delivered.[67] Nationalization of the EMBRAER Piper product line continued under Neiva, with participation of Sociedade AEROTEC Ltda and MOTORTEC Indústria Aeronáutica S.A. Additionally, firms such as FORTEPLAS, producer of the fiberglass components and AEROMOT, maker of chairs and benches, also produce equipment. Based upon the learning process acquired with Piper aircraft, in concert with CTA EMBRAER designed an indigenous agricultural aircraft the EMB-210 Ipanema.[68]

EMBRAER's engineers do not regard the Piper line to be as sophisticated as the planes they designed or will bring out in the near future. One engineer said, "We don't think of Piper products as part of EMBRAER."[69] Indeed, EMBRAER wanted to sell Neiva because "the technology of NEIVA is incompatible and disproportional with that of EMBRAER today," according to engineer Ozílio Silva.[70] The incompatibility was accentuated by EMBRAER's need to expand in the high technology arena but was constrained by indebtedness limits as a state enterprise.[71] However, a suitable buyer was not found for the asking price. The offers made included as part of the terms the continued participation of the state enterprise.[72] Under these terms the objective of privatizing the firm was not met and the deal fell through.

Instead of selling the subsidiary EMBRAER chose to re-export the production technology. The May 1989 agreement transferring the bulk of the production of the Piper line to with Chincul Fábrica de Aviones of Argentina reflects this position. In accordance with that agreement, EMBRAER will only produce two of the six licensed Piper aircraft and

TABLE 6.3
Factors Influencing the Piper Technology Transfer

FACTOR	+/-	APPLIED TO BRAZIL
Large domestic market	+	2nd largest outside U.S.
Protectionist state	+	Brazil imposes 50% levy
Potential to surpass	o	Limited by contract
Competition	+	Piper could overtake Cessna
Technology type	+	Intermediate, with high obsolescence

the indigenous Ipanema; Chincul will expand the Piper line production in Argentina. Marketing and sales will be carried out by both the Argentine and Brazilian producers, with financing available from both nations as well.[73] Part of this package is an open line of credit covering 85% of the plane's price with a low interest rate of 6.75% over eight years.[74] The joint production agreement should also allow EMBRAER and Chincul to take advantage of economies of scale.[75]

That EMBRAER moved from a licensee of technology to a licensor reflects the dynamism of this technology transfer model. The Piper-EMBRAER agreement is a case of effective government-enterprise partnership. Table 6.3 summarizes the beneficial conditions favoring the transfer. The state threatened and carried through on protective tariffs, closing the market to other competitors, enabling EMBRAER to negotiate an agreement minus restrictive and expensive royalties and fees. Nevertheless, while facilitating the technology exchange, it left the choice of the product and the transnational partner to EMBRAER. The transfer also benefitted from EMBRAER's production experience on the Bandeirante, Xavante and Ipanema projects. It had the expertise not only to negotiate for the appropriate product and process, but also to bring the aircraft quickly into production. Because of EMBRAER's knowledge in the area, the firm was able to nationalize a high percentage of the aircraft rapidly. Furthermore, as the capabilities of the firm matured, the agreement allowed EMBRAER to move out of this line, further recycling the technology.

CASE 3:
ENGESA's Indigenous Development of a Unique Technology and the Further Development of a Science and Technology Infrastructure in the Armored Vehicle Sector

ENGESA became a leading world manufacturer of armored vehicles not by design but by circumstance. The firm was formed in 1956 as a supplier of pieces and components utilized in discovery and extraction of oil by the state-owned oil firm Petrobras.[76] In the early 1960s the company was a small shop in São Paulo adapting civilian Ford, Chevrolet and Dodge trucks to the rigorous Brazilian terrain. ENGESA engineers, however, developed a unique suspension system giving forward propulsion to all wheels, enabling off-road maneuvers. This system, baptized "boomerang suspension," was patented and formed the core around which a family of military vehicles was subsequently developed.[77] Thus, a specialized civilian technology with key military applications made ENGESA competitive in the military market. An ample civilian market, including construction companies, Petrobras, and wood firms in the Amazon, gave the firm valuable manufacturing experience. Therefore, in its initial stages, the firm was not dependent upon government orders, but solidified production outside the military umbrella.

The firm became well integrated into the existing automobile industry, using readily available parts and components to reconstruct Fords and Chevrolets with the boomerang system. Unlike the aeronautical industry, forced by the exacting nature of aviation technology to import, ENGESA built upon an existing set of automotive suppliers. Moreover, incentives for doing so were strengthened by strict import quotas. This standardization of materials and off-the-shelf availability incorporated into ENGESA tanks significantly contributing to the firm's success.

In the late 1960s the Army looked to replace jeeps, trucks, tractors and aging heavy combat M-8 "Greyhound" tanks acquired through U.S. military assistance programs. However, limited foreign exchange and international scarcity made international purchases problematic. With the Brazilian economy in the throes of what the Armed Forces had defined as chaos, costly imports were discouraged. But even if currency had been plentiful, equipment was not, with supplies being channelled to Vietnam. Finally, the Brazilian economy had reached a level of industrialization that made possible domestic procurement. Thus, political and military sentiment was to promote industrial expansion and military security through arms production.

The idea for ENGESA to build army tanks came not from any grand government strategy, but from good personal relations between people in the firm and those in the Army.[78] The Army solicited from ENGESA a prototype of a wheeled reconnaissance vehicle and an amphibian personnel transport to replace old American tanks. Unlike the aerospace sector where technology was firmly rooted at the CTA and a state firm formed to commercialize this technology, the armored vehicles sector was more decentralized and relied heavily on private enterprise. Said General Alves Martins, director of the Army's Research and Technical School:

> We are looking to work with the participation of civil industry in all of our projects, not only because we do not have sufficient funding but also because civil industry is ready and capable to participate in the plans. This integration promotes the exchange of experience, reduces the costs and elevates the results both in terms of profits for the industries as well as in total knowledge gained.[79]

After several revisions of the prototype, ENGESA began production in 1972 of the EE-9 Cascavel and the EE-11 Urutu. The Navy, duly impressed, ordered a modified version of the amphibious Urutu and ENGESA began amplifying military deliveries. Reflecting on the move from civilian to military production Carlos Alberto M. Barbarosa, the director of commercial planning for ENGESA, said:

> ENGESA began producing armaments as the result of a natural process. The civilian vehicles of the firm had been utilized by the Armed Forces and had consistently been improved to perform with adverse conditions such as difficult roads, streams, mountains, holes and other obstacles. The group then developed its own armament technology, which today is being exported. We also import technology, but for aspects far more complex such as ballistic equipment.[80]

ENGESA successfully developed an indigenous technology which has been applied to civilian and military vehicles domestically and abroad. What were the characteristics which made for effective technological applications? Given that the technology was developed in-house, there was no difficulty with the flow between the technology donor and the intermediate producer. The benefit came in the effective flow of information between the final user, the Armed Forces and the producer. In the civilian market ENGESA's already strong connections with the automobile and oil industries facilitated the feedback from civilian customers on specific needs. Thus, the Brazilian Armed Forces provided both the incentive to produce the new tanks with ENGESA's boomerang system and a guaranteed final demand.

The domestic political economy was conducive as the national industrialization policy complemented the strategy of the firm. Although the technology was innovative, it was not radically different from well known products. Thus, adoption of the boomerang system was simplified by the existing pool of technical knowledge. But this intermediate technology still had a lucrative and untapped developing country market. Without tough international competition, ENGESA was able to commercialize the tank in Brazil and abroad.

ENGESA's technological development contrasts with the aeronautical sector in two respects: technology type and technology source. ENGESA began with a civilian technology type. The product which launched EMBRAER's military line was the military Bandeirante, although it later found a strong civilian market. Nevertheless, that ENGESA began with a civilian product which later found a military market in contrast with EMBRAER's beginning with a military prototype seems to have made little difference in the behavior of the firm. However, technology source has been more influential. While ENGESA developed its own technology, EMBRAER received the Bandeirante from CTA and licenses for commuter and military models from Piper and Aermachi. The independent sourcing of ENGESA, in addition to the important fact that the firm began and remains a private entity as opposed to EMBRAER's mixed enterprise status, allows ENGESA more leeway in marketing its military goods in international markets and makes it less accountable to domestic public policy. Private, independent technology sourcing has made for more private, closed behavior on the part of the firm. Nevertheless, the state still played a critical role in shaping the development of technology in the armored vehicle sector. Without the incentive offered by the Army for a prototype and the support of its research and technical school, the boomerang system would not have been refined for use in military vehicles. Thus, while the firm directly developed and controlled the technology, the flow of information between the purchaser and the producer promoted rapid development.

Ongoing Technological Development
in the Army Sector

While ENGESA was able to develop the technology for the boomerang system within the firm and commercialize the product domestically and internationally, as a whole the sector has become constrained by weaknesses in the technological system. In particular, the need for increasingly sophisticated electronic subsystems has forced greater dependence on imports, compromising autonomous procurement. With the goal of promoting domestic technology sources the Army has reorganized its science and technology structure.

But before discussing the new system it is instructive to differentiate technological development under the auspices of the Ministry of the Army over time as compared to the Ministry of Aeronautics. Up until recent years technology has not been at the center of Army procurement policy. In light of an almost nonexistent external threat, Army commanders have been more concerned with equipping foot soldiers and less interested in the latest in technological gadgetry. Indeed some army officials have even been characterized as techno-phobic. Part of this might be explained by the fact that Army personnel are less directly dependent on technology than those in the Air Force. For example, if a tank breaks down, the soldier can simply get out and walk; if there is failure in an aircraft system, however, the likelihood of death is high.[81]

Despite the lack of a central focus, the history of technological activity in the Army can be dated prior to the formation of the Republic. In 1762 the first facility to provide war material was built by the governor of Rio de Janeiro. A gunpowder factory was built in 1808 and in 1811 the Real Military Academy was created to organize all of the engineering faculties in the country.[82] By the turn of the century factories were set up in Realango and Piquete to produce small arms and explosives. The basic directive of the time was to import the equipment necessary to produce domestically.[83] When World War I shortages interrupted supplies and the 1930 civil revolution demonstrated the weaknesses in national procurement, factories in Adarai, Curitiba, Itajubá, Juiz da Fora, and Bonsucesso were built. All continued to produce under license, with engineering capabilities limited to "knowing how" to produce but not "knowing why."[84] Formation of qualified engineers became a priority in 1928 with the opening of the Military Engineering School, which in 1942 became the well respected Military Engineering Institute, IME. At this point in Army technological history the primary activity was production, with formation of human resources secondary, and research and development practically nonexistent.[85]

Note the contrast with the CTA and the aeronautics model where human resource development came first in ITA, research and development was closely allied in the IPD, and production was the very last step in the chain. In the Army sector production, principally under foreign license, preceded human capital formation. Rather than

FIGURE 6.9
Army Ministry Structure of Research and Development

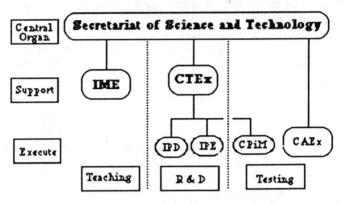

Source: Based on information presented in Coronel José Carlos Albano do Amarante, "O Papel do Setor de C&T do Exército na Interação Universidade-Empresa," Paper presented in the Universidade-Empresa (University-Firm Seminar), COPPE-UFRJ, Rio de Janeiro, June 5-8, 1989.

building upon the experience of a core group of scientists and engineers heavily invested in developing military technology, technology advocates in the Army had to overcome vested interests in the status quo. Furthermore, while the Air Force could build the productive structure from the ground up, as technology began to assume greater importance for the Army it was saddled with outmoded and inefficient plants constructed as early as the mid-eighteenth century.

By the late 1960s the Army at least recognized the deficiencies in its program and the high degree of dependency on imported technology. The Three Year Plan for the 1968-1970 period attempted to redress these weaknesses. In 1969 the first post graduate courses were offered at IME and two years later the Institute for Research and Development, IPD was formed. The Army factories were brought under the administrative responsibility of IMBEL (the Brazilian Industry for Military Material) in 1975 and in 1979 CTEx, the Army research and technical center was created on the CTA model. The systematization of the Army research and development model was formalized with the creation of the Secretariat for Science and Technology in 1984; in that year the testing center CAEx was also formed. Completing the institutional structure was the addition of the IPE, the Institute for Space Projects, in 1986.[86] Thus, the current structure of research and development under the Army Ministry is shown in Figure 6.9.

The principles guiding research and development under the Army Ministry strictly adhere to the precepts of a public-private partnership. In a paper describing the role of research and development in the Army, Amarante highlights several points:

- The focus of activity is in human resource development in areas closely aligned with the operational needs of the Brazilian Army.
- Research and development should always take place in national firms where possible, with the research centers providing a supportive role.
- The Army Ministry will only develop those projects that do not interest national firms, national firms are not capable of performing, or those that demand a high degree of secrecy.
- Imported technology should only be used to burn steps in the technology acquisition process.[87]

Accordingly, research in the sector is not scientifically open-ended but grounded in human capital development with concrete benefits for Army procurement needs. The locus of research activity is domestic private firms, with state research centers and international technology sources supporting efforts only when the private sector fails to achieve desired results.

Amarante further delineates the spheres of public and private interaction in the technological camp. First, state research and development agencies should act as generators of technology. This can do accomplished by working closely with a firm such as in the case of D.F. Vasconcellos in the development of night vision equipment or in supporting the development of more independent research within firms as was the case with ENGESA's Osório project. Alternatively technology may be developed within the research institutes of CTEx and later transferred to industry. This, however, should only occur when private firms cannot be induced to generate the product. Other services of CTEx include quality control, technical testing and operational evaluations—all functions which supplement the workings of the private market.

Thus, in terms of our technology flow diagram we can see in Figure 6.10 that the final user, the Brazilian Army, has a central role to play in product definition. Furthermore, research and development is primarily performed by private industry, with state research and development centers assuming only those tasks outside the capabilities of the private sector. Finally, in contrast to the strong reliance on

FIGURE 6.10
Armored Vehicles Sector Technology Flow

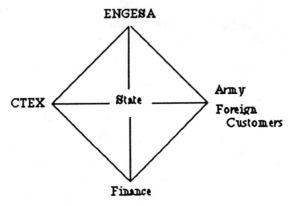

imported technology in the past, foreign sourcing should only be considered when the national industry would take so long to develop the technology that the gain in time would outweigh the cost of dependency.

The emphasis on participation of the private sector is reinforced by General Theodomiro, the chief of CTEx:

> I think that working together is necessary. In the past many errors were made from the premise that the Army had production as its mission. Independently of what private industry could do or not, there wasn't dialogue. Today, the situation is different.[88]

In addition to a central role for private industry Theodomino also underscored the need for exports, arguing that the Brazilian Army cannot be seen as the sole final user of the product:

> Above all, from the moment that a firm is invited to work with us, the first thing that we say is that they cannot live only with the orders of the Armed Forces of Brazil—at least not the Army, about which we can make this statement with certainty and very possibly not with just the Navy or Air Force. For economic reasons, Brazil is a country that does not have the conditions to maintain an Armed Force equipped in a manner that would perhaps be ideal.[89]

Despite the systemic conceptualization of the science and technology system in the Army sector, in practice the structure has not matured as planned. The principle problem is the lack of resources. Expansion of research and development under the new Secretariat happened at the same time that the federal budget in Brazil was subject to severe cutbacks because of external debt service burdens. CTEx is weak, without the necessary equipment or personnel to undertake substantial research projects. As the director of CTEx, General Theodomiro Serra Filho notes,

> Research, development, science and technology are areas that only live with financial resources; to obtain satisfactory results it is necessary to acquire equipment and contract good professionals. We believe that this [current crisis] is a passing stage, that the country is going to pass out of this economic crisis and then we will find that we can produce and develop all that we want.[90]

Nevertheless, while it may be argued that the CTEx installations merely await a better financial environment, this short run resource problem may have long run repercussions. The program to expand the research and development activities of the state came about precisely because the private sector was unable to absorb the growing costs. With the State compromised financially, the firms may be unable to continue to explore technological niches in the international market. More will be said of this contemporary crisis of the defense sector in the final chapter of this book.

Conclusion:
The State as Technology Promoter

> The secret of the success and of the growth of the Brazilian armaments industry is simple: the Brazilian armed forces, instead of following the inefficient solution in the majority of cases of maintaining its own production line for military equipment, came to invest larger sums in research and development in the Military Engineering Institute, in the Marine Research Institute and in the CTA. The technology developed is transferred to private industries which receive regular orders from the Government and can, with these new techniques, improve the quality of the products destined to the civilian arena. Through this process the firms are able to compete fairly in terms of quality with traditional suppliers of defense materials.[91]

Achievements in the defense sector underscore the benefits of this technology policy. The state, by supplementing and supporting the activities of the firm, facilitated national research and development. Rather than controlling the entire process, the government performed

TABLE 6.4
Elements of an Effective Technology Policy:
The Armaments Industry Case

Elements	Role of the State	Activity of Defense
Define Objectives	Ideology of Segurança e Desenvolvimento	Set micro production goals
Search for alternative technologies	Decided to develop internally	Began search
Obtain disaggregated information about the technology	Done in research institutes as well as through human capital investments	Engineers able to assimilate due to strong training
Comparison of different options	Defense Ministry	Strong firm input
Discussion of acquisition contract	Entertained between the producers, technology donor, military and government. Free flow of information.	
Government approval & support	Political and financial	Strong personal contacts
Reformulation and adoption	Financing schemes; guarantee final demand	Begin production planning
Line up suppliers of equipment and material	Support of IFI, GPMI, FIESP	Firm chooses suppliers
Acquisition of physical plant	CTA & Army lend/donate	Firm purchases the rest
Initiates operations		Start-up at firm
Product and process control	Research Centers-CTA, CTEX	In firm quality control
R&D to modify, adapt, innovate	Research Centers-CTA, CTEX	In firm innovations

Source: Column 1 from Plitzer and Arroz, "Transferência do Tecnologia para Desenvolvimento Autônomo," in Merlo, "Ciência e Tecnologia no Expressão do Poder Nacional," Lecture in ESG, Rio de Janeiro, September 12, 1983 (Unpublished paper).

the functions of technology acquisition beyond the capability of the firm. The degree of state support was a function of the technological requisites of each weapons program. It granted protection, exemption from tariffs and taxes, and was a guaranteed source of final demand. Domestic strength then promoted international competitiveness. The economic need for new markets was made clear. Exposure to broader markets encouraged further in-house research as well as providing the scale to engage in costly R&D.

Figure 6.13 illustrates this efficient division of labor between the state and defense firms. Using criteria developed by Plitzer and Arroz which are presented in column one, the complementary division of labor promoting effective technology transfers in the sector are illustrated.[92] The state, by providing technical and institutional support for R&D throughout the acquisition process, allowed the firm to maximize returns, in turn enhancing domestic procurement capabilities.

The objectives for the sector were broadly defined by the policy of "segurança e desenvolvimento" and institutionalized through the Superior War College (ESG). Institutional support played a critical role in implementing a high technology industry.[93] The armaments sector was promoted by a core of technicians, bureaucrats and entrepreneurs with a vested interest in achieving economically viable autonomy from import dependence in the sector. Through training in the Air Force Institute (ITA) and the army engineering school, entrepreneurs and technicians possessed the requisite skills to evaluate alternative technologies. This state support by pragmatic decision makers with clearly communicated objectives provided the firm with the direction and foundation critical to establishing production goals and techniques. Together, the state worked with firms in the industry to determine which technologies are feasible within the Brazilian industrial infrastructure as well as suitable for the domestic armed forces and international marketing. Furthermore, the state provided financial support, supplied physical factors of production and guaranteed the minimum level of purchases for viable production. Finally, we note cooperation and complementarity between the state and the firm in improving quality and efficiency in production.

The partnership between the state and the firms throughout each step of the process allowed Brazil to develop military technologies indigenously. Control over technologies developed specifically for Third World conditions promotes the dual use of these products in other sectors, an increased rate of "spin-offs" of research on both products and processes into other industries and conserved foreign exchange.

In partnership with the state, Brazilian firms were able to develop indigenous technologies appropriate to national economic constraints as well as military demand. With a clear view of the objective of autonomy, international transfer agreements were negotiated which maximized the bargaining power of the Brazilian firm to control the imported technology. In conclusion, the complementary, supportive role of the state in technology policy promoted autonomous technological development, increasing the benefits for the firm as well as for the Brazilian society as a whole.

Notes

1.   For a broad overview of the problem of technology in Latin America, see Jack Baranson, *North South Technology Transfer*, (Mt. Airy, MD: Lomond Publications, Inc., 1981), pp. 1-12. Adler gives a particularly lucid overview of the development of science and technology policy including a very useful chronological summary of institutional developments from 1962-1980 (pp.156-162). Emanuel Adler, *The Power of Ideology: The Quest for Technological Autonomy in Argentina and Brazil* (Berkeley, Los Angeles and London: University of California Press, 1987).

2.   Carl Dahlman and Larry Westphal, "Technological Effort in Industrial Development—An Interpretive Survey of Recent Research," *The Economics of New Technology in Developing Countries*, F. Stewart and J. James, eds. (Boulder, CO: Westview Press, 1982).

3.   *O Plano Básico do Desenvolvimento Científico e Tecnológico*, A Presidência da República, Fundação IBGE, Servico Grafico.

4.   Candido Pereira, "Reflexões Sobre o Estado, Ciência e Tecnologia no Brasil," FINEP working paper, O Centro de Estudos e Pesquisas (CEP), Grupo de Estudos Sobre O Setor Público, November 1976

5.   Ibid.

6.   See Werner Baer, *The Brazilian Economy*, 3rd edition (New York: Praeger Press, 1989), Chapters 2, 3, and 4.

7.   Candido Pereira, "Reflexões Sobre o Estado."

8.   Adler, *The Power of Ideology*.

9.   Candido Pereira, "Reflexões Sobre o Estado."

10.   Yet Brazil led developing countries in technology planning. OECD countries set the goal of technology planning in 1963; Brazil, with the Strategic Economic Development Program (PED) in 1968 was the first in Latin America to plan technology.

11.   José Murilo Carvalho, "A Política Científica e Tecnológica no Brasil," *Revista da Finanças Públicas*, 39 (No. Especial), March 1979.

12.   *Plano Basico de Desenvolvimento Científico e Tecnológico*.

13.   Ibid.

14.   Ibid.

15.   *O Globo*, May 29, 1985.

16.   Delfim Neto was Minister of Finance under the Costa e Silva and the Medici governments. Enormously powerful, he was behind the so-called

"Brazilian Miracle." See P. Flynn, *Brazil: A Political Analysis* (CO: Westview, 1978)

17.   Carvalho, "A Política Científica e Tecnológica no Brasil."
18.   Ibid.
19.   Ibid.
20.   Ibid.
21.   Ibid.
22.   Fabio Stefano Erber, "Política Científica e Tecnológica no Brasil: Uma Revisão da Literatura," *Resenhas da Economia Brasileira*, Editora Saraiva, J. Sayad, ed. (Rio de Janeiro, 1979).
23.   Carvalho, "A Política Científica e Tecnológica no Brasil."
24.   Ibid.
25.   Erber, "A Política Científica e Tecnológica no Brasil."
26.   Waldir Pirro e Longo, "Ciência e Poder Militar," *Defesa Nacional*, No. 576, March/April 1978.
27.   Erber, "A Política Científica e Tecnológica no Brasil."
28.   Adler describes the Sabato Triangle as "an almost mystic metaphor informing contemporary discussion [of technology policy]. Adler, *The Power of Ideology*, p. 58.
29.   Adler, *The Power of Ideology*, p. 58
30.   Adler, *The Power of Ideology*, pp. 191-192.
31.   Saadat Deger and Somnath Sen, "Technology Transfer and Arms Production in Developing Countries," *Industry and Development*, (Nov. 15, 1985; also see Deger and Sen "Military expenditure spin-off and economic growth," *Journal of Development Economics*, 1983; and P. Lock and H. Wulf, "The Economic Consequences of the Transfer of Military Oriented Technology," *The World Military Order*, M. Kaldor and A. Eide, eds. (London: MacMillan, 1979).
32.   Deger and Sen, 1985, p.4.
33.   *Jornal da Tarde*, "Nossos aviões já voam em 45 países," September 18, 1987.
34.   Ozires Silva, "Pesquisa, Tecnologia e Desenvolvimento Nacional," Conferência proferida na Faculdade Tibirica 1980, Texto No.1. Also see Ozires Silva, "O Vôo da EMBRAER," *Revista Brasileira de Tecnologia*, V.13(1) Jan/Mar 1982, pp20-30.
35.   *Jornal do Brasil*, "Brasil testa Sonda IV, seu maior foguete, para 1982," July 20, 1982; *Jornal da Tarde*, "CTA planeja exportação de peças de avião," May 20, 1975; *Estado de São Paulo*, "Em teste a primeira turbina a jato nacional," August 27, 1983; "Brasil na era espacial," Publication of the Ministry of Aeronautics, Public Relations Center; *Jornal do Brasil* "EMB quer avião militar," July 16, 1980; J. Damiani, "O EMB-110 Bandeirante e o Processo de Inovação Tecnológica," paper given at the VII Simpósio Nacional de Pesquisa em Administração de Ciência e Tecnologia, São Paulo, 1983; João Alexandre Viegas, in "Algo além dos aviões no campo da aeronáutica," *Dados e Idéias*, 5, Apr/May 1979 discusses several of these projects in depth.
36.   "O salto tecnológico da indústria nacional," *EXAME*, November 28, 1984, p. 85.

37.   *Folha de São Paulo*, "Governo investirá mais na área de armamentos," May 18, 1982.

38.   *Jornal do Brasil*, "Brasil testa Sonda IV, seu maior foguete, para 1982," July 20, 1982.

39.   Ibid.

40.   "As que mais gastam em pesquisa," *EXANE* October 2, 1985, p. 40.

41.   *O Globo*, August 8, 1987, "Moreira Lima não confirma inclusão do AMX no PND," p. 18.

42.   *Folha de São Paulo*, "EMBRAER investe US$350 mil em novos projetos até 1992," Aug. 30, 1987.

43.   *EMBRAER News*, Press Release 039/88, September 4, 1988.

44.   *Folha de São Paulo*, "EMBRAER investe US$350 mil em novos projetos até 1992."

45.   The purpose of the FND is to create an organization to answer the country's need for resources to finance vital works in the areas of energy, steel production, and telecommunications, and to help the country's economic development.

46.   FBIS LAT, August 6, 1987 p m1 from "State Development Fund to Finance AMX Plane," *Folha de São Paulo* August 5, 1987 p. 1.

47.   *Jornal do Brasil*, "Fundo de Desenvolvimento não vai financiar O AMX." Sept. 24, 1987. Also *Jornal do Brasil* "Fundo social é usado para pagar projeto do caça AMX," August 8, 1987.

48.   FBIS LAT Aug. 7, 87 p. M2 from "Air Force Minister Favors Construction of AMX."

49.   Ibid.

50.   All information on the PIC is taken from an internal document from the CTA entitled "O Esforço de Nacionalização da EMBRAER e do Ministério da Aeronáutica;" "EMBRAER , A Estrela Solitária" INFO, April 1987 p. 32 can also be consulted for a description of the program.

51.   Interview with Engineer Paulo Vieira Alves, Head of the Industrial Promotion Division, IFI, CTA, July 19, 1989.

52.   Ozires Silva, "O Vôo da EMBRAER ," *Revista Brasileira de Tecnologia*, V.13(1) Jan/Mar 1982, pp20-30.

53.   Thomas Guedes da Costa, "Uma Dependência Relativa," *Jornal do Brasil*, January 3, 1982.

54.   "Brasil na era espacial," Ministry of Aeronautics, Public Relations Center; Also R. Ramamurti, "High Technology Exports by SOEs in LDCs: A Brazilian Case Study," a paper presented at The Conference on Latin American Public Enterprises, ISEA, Caracas Venezuela, Nov. 10-13, for a discussion of the benefits of human capital development in the sector.

55.   Single and twin motor general aviation class which, in addition to turboprops and small jets, are used for agriculture, business executives, commuter airlines, recreational flyers and some defense departments.

56.   World Bank, *Industrial Policies and Manufactured Exports* (Washington, DC: World Bank Publications, 1984).

57.   Ramamurti, Ravi, Harvard Business School, Case Study: EMBRAER .

58.   508 planes were imported in 1973; multiply this by the lowest price in

the class, $20,000.

59. Baranson, Jack, *Technology and the Multinationals*, (Lexington, MA: Lexington Books, 1979), pp. 34-39.
60. See Table 6.7
61. *O Globo*, April 15, 1975.
62. Ramamurti, Ravi."EMBRAER ," Harvard Business School, Case #0-383-090, 1982, p. 11
63. Jack Baranson, *Technology and the Multinationals.*
64. Ibid.
65. *Armada International*, May 1978.
66. Company report, "Informações de Caráter Geral."
67. *Jornal do Brasil*, "FAB começa receber da EMBRAER ainda este ano o avião Tucano," April 15, 1982.
68. EMBRAER Press Release 058/87 "Light Aircraft Subsidiary NEIVA Reaches 2000 Aircraft Produced, *EMBRAER News*, November 16, 1987.
69. Ramamurti, Ravi, Harvard Business School Case Studies.
70. *Gazeta Mercantil*, "A EMBRAER decide vender a Neiva, sua subsidiária de aviões leves," December 23, 1986.
71. "Investir em alta tecnologia é prioridade da empresa," *Folha de São Paulo*, March 20, 1987.
72. "Privatização só com sociedade," *Jornal do Brasil*, August 8, 1987.
73. EMBRAER *Press Release* No. 009/89 "EMBRAER and Chincul Sign Agreement for Light Aircraft Production and Marketing," EMBRAER *News*, May 17, 1989
74. *Folha de São Paulo*, "EMBRAER divide produção de aviões Piper com Argentina," May 20, 1989.
75. *Estado de São Paulo*, "EMBRAER se associa a Argentinos," May 13, 1989.
76. *O Globo*, "ENGESA fatura 18 bh Cr$," February 15, 1982.
77. *Tecnologia e Defesa*, "Os Venenosos Tanques ENGESA," No.3, 1983.
78. ENGESA Interview, São Jose dos Campos, July 6, 1989.
79. *O Globo*, "Exército quer garantir a segurança nacional com tecnologia própria," April 18, 1973.
80. *Jornal do Brasil*, "As Serpentes Blindadas," March 15,1977.
81. Described by Colonel José Carlos Albano do Amarante, Military Engineering Corps, Secretariat of Science and Technology, discussion with the author, Rio de Janeiro, July 17, 1989.
82. Coronel José Carlos Albano do Amarante,, "O Papel do Setor de C&T do Exército na Interação Universidade-Empresa," Paper presented in the Universidade-Empresa (University-Firm Seminar), COPPE-UFRJ, Rio de Janeiro, June 5-8, 1989. Published papers by Amarante covering CTEx include "A Capacitação Tecnológica de Empresa Nacional no Desenvolvimento de Sistemas de Armas," *Defesa Nacional*, No. 718, March/April 1985. A discusison of CTEx may also be found in Antonio Cunha de Oliveira, "Desenvolvimento de Sistema de Armas: Absorção de Tecnologia Específica," *Defesa Nacional*, September-October 1986.
83. Amarante, "O Papel do Setor de C&T".

84.   Ibid.
85.   Ibid.
86.   Ibid.
87.   Amarante, "O Papel do Setor de C&T", p. 10.
88.   Interview published in *Segurança e Defesa*, "O Chefe do Centro Tecnológico do Exército," No. 20 1988, p. 26.
89.   Ibid.
90.   Interview published in *Segurança e Defesa*, p. 25.
91.   *Tecnologia & Defesa*, Edição Especial, "Brazilian Defense Industry," 1983, p. 38.
92.   Plitzer, and Arroz, "Transferência da Tecnologia para Desenvolvimento Autônomo," cited in Merlo, "Ciência e Tecnologia na Expressão Militar do Poder Nacional," Lecture in the ESG, Rio de Janeiro, September 12, 1983. (Unpublished paper.) p. 21.
93.   *International Organization*, Vol. 40, No. 3, Summer 1986. Adler describes the critical role of institutions in the case of the computer industry in Brazil.

7

Exports of
Brazilian Armaments

In addition to an active partnership with the state and a dynamic technological system, the third element which distinguishes the Brazilian armaments industry from other third world producers is its emphasis upon exports. The pragmatic relationship between the state and the firms made export promotion possible. The Brazilian military appreciated that defense production was only viable through exports. International marketing favored economies of scale, and competitive, efficient production; the domestic market was simply too small to support the industry. Additionally, armaments exports were consistent with Brazil's broad foreign policy goals of power projection, debt reduction, and offsetting the burden of oil imports. Arms exports between $US 1 and 2 billion annually contributed to debt service as well as led the way for marketing a range of non-defense products from tractors to chickens, often in countertrade agreements for oil.

This chapter illustrates how the partnership between the state and the firms described in Chapter 5 favored defense exports. It begins with a profile of armaments exports, including sketches of EMBRAER's, ENGESA's and AVIBRAS' performance. To explain the success of the sector, the effective division of labor between the state and the private sector is then examined as are other sources of comparative advantage. It is concluded that in addition to the relationship between the state and the firm which allowed arms exports as economic goods rather than political tools, successful international performance may be explained by lower labor costs, reasonable prices and a unique, appropriate technology.

TABLE 7.1
The Range Reported of Brazilian Export Performance

source	(US billion dollars)						
	1980	1981	1982	1983	1984	1985	1986
1980: Financial Times	1						
1981 Jornal do Brasil	1-2						
1981: Christian Science Monitor		3					
1981: The Review of River Plate	1			1.5			
1982: International Defense Review	1	1.2					
1982: International Herald Tribune				0.7			
1982: O Estado de S. Paulo			0.5	1			
1984: International Herald Tribune				1	1	2	2
1984: Brazilian Foreign Ministry			1.4				
1984: Brigagão				1			
1984: Defense and Foreign Affairs					2		
1984: Fontanel					1		
1984: Jornal do Brasil					0.8	1	1
1984: Latin American Defense	1				3	3	
1984: O Globo					1	1.5	1.5
1984: U.S. Department of State				2.6	2.6		
1984: Veja					1		
1985: Christian Science Monitor					1		
1987: Brigagão							2
1987: Bustamante		1.2					

Source: Adapted from Renato Dagnino, "A Indústria de Armamentos Brasileira: Uma Tentativa de Avaliação," Doctoral Thesis, Institute of Economics, UNICAMP, Campinas August 1989.

A Profile of Brazilian Arms Exports

Much has been made in the international press of Brazilian defense exports. That a less industrialized country cracked the competitive international arms market piqued the curiosity of defense analysts and concern among policy makers in arms control circles. But there is confusion over the true magnitudes the Brazil's foreign military sales. It is difficult to arrive at accurate estimates of Brazilian armaments exports. As noted earlier in this book, data on the Brazilian armaments industry is suspect. Dagnino, in his doctoral thesis, presents the most systematic attempt at uncovering the inconsistencies in export and production data on the Brazilian defense industry.[1] As shown in Table 7.1, reports of armaments exports from Brazil for 1983, for example, ranged from $US 1 to 2.6 billion. The annual average export over the period 1979 to 1986 was 1.29 billion dollars.

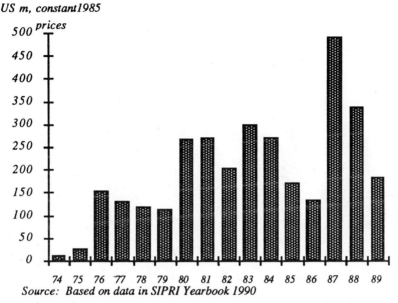

FIGURE 7.1
Brazil's Exports of Major Weapons Systems

US m, constant1985 prices

Source: Based on data in SIPRI Yearbook 1990

Dagnino argues that Brazilian firms have systematically inflated export numbers to project a well developed defense industry. He contends that some in the military and industry thought more countries would purchase Brazilian arms if they believed there was a wide acceptance of the systems in the international market. But the variation in estimates of the size of the exports is not necessarily particular to the Brazilian case. Armaments exports are difficult to report because, in addition to often being secret, deals are customarily signed for a multi-year period. For example, as is shown table 7.2, arms transactions recorded by SIPRI, the Stockholm International Peace Research Institute, the sale of 120 Cascavels negotiated in 1982 took place over a four year period beginning in 1984. The same sale is sometimes counted twice in the press--once when negotiated, and then again when actually delivered. The SIPRI tables avoid this double-counting problem by distinguishing negotiation from delivery.

Dispersion in reporting on defense exports does not prevent us from identifying trends in Brazilian foreign military sales performance. Figure 7.1 uses SIPRI data to demonstrate the growth in Brazil's foreign military sales from 1974-1989. With an overall upward trend, the

TABLE 7.2
Exports of Brazilian Armaments
1987 through 1989

Recipient	# Weapon Delivered	Order Year(s)	Delivery Year(s)	Comments
Cyprus	120 EE-3 Jacara	1982	1984-88	120
	120 EE-9 Cascavel	1982	1984-88	120
France	20 EMB 312 Tucano	1988		
Algeria	2 EMB 111	1987	1988	2
	EE-9 Cascavel $400m including	1987		negotiating package technology transfers
Angola	2 EMB 111	1987	1988	2
Argentina	30 EMB 312 Tucano	1987	1987-88	30; deal worth 50m, partially offset by tech purchases
	20 CBA 123	1989		order for 36; 16 for civilian users
	10 HB-355 M Esquilo	1987	1989	10
Bolivia	3 HB 315 Gaviao	1985	1987-88	3 worth 3.8M
Ecuador	10 EMB 312 Tucano	1988		worth 19m
Eqypt	125 EMB Tucano	1983	1985-9	125; kits in addition to 10 delivered direct. 95 for Iraq, option for 70 more, 45 for Iraq
Iran	50 EMB 312 Tucano	1988	1989	15; deal worth $15m
Iraq	Astros II SS-30	1983	1984-88	78
	Astros II SS-60	1985	1987-88	20
	200 EE-3 Jacara	1987		
	Astros II SS-60	1985	1987-88	20
	250 Cascavel	1986	1987-88	250

TABLE 7.2 (Continued)

Recipient	# Weapon Delivered	Order Year(s)	Delivery Year(s)	Comments
Iran	Astros guidance	1983	1984-88	13
	SS-60	1985	1987-89	960
Jordan	EE-11 Urutu	1986	1987	180 spec. forces
Libya	30 Astros SS 40	1985	1986-88	30
	15 Astros SS 60	1987	1987	15
	3 Astros Guidance	1985	1987-88	3 (denied)
	SS-6	1987	1987-88	450
	8 EMB-111	1987		negotiating
	25 EMB 121 Xingu	1987		negotiating
	100 EMB 312 Tucano	1987		negotiating
	EE-11 Urutu	1987		negotiating
	EE-3	1987		negotiating
	EE-9 Cascavel	1987		negotiating
	100 X-20 180 mm	1987	1987	50
Morocco	60 EE-11 Urutu	1985	1986-7	60
Paraguay	6 EMB 312 Tucano	1988		
	10 EMB 110	1985	1986-7	10
Peru	3 EMB-111 1986			
	20 EMB 312 Tucano	1986	1987	20 worth $32 m
S. Arabia	Astros SS 30	1987	1988	10 part of 500m
	Astros SS -40	1987	1987-88	30 part of 500 m
	Astros guidance	1987	1987-88	4 part of 500 m
	EE-9 Cacavel	1987		allegedly ordered
United Kingdom	128 EMB 312 Tucano	1985	1987-89	41 delivered; deal worth $145-50m; option on 15 more Coproduction arrangement
Venezuela	30 EMB 312 Tucano	1986	1986-7	worth $50m
	6 EMB 312 Tucano	1988	1988-9	attrition replacement
	100 EE Urutu	1988	1989	30

Source: Extracted from SIPRI Yearbook World Armaments and Disarmament 1988, 1989 & 1990.

chart also shows the annual fluctuations in sales. However, when these numbers are analyzed in the context of total world sales, it can be shown that dips in Brazilian sales largely reflect global troughs in weaponry sales.[2] Brazil's share of the world market increases over the period, doubling from .5% in the late 70's to an average of 1.18% of world sales in the 1980's. The SIPRI tables are particularly instructive for identifying weapon type and recipient. From table 7.2 we can see that defense exports from Brazil are heavily concentrated in three nations: Iraq, Libya and Saudi Arabia. With the exception of 100 tanks to Venezuela, from 1987 through 1989 only EMBRAER sold to other Latin American countries. This concentration by AVIBRAS and ENGESA on a narrowly defined market was a major factor in the crisis faced by the firms discussed in the next chapter.

Official Brazilian sources for defense export data can be used as an indication of the export capability of the firms, albeit with caution. Numbers published by CACEX, the export agency of the Bank of Brazil, are difficult to interpret because of the nomenclature used to identify products. For example, according to CACEX, ENGESA does not export tanks but rather heavy trucks. Exports are not designated by civilian or military market type. EMBRAER on average exports 50% military products and 50% civilian products; ENGESA and AVIBRAS are almost exclusively military exporters. Thus, CACEX data picks up both EMBRAER's military and civilian exports and is not specifically representative of defense products. However, this is not a constraining data problem if one looks at the CACEX totals as a rough measure of the firms *potential* export production should the demand warrant a conversion to entirely defense production.

Figure 7.2 tells a dramatic story of defense exports from Brazil. Allowing for the 83-84 period when the Bandeirante had reached the end of its export cycle and the Brasília's sales had not yet picked up, EMBRAER's exports have grown steadily over time. But the source of growth was not always the military line. Applying the revenue breakdown from EMBRAER's annual report for 1989 of 48% Brasília, 25% AMX, 8% spare parts, 6% Tucano, 5% Bandeirante, 5% Light aircraft and 3% others, total military exports for 1989 were on the order of US$ 191.71 million, well off from the estimates of 4 to 5 billion dollars that the press proliferated as the likely target for 1990. ENGESA's and AVIBRAS' sales have been far more erratic than EMBRAER's. ENGESA experienced a surge in exports in the first part of the 1980s which was matched by an even greater decline in the second half of the decade. AVIBRAS had two banner years, 1985 and 1987,

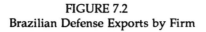

FIGURE 7.2
Brazilian Defense Exports by Firm

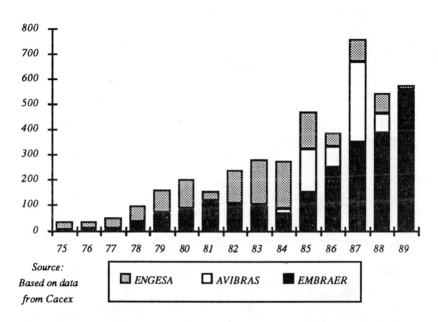

leaving other periods with mediocre performance.   By 1989 the exports
of both AVIBRAS and ENGESA were both negligible.

Even for earlier years when defense exports were robust, reconciling
the CACEX figures with the media reports takes some imagination. For
example, where the reported size of Brazilian exports ranged from US$
1 to 3 billion in 1985, CACEX data places the total at a more
conservative $466 million, before discounting for EMBRAER's civilian
exports. In addition to the multi-year reporting problem, some of the
difference between the total for the three firms and the figures
presented by the press may be accounted for by exports of smaller
defense producers. However, few are listed in the CACEX registry of
principle exporting firms. In 1985, for example, only three firms
traditionally known as producing defense equipment are on the list of
the top 250 exporters. The total of their exports only reach $43 million,
and this does not discount for the fact that military products are not
their sole product line. Thus, while it could be argued that the CACEX
export totals for EMBRAER, AVIBRAS and ENGESA underestimate
defense exports, the addition of exports from the smaller international

TABLE 7.3

Largest Exporters of Non Food Manufactured Products 1979,
US Million, fob

Enterprise	Main Product	Exports 1979
Petrobras	Gasoline	323.8
Volkswagen	Motor Vehicles	213.3
Interbras	Alcohol	133.2
General Motors	Motors	128.4
Mercedes Benz	Trucks	126.9
Saab	Trucks	71.5
Aracruz Cellulose	Pulp	68.8
EMBRAER	*Aviation Equipment*	*68.5*
Comex	Trucks	64.4
Fiat Diesel	CKD cars	59.9
Cellulose Nipo	Cellulose	56.4
Comp. Navegacao	Freight Ships	49.3
Verolme Etal	Freight Ships	47.9
ENGESA	*Armored Vehicles*	*47.2*
Caterpillar	Earth Moving Equipment	42.5
ENGEXCO	*Optical Instruments*	*41.4*
Pirelli	Car Types	34.1
Estonefera	Steel Pipes	33.7
Chrysler	Motors	33.3
EMBRAER as a percent of non food exports:		1.0546 %
ENGESA as a percent of non food exports:		.7267 %

Source: Extracted from Table 3.15, "Largest Exporters of Non-Food Manufactured Products," World Bank Country Study, *Brazil Industrial Policies and Manufactured Exports*, p. 195.

suppliers of armaments is unlikely to bring the total to some of the grander estimates presented in the press.

Despite the fact that it is difficult to arrive at a consistent set of export figures, the relative importance of defense exports among manufactured goods exports in Brazil can be distinguished. Table 7.3 illustrates the importance of ENGESA and EMBRAER as manufactured goods exporters in Brazil. In 1979 the combined exports of ENGESA and its trading company ENGEXCO made it the eleventh largest nonfood exporter in Brazil; EMBRAER was sixteenth. The larger exporters are subsidiaries of multinational ventures: Volkswagen, General Motors, Mercedes Benz, Ford, Philco, Fiat, IBM and Saab. That ENGESA and EMBRAER, without multinational parentage, have become major

TABLE 7.4
Ranking in Top 100 Exporting Brazilian Firms

	EMBRAER	ENGESA	AVIBRAS
1985	25	24	22
1986	8	86	40
1987	9	52	5
1988	10	na	na
1989	7	>100	>100

Source: Drawn from CACEX (Export division of Bank of Brazil) Principais Empresas Exportadoras, compiled from various years.

exporters so quickly reflects the strength of these firms and their contribution to the economy. In total, EMBRAER's and ENGESA's exports accounted for approximately 2.3% of total nonfood manufactured exports in 1979.

The crisis of the industry is reflected in recent export rankings. Table 7.4 shows the ranking of the defense firms among Brazilian exporters from 1985 through 1989. While EMBRAER has consistently ranked in the top 100, AVIBRAS and ENGESA have had difficulties in recent years as the demand for armaments by their principle clients, Third World nations, has decreased. In contrast, EMBRAER's exports are steadied by its exports of civilian products. Because of the difference between EMBRAER, AVIBRAS and ENGESA in market type and export strategy, a detailed consideration of the international performance of each firm is instructive.

EMBRAER's Exports

Focus on the international market has been a key ingredient in EMBRAER's growth strategy. This external orientation sets EMBRAER apart from the typical State-owned enterprise. Indeed, Jones and Wortzel, in their study of exports by public enterprises in less-developed countries, cite EMBRAER as an exception to the general observation that public enterprises are not strong exporters.[3] EMBRAER was export driven from the start. Its first products were introduced to the domestic market in 1971; full production began in 1974. By 1975, Brazil entered the international aviation market with the sale of five EMB-110C military Bandeirantes and ten EMB-201 agricultural Ipanemas to Uruguay for US$5 million. In the following year EMBRAER delivered three Bandeirantes to the Armed Forces of Chile and three Xavante to the Air Force of Togo. Export to sales ratios

TABLE 7.5
Brazilian Aircraft Exports

Year	US $million (current $) Amount	% of Sales
1975	5.0	6%
1976	20.7	18.7%
1977	12.1	1.7%
1978	38.0	33.0%
1979	70.0	40.8%
1980	85.0	49.6%
1981	102.4	43.4%
1982	95.1	46.2%
1983	81.0	36.9%
1984	74.3	40.8%
1985	137	62.56%
1986	247	65.34%
1987	333	70.25%
1988	323	61.76%
1989	450	64.19%

Source: Drawn from EMBRAER company report, *Informações* . . . and EMBRAER Press Releases No. 021/85 and 059/90.

for these two years were 6.0 and 18.7% respectively;[4] by 1978 exports accounted for 33% of EMBRAER's production.[5]   Approximately half of EMBRAER's sales were made abroad by 1980.[6]   Of the fifty Bandeirantes produced in 1981, 80% were shipped overseas.[7] From 1985 through 1989 exports as a percent of sales exceeded 60%. EMBRAER's ability to establish the firm as an international competitor rather than a protected state enclave was critical to its success.

In addition to expanding exports as a percent of sales, EMBRAER's exports have grown in absolute terms over time. Table 7.5 and Figure 7.3 show Brazilian aviation exports increased substantially in 1976 with full production of the Bandeirante. From 1976 to 1980, exports quadrupled; over the 1980s, foreign sales increased again fivefold. There was, of course, annual variation.

1977 was a   difficult year   for all aviation   exporters.   Sales recovered in the late seventies as the oil crisis was a disguised blessing. The fuel efficient Bandeirante became a popular choice for regional airlines desperate to cut oil costs and maintain profitable operations. In 1978 the aircraft was certified by the FAA; the next year 31 planes were sold in the United States. Weak export performance was registered in

FIGURE 7.3
EMBRAER's Exports

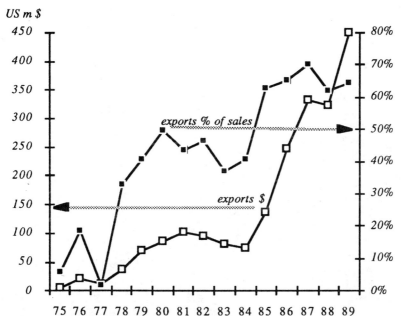

Source: Data from EMBRAER's company reports

1983 and 1984 both absolutely and as a percentage of total sales. Although the world economic picture had improved, this dip in sales represents the phasing out of the Bandeirante before the Brasília ready to replace it. However, during this period the Brazilian Air Force took delivery of Tucano trainers, increasing domestic sales and thus decreasing exports as a percentage of the total. Exports as a percent of sales therefore fall well below the historical levels for 1983 and 1984. This was consistent with the Armed Forces' policy to intervene to soften declines in the international market. The later part of the 1980s continue to exhibit an upward trend in growth of exports, with the exception of a slight fall in 1988. A soft year internationally, the firm also had difficulties selling its planes as the economic crisis mounted at home. Nevertheless, overall EMBRAER's export performance in the competitive general aviation field is certainly impressive.

EMBRAER's export growth did not rely on a single customer or a

TABLE 7.6
EMBRAER's Exports by Region

country	1982	1987	JanSep1988[8]
North America and Europe			
Canada		327	
Belgium	165,600	4,630	20,256,761
Denmark		4,330	3,730
Finland	133,447	346	492
France	19,258,691	26,995,667	13,461,782
Ireland		506	7,974
Italy		2,977,922	29,155,660
Malta	4,270,136		
Norway		5,778,540	209,563
Sweden		1,207	8,371
UK	6,850,845	1,159,161	11,860,751
USA	50,659,617	131,483,119	109819263
West Germany	1,837,425	41,277,042	5,617,429
Latin American and the Caribbean			
Argentina	15,519,422	29,202,137	23,762,333
Bahamas	5,700		
Chile	233,528	71,830	38,284
Columbia	4,897,285	888	21,745
Domican Republic		1,650,000	
Grenada	5,572		
Hondoras		32,172	10,920
Mexico	972	29,296	
Panama	186,571		10,578
Paraguay	2,820,030	5,828,872	12,363,399
Peru	1,191	45,176,381	717,568
Uruguay	238,012	23,747	1,688,465
Venezuela		27,793,799	2,269,837
Africa and the Middle East			
Angola		2,236	34,844
Egypt		26,214,909	8,126,903
Gabon	2,018,067	681	
Iraq			7,887
Nigeria	2,023,825	174,899	3,617
Somalia	894		
Togo	9,1895	191,302	262,874
Upper Volta	59,659		

TABLE 7.6 (Continued)

country	1982	1987	JanSep1988[9]
Japan and the Pacific			
Australia	2,329,549	405,010	290,842
Fiji	92,799	8,269	194
Japan		478,940	77,985
New Guineau	2,368,088		
New Zealand	20,731		126
Total	116,089,571	346,968,165	240,090,177

Source: Calculated from data in Banco do Brasil, CACEX, Carteira de
Comércio Exterior, Transações por Empresa/Mercadoria/ Pais.

narrow regional market. Figure 7.4 and Table 7.6 portray the regional distribution of EMBRAER's sales. Given that EMBRAER aircraft are promoted in international trade journals and the Brazilian press as designed specifically for Third World needs, the strong performance in the U.S. and Europe is striking. EMBRAER officials estimate that almost one fifth of U.S. commuter passenger seats flown in 1982 were in Bandeirantes, with the turboprop comprising 46% of new acquisitions.[10] 17% of the aircraft produced were sold in Central and South America. In the Latin American market purchases of a small number of Bandeirante patrol aircraft were made to police the border region Essequibo in dispute with Venezuela. This agreement was in tandem with one signed with ENGESA for the delivery of personnel carriers equipped with 90mm cannons.[11] EMBRAER's planes, sold through the Brazilian Air Force, also flew in the Falkland-Malvinas conflict, indicating a new role for the Brazilian Armed Forces—weapons supplier in wartime.

Table 7.5 ranks the major customers of EMBRAER by sales volume in 1982. The U.S. tops EMBRAER's slate of major customers, registering twice the next largest customer's purchases. The United States accounts for approximately 45% of EMBRAER's exports. In 1982 this reflected purchases of 100 Bandeirante regional aircraft. By the late 1980s US regional carriers began to supplement the small Bandeirante with the larger, more comfortable Brazilia. In Latin America, Uruguay ranks highest over the eight year period, while Argentina was the major regional purchaser in 1982. The volume of Argentina's purchases was an anomaly due to the Falklands-Malvinas conflict. Uruguay, Paraguay and Chile have been EMBRAER's most consistent Latin customers. Latin

TABLE 7.7

EMBRAER's Major Customers,1982 by Country, US $, fob

Country	Total Purchase
US	50,659,617
France	19,258,691
Argentina	15,519,442
Bahamas	7,005,000
UK	6,850,845
Colombia	4,897,293
Malta	4,270,136
Paraguay	2,920,030
N. Guineau	2,368,088
Australia	2,329,549
Nigeria	2,023,825
Gabon	2,018,067
W. Germany	1,837,425
Total.	**$121,958,010**
% of all Exports: 98.9%	

Source: Calculateed from data in CACEX, Carteira de Comércio Exterior, DEPEC, EXPORTAÇÃO, Transações por Empresa/ Mercadoria/Pais, pp. 01330–01335. "Major" was differentiated by 1% of EMBRAER's international sales by U.S. dollar value in 1982.

purchases were military, accounting for one-half the military sales of EMBRAER aircraft in the Third World.

The regional distribution of EMBRAER's sales to developing countries shifted toward the Middle East in the mid eighties. In 1983 EMBRAER signed a three-year contract for 150 Tucanos and 10 Bandeirantes with the Libyans; including spare parts and technical assistance the total package reached $250 million, twice the firm's exports in 1982.[12] Moreover, this deal paved the way for additional exports by AVIBRAS to fortify the planes with missiles and rockets.

Table 7.8 shows that EMBRAER exported more than one quarter of both military and civilian models from 1975-1983. However, the 25% ratio does not hold evenly across each product. Designed for civilian applications, military Bandeirantes did not sell well internationally. It is possible, however, that some civilian models are used militarily. For example, the Gabonese employ 110P1s with the National Air Force.[13] However, such deviations from civilian use are not likely to change the low percentage radically, since many civilian Bandeirantes are flown in U.S. commuter airlines. Exports of agricultural use

FIGURE 7.4
Regional Distribution of EMBRAER's Exports, 1988

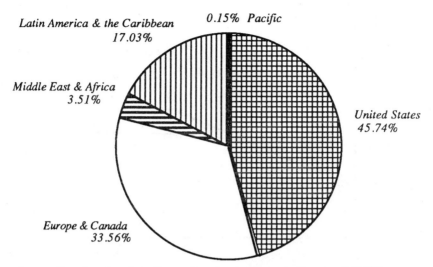

Source: Based on data from Cacex, Carteira de Comercio Exterior, DEPEC,
Exportação, Transações por Empresa/Mercadoria/Pais, pp. 01330-10335.

Ipanemas were negligible at 2.6% of production. Military exports were
buttressed by the Xingu, a civilian trainer which found its niche in
military applications, and the Xavante, with 68.9 and 14.8% of
military exports respectively. EMBRAER introduced the versatile
Tucano trainer in the international market in 1982 with the sale of ten
to Honduras. In addition to licensing agreement with Egypt and
England discussed below, other sales include Venezuela (30), Peru (20)
Argentina (30), Paraguay (16) and 15 to an undisclosed customer.[14]
   In the second half of the 1980s the civilian line gained greater
ascendancy. As shown in figure 7.5, after 1986 the civilian line
outstripped the military in the export market. According to EMBRAER
CEO João da Cunha, this trend is likely to continue in the 1990s.[15]
EMBRAER is focusing on the regional market, offering a flexible
combination of three aircraft for commuter lines: the 19 seat CBA 123
Vector, the 30 passenger EMB 120 Brasília and the 50 seater EMB 145.
Commonality of parts, structure and systems will keep production costs
low for EMBRAER and should enhance operational efficiency for
clients.[16]

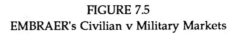

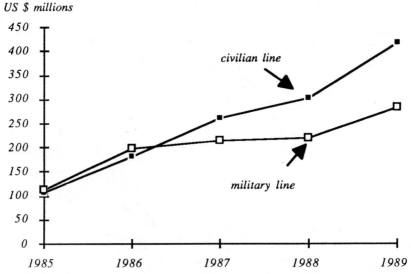

FIGURE 7.5
EMBRAER's Civilian v Military Markets

US $ millions

Source: Based on data in EMBRAER Press Release, Sept. 2, 1990.

By August 1990 200 Brasílias were flying in 15 countries including the US, France, Norway, Britain, Belgium, Aruba, Brazil, Panama, Canada, Cabo Verde and Australia.[17] The Vector turboprop, produced in collaboration with Argentina, is forecasted to have a market of 2000 aircraft through 2005, of which EMBRAER hopes to capture 30%; the EMB 145 jetliner is projected to capture 50% of the market for 1000 regional jets over the next fifteen years.

EMBRAER has ventured into a new area of international sales: licensing abroad. The Tucano is at the center of this development, with production lines in Egypt and Ireland. By licensing abroad, Brazil amortizes research and development   costs and gains entry into important markets. In 1983 the Egyptians signed a $181 million licensing agreement to produce the Tucano.[18] Ten assembled Tucanos were shipped from Brazil, with 110 to be completed in Egypt at the Arab Organization for Industrialization's Kader Factory. Of the 110, forty are marked for the Egyptian Air Force Academy and 70 have been resold to Iraq. In addition to signing the largest contract in company history, the Brazilians hope to open the Middle East market through the Cairo facility. This agreement has also spun off benefits for

TABLE 7.8

Exports of EMBRAER's Product Line, 1975–July 1983

Model	Export Contracts	Total Production	Exports/Total (%)
Civil Line			
EMB 110P1 Bandeirante	164	201	81.6
EMB 110P2 Bandeirante	32	35	91.4
Civil Bandeirante	not exp.	45	0
All Civ. Bandeirante	(196)	(281)	69.7
EMB 201 Ipanema	13	488	2.62
Subtotal	209	769	27.17
Military line			
EMB 110C,A,B1	09	103	8.7
EMB 111 Bandit	16	19	84.2
Mil Bandit not exp.	0	21	0
All Military Bandit	(25)	(143)	17.5
EMB 121 Xingu	51	74	68.9
EMB 326 Xavante	27	82	14.8
Subtotal	103	399	27.24
Total Civilian and Military	312	1168	26.7%

Excludes Piper models because by agreement they are not freely exportable and because they are produced by NEIVA.

Bandit=Bandierante

exp=exported

Source: Calculated from table 7, p. 33 *Informações de Caráter Geral.*

another Brazilian firm, the ABC Group based in Belo Horizonte, which will supply five Tucano flight simulators for US$10 million.[19]

A second Tucano development was the sale to the Royal Air Force (RAF) in the U.K. The RAF choice of the Brazilian trainer was economic and political.[20] Economically, EMBRAER teamed up with Short Brothers of Belfast, Northern Ireland. The prospect of jobs for depressed Northern Ireland was a factor in the decision. An additional economic reason was the product readiness of the Tucano. While competitors remained on the drawing board or prototype stage, the Tucano is flying in Brazil and abroad.[21] Politically, the British purchased a Latin ally in the wake of the Falklands-Malvinas. Aircraft from competitors such as Pilatus were deemed superior by the evaluation team; the procurement decision went to the Cabinet level in the Thatcher government. In the wake of the Falklands, the deal for an

TABLE 7.9
Brazilian Imports of U.S. Aeronautical Products 1971-1981
US$ 1000cif

Category	1971	1972	1973	1974	1975	1976
Jet Aircraft	32469	30333	50675	172638	126329	31623
Helicopters	1019	2543	10058	2951	6415	8602
Piston Aircraft	7365	9568	18989	31735	11573	2020
Turboprops	2185	8063	6437	3237	311	41
Parts& components	10526	9725	16647	27552	35553	43736
Piston Engines	332	570	1006	1254	1815	1794
Turboprop Engines	54	112	30	3	1432	355
Jet Engines	1349	216	1334	9685	9365	5307
Engine Parts	4716	5080	7285	11249	13704	11377
TOTAL U.S.	60015	66210	112461	260304	206497	104855
TOTAL U.S./ + OTHERS	83848	103493	149988	287257	237635	135938
%U.S./OTHERS	72%	64%	75%	91%	87%	77%

Category	1977	1978	1979	1980	1981
Jet Aircraft	3472	3438	3610	249926	40788
Helicopters	2975	7663	9502	13612	13008
Piston Aircraft	82	–	--	194	636
Turboprops	--	78	1637	--	2520
Parts&Components	39442	23093	37131	54567	114109
Piston Engines	1602	1286	2303	1423	725
Turboprop Engines	167	360	918	971	366
Jet Engines	2352	281	1516	15383	3666
Engine Parts	12820	18885	22224	24142	17016
TOTAL U.S.	62912	55084	78841	360218	192834
TOTAL U.S./OTHERS	99148	112253	109042	503047	275286
%U.S./OTHERS	63%	49%	72%	72%	70%

Total U. S. 1971-1981	$1,560,231
Total U. S. + Others, 1971-1981	$2,096,935

Source: "Manufacturing Aircraft in Brazil-Some Fair Trade Issues"-
presentation made by Engineer Ozires Silva, EMBRAER's
Chairman and Chief Executive Officer, at the Aviation/Space
Writers Association Conference, Ft. Lauderdale, May 4, 1982.

initial order of 130 units was closed to improve ties in Latin America. Over three years, the Royal Air Force will receive 200 Tucano and the British government will receive the good will of million dollars worth of the well designed but perhaps not superior Brazilian aircraft.

Both the Egyptian and Irish licensing agreements herald a new phase for EMBRAER's international marketing strategies. These technology sales show a keen appreciation of the new trend in aviation: countertrade.[22] Rather than covet a technology which could be obtained elsewhere, the Brazilians are selling their know-how for market entry. Indeed the use of licensing indicates the sophistication of the Brazilian industry, providing evidence that EMBRAER has technologies desirable for international production.

In addition to international licensing, EMBRAER has entered into collaborative agreements with foreign partners. The production of the AMX dedicated ground attack aircraft is a coproduction effort with the Italian firms Aermachi and Aeritalia. As the requirements of the Italian Air Force were close to those of the Brazilians, a joint effort was undertaken. EMBRAER has a 30% share in the program, including design, development testing and manufacturing of the aircraft's wings, air intakes, ordnance pylons, fuel tanks , landing gears and parts of the electric system.[23] The initial requirement for the Italian Air Force was 187, with the Brazilians forecasting a need for an additional 79. In 1989 23 aircraft were delivered to the Italian and Brazilian Air Forces. The partner companies have formed AMX International to promote foreign sales. However, the prognosis is uncertain as the price of the AMX exceeds that originally forecasted.

As noted above, in the civilian field EMBRAER is developing a small commuter aircraft with Argentina, the CBA123 Vector. This nineteen seater aircraft is the replacement for the Bandeirante, making use of the technological experience gained in the Brasília. EMBRAER is responsible for 80% of the program, with FAMA, the Argentine firm, holding the balance. EMBRAER is also participating with McDonnell Douglas in the production of the MD-11 widebodied jet. EMBRAER is responsible for providing 200 ship sets of advanced composite outboard flaps with options for 100 more in an agreement worth approximately $120 million for EMBRAER.[24] Collaborative production not only allows the firms to take advantage of economies of scale in production, but also divides the development risk and broadens the market. CEO da Cunha's strategy for the nineties includes greater reliance on collaborative programs to exploit these advantages.

To complete EMBRAER's international profile, imports must be considered. Any aviation industry outside the U.S. or Europe is faced with importing pieces and components. To be marketed in the U.S. or Europe, aircraft must pass strict certification requirements; each *piece* must be aviation board approved. Thus, it is easier to import than risk individual certification. Secondly, some parts and components, particularly avionics systems, are beyond the technological reach of individual firms. Even if the primary producer, such as EMBRAER, is technologically capable, it may not be economical to internalize all stages of production. In particular, this condition applies to the highly concentrated transnational engine industry where four producers, Pratt & Whitney, Avco Lycoming, Rolls Royce and General Electric, hold 77% of the market.[25] The possibility of circumventing engine imports for nations with limited aerospace industries is unlikely in the medium term.

Table 7.9 shows imports of aeronautical equipment from the U.S. from 1971 to 1981. Turboprop and piston aircraft imports fell due to tariff restrictions from 1975-1980; they revived in 1981 with tariffs reductions in response to General Agreement on Tariffs and Trade (GATT) negotiations.[26] Imports of parts and components have risen dramatically as EMBRAER expanded production. In the first years Piper kits weighed heavily, but as Piper production declined, the import intensive Brasílias and Tucanos came on line. As these two aircraft and the AMX go into full production, imports can be expected to increase as sophisticated military electronics are unavailable in Brazil. The large Brazilian engine and engine components market accounts for 13.9% of all aeronautical imports from the U.S.—and the producer of engines represented, Avco-Lycoming, is not the major supplier to the Brazilian industry. Adding to the U.S. figures, imports from Pratt & Whitney and Rolls Royce, engines & engine components account for 50% of imports. Despite substantial progress in the Brazilian industry, the import ratio for engines will remain high.

Table 7.10 analyzes Brazilian imports by country of origin. Imports from the U.S. fell from 70% in 79-81 to 40% in 1982. However, they recovered again in 1988. The United States and Canada together account for over 87% of EMBRAER's total imports. This, in conjunction with the importance of the two countries as export markets, is an important to bear in mind as US policy towards the Brazilian defense industry is considered later in this book. The United States is very important to EMBRAER, and it is unlikely the firm would behave in ways far outside the scope of US policy interests, for fear of retaliation and market loss.

TABLE 7.10
EMBRAER's Imports by Country of Origin, U.S. dollars, fob

	1982	(%)	1988	(%)
USA	25,927,097	40.44	185,835,759	52.08
UK	3,052,827	4.76	5,267,553	1.48
France	7,573,183	11.81	24,016,863	6.73
Italy	4,261,334	6.65	11,607,444	3.25
Netherlands	0	0.00	27,514	0.01
Canada	22,868,839	35.67	126,140,092	35.35
Japan	20,569	0.03	319,742	0.09
Belgium		0.00	10,078	0.00
Denmark	4,410	0.01	72,087	0.02
Switzerland	135,320	0.21	157,975	0.04
Germany	270,569	0.42	2,593,209	0.73
Argentina		0.00	684,766	0.19
Yugoslovia		0.00	52,064	0.01
Sweden	2,106	0.00	24,809	0.01
Total	64,116,254	100.00	356,809,955	100.00

Source: Calculated from data in Banco do Brasil, CACEX, Carteira de Comércio Exterior, Transações por Empresa/Mercadoria/ Pais, 13.07.83, pp.1651-1654, Importação.

In 1982 imports comprised 52% of the exports of EMBRAER. Thus for every dollar of imports, the industry generated two dollars of export earnings. By 1988 these gains had decreased. Imports were 64.5% of exports, yielding 1.55 dollars in exports for each dollar of imports. This is not surprising given the higher import demands of the more sophisticated aircraft. The requirement for more sophisticated technological subsystems as a constraint in the firm's development is discussed more systematically in the following chapter. Nevertheless, EMBRAER is likely to balance these high costs with its stronger focus on civilian exports to industrial country markets.

Although EMBRAER's requirement for imports will remain high, its prospects in the international market are positive. Under da Cunha's leadership, there appears to be a very realistic assessment of the firm's capabilities which should contribute to sound international marketing. EMBRAER's diverse customer base is likely to withstand the vagaries of international aviation sales, and concentration on civilian market segments will cushion the volatile defense market. This stands in contrast to ENGESA, whose prospects are less sanguine.

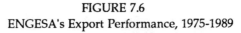

FIGURE 7.6
ENGESA's Export Performance, 1975-1989

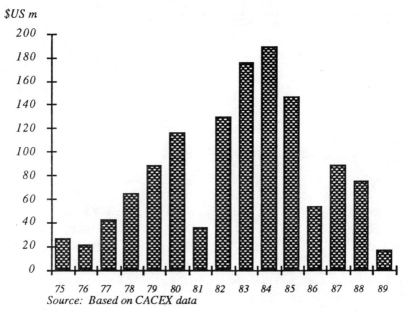

Source: Based on CACEX data

ENGESA's Exports

ENGESA's export performance has been decidedly different from EMBRAER's in both its client base and product line. What appeared to be a magical formula of selling simple to maintain and operate military equipment to clients in the Middle East ground to a halt in the late 1980s as markets were saturated and demand declined. As Figure 7.6 graphically demonstrates, ENGESA's foreign military sales grew dramatically and then fell precipitously. This section will consider both the successes and the difficulties of ENGESA's export performance.

A simple formula for international marketing contributed to ENGESA's early success in export markets: sell standard, durable products on commercial terms. Its rapid growth from a small enterprise re-equipping trucks with the boomerang suspension system to a thirteen-firm conglomerate was a function of strong international presence. Although the domestic market provided the impetus to Table 7.11 summarizes ENGESA's international sales to 24 countries from 1975 to 1985.[27] Its first international clients were Chile and Bolivia.

TABLE 7.11
International Transactions by ENGESA, 1975-1985

Country	Description of Transaction
Algeria	Negotiating Sale of $400m worth of Cascavel, for delivery in 1983; Defense Ministry approval granted.
Angola	Sale of 20 ENGESA trucks in 1980.
Argentina	Delivered 10 Cascavel for evaluation in 1982
Bolivia	Undisclosed number of Cascavel in mid 1970s.
Chile	Ordered 30 Cascavel; 15 delivered in 1978. Delivered 50 Urutu in 1981; Delivered 40 Sucuri in 1981
Colombia	Ordered 100 Cascavel in 1981; Delivered 20 in 1982. Ordered 100 Urutu in 1982; Delivered 15. New contract reported for further deliveries in April 1985.
Cyprus	Ordered 20 Cascavel in 1982.
Ecuador	Reported of deal for undisclosed # armored cars April 1985.
Gabon	Ordered 12 Cascavel in 1980; 16 delivered in 1981. Delivering Urutus in March 1984
Guyana	Ordered undisclosed number of Urutu in 1982
India	Testing Cascavel & Urutu in April 1985.
Iraq	Delivered 150 Cascavel in 1979; 200 delivered in 1980; 200 delivered in 1981; 200 delivered in 1982. Delivering a total package of Urutu, Cascavel missiles & rocket launchers worth $30m in Dec 1984. Ordered 150 Urutu in 1979; 50 delivered in 1979; 50 delivered in 1980; 50 delivered in 1981; 300 ordered in 1982; 50 delivered in 1982. Delivered 50 Sucuri in 1979; 100 delivered in 1980; 100 delivered in 1981; 50 delivered in 1982. Delivered 300 Jararaca in 1982.
Libya	Ordered 200 Urutu in 1978; delivered 100 Urutu in 1979 and 100 in 1980; Ordered 700 Urutu in 1981. Ordered 200 Cascavel in 1977; 100 delivered in 78 & 100 delivered in 79; Planning $280 m of Cascavel in 1983.
Morocco	Negotiating for Urutus and Cascavels in 1981.
Nigeria	Ordered 100 Cascavel in 1981.
Portugal	Negotiating for Urutu & Cascavel in 1981 & 83
Qatar	Ordered 20 Urutu in 1977
Saudi Arabia	Cascavel and Osórios included in 1984 armaments transfer contract worth approx US$ 1 b; However, Osório deal never concluded.
Suriname	Delivering undisclosed number of Urutu & Cascavel in 1984.
Thailand	Delivered 56 Cascavel in 1981.
Turkey	Negotiations for 700 Cascavel & Urutu in 1977.
United Arab	Ordered Cascavels in 1980; Delivering 30 Urutu in Emirates March 1985 as part of earlier deal for 66 worth $7.1m.
(Abu Dhabi)	Ordered 200 Cascavel; 50 delivered in 1977.

TABLE 7.11 (Continued)

Country	Description of Transaction
Venezuela	Delivering 30 Urutu in July 1984.
Zimbabwe	Negotiating in 1981; order for Cascavel reported August.1984.

Due to the scarcity of verifiable sales data for the firm, this table is important for its heuristic value. Negotiations for transfers and orders are included as well as deliveries. This is justified since negotiations often materialize into sales without public knowledge and all deliveries are not capable of being tracked from orders. Additionally, there is a long lag between negotiations, orders and deliveries due to the bureaucracies involved. For example, negotiations began with Zimbabwe in 1981, orders were placed three years later with deliveries as yet incomplete. Some international monitoring agencies consider orders and not deliveries the significant criterion for arms transfers. Congressional Research Service figures maintained by the U.S. Library of Congress differ from U.S. Arms Control and Disarmament numbers this way. Moreover, given that even the extended picture including orders and negotiations is most certainly an understatement of actual transactions, the additional information helps round out the picture, giving a feel for the global presence of the industry.

Sources: *SIPRI Yearbooks* for 1977, 1978, 1979, 1980, 1981, 1982, 1983, Appendix entitled "Arms Trade in Conventional Weapons"; *Defense & Foreign Affairs Monthly* for June 1982, Sept 1982, Jan/Feb 1983, April 1983, June 1983, August 1983, April 1984, June/July 1984, August 1984, Nov 1984, Dec. 1984, Jan 1984, Feb 1985, Mar 1985, April 1985 Many 1985 June 1985 and July 1985; *Defense and Foreign Affairs* Daily, 11-21-85; 3-22-85; 4-23-85; *Latin American Political Report*, March 4, 1977.

Although these two countries initially purchased small quantities of the Cascavels, this foray into the international market opened doors to ENGESA, as these armies gave the equipment positive reviews for operational efficiency. Arms embargoes by traditional suppliers made Brazil Chile's major source of light tanks. With over 200 Cascavels and 250 Urutus, more than half the armored vehicles employed by the Chilean military are from ENGESA.[28] Given that the Brazilian army only maintains 138 Cascavel and 120 Urutus in its battle order, the Chilean inventory of Brazilian equipment is significant.[29] In addition to the apolitical terms upon which the tanks are offered, (discussed below) transactions with Chile were facilitated by barter payments in copper in exchange for the arms.[30] Other clients include Argentina, Colombia, Ecuador, Guyana, Suriname and Venezuela.

The Middle East and Africa are ENGESA's largest markets; Iraq is the major purchaser. In 1977 ENGESA signed a $US 200 million contract to supply 400 armored vehicles.[31] A large agreement with Iraq was a package including not only twenty-six ENGESA armored vehicles but also four rocket pod resupply vehicles, twenty-two Brazilian AVIBRAS multiple rocket launchers, 1,008 ballistic rockets, 32 rocket launchers plus numerous space parts and machine guns, submachine guns and ammunition[32] valuing $30 million.[33] Astros II systems were reported to have been purchased by Iraq at an estimated cost of US$10 million apiece in addition to 9 accompanying specialized vehicles.[34] The importance of this sale, however, goes beyond the monetary value in its significance for joint marketing of major firms in the Brazilian defense sector. The late 1980s saw more cooperation between ENGESA, EMBRAER and AVIBRAS to facilitate the exports of all firms in the sector.

Large deals were negotiated with Saudi Arabia and the United Arab Emirates. The Saudi Arabian Defense minister signed a protocol agreement with Brazil in October 1984 to enhance military cooperation between the two countries. This agreement may foreshadow extensive Brazilian participation in the development of a Saudi or a Gulf Cooperation Defense Council, also engaging the armored vehicle industry in licensing abroad.[35] ENGESA continues to pursue a billion dollar deal with the Saudis, although the possibility for conclusion is slim. This prospective sale includes the Cascavel and Osório models as well as munitions and is part of a larger package of tanks, missiles, naval and aircraft equipment the Saudis purchased. The fact that this sale has not been closed over the past six years is a major factor in ENGESA's instability. Other Middle East purchasers include Cyprus and Qatar. Further to the East, India has demonstrated an interest in Brazilian tanks and Thailand has purchased over 50 Cascavels.

Libya leads the list of African customers. The first sale to Khadafi was in 1977, not so coincidentally announced 24 hours after Brazilian president Geisel broke off relations with the United States.[36] Nigeria is cultivated as an important trade partner as it is prepared to barter arms for oil. A billion dollar countertrade agreement including armaments makes Brazil Nigeria's primary trading partner.[37] Algeria, Angola, Gabon, Morocco and Zimbabwe complete the list of African nations familiar with Brazilian weaponry. These trade agreements strengthen relationships between Brazil and Western African nations, important in achieving what Brazil considers her natural destiny: Southern Basin Superpower.

Table 7.12 profiles ENGESA's exports for 1987 and 1988. The most striking aspect of this table is the low dollar value of exports for these years. Total sales of US$50 million are on an entirely different order of magnitude than the multi-billion dollar deals forecasted for the period. Furthermore, the sales registered principally reflect small purchases of parts and components. With the drying up of the Middle

TABLE 7.12
ENGEXCO Exports, by Country 1987 and 1988 US $

Country	Exports 1987	Exports 1988
		(January -September)
Angola	73,682,335	21,790,733
Libya	5,260,510	1,384,703
Chile	352,136	501,617
Equador	18,587	213,540
Suriname	213,540	146,376
Cyprus	2,310	118,108
Saudi Arabia	272703	168,731
Jordan	3,869,767	26,361,208
Gabon	191,143	245,088
undeclared	849,981	
Columbia	32,749	32,273
Venezuela	442,414	142,471
Zimbabwe	1,663,832	
Uraguay	3,443	35,855
Iraq	537,939	
Canada	4,634,417	
Togo	6,147	
USA	48,149	
Cameroon		656,993
Paraguay	78,530	194,711

Source: Calculated from data in   Banco do Brasil, CACEX, Carteira de
Comércio Exterior, Transações por Empresa/Mercadoria/ Pais.

East arms market in the late 1980s, ENGESA suffered a major
contraction. As shown in table 7.12, it did not have the civilian market
as a cushion for hard times in the military sector. Exports of civilian
goods only amounted to 1.40% of the firm's production in 1987.
Although the firm did compensate for soft international military
markets by expanding the sale of civilian products to the domestic
market, this was too little too late. ENGESA's limited civilian line and
narrower range of clients made it more susceptible to the instability in
Third World arms markets.

In addition to the difference from EMBRAER in emphasis on civil
versus military exports, ENGESA has not sold finished products to
industrialized countries. This may be attributed to several factors.
Procurement needs in industrialized countries are more sophisticated.
Military technology demanded in tanks and armored vehicles in

TABLE 7.13
ENGESA's Civilian versus Military Production

Year	domestic market		export market	
	civil	military	civil	military
1980	0.0	5.0	95.0	0.0
1981	0.0	5.0	95.0	0.0
1982	0.0	5.0	95.0	0.0
1983	3.08	4.35	92.57	0.0
1984	6.79	4.51	88.7	0.0
1985	8.2	.30	91.5	0.0
1986	17.2	61.2	21.6	0.0
1987	18.7	10.7	70.6	1.4

Source: Adapted from Renato Dagnino, "A Indústria de Armamentos Brasileira: Uma Tentativa de Avaliação," Doctoral Thesis, Institute of Economics, UNICAMP, Campinas, August 1989.

Western nations is superior to the capabilities of the Brazilian industry. In developing nations, however, standard technology and easy maintenance are strong selling points of the equipment. Secondly, the placement of many EMBRAER aircraft in the industrialized world was in civilian markets and not in the electronically sophisticated military segment. Moreover, military markets, in addition to technological barriers to entry, are protected by national security regulations governing the import of defense material. Finally is the issue of offsets. In the aeronautical industry, Brazil continues to purchase advanced aviation equipment such as Boeings and Mirages for civilian and military use. While contracting for this equipment, it negotiates the offsetting purchase of Brazilian planes, as demonstrated in the Mirage-Xingu transaction with France. However, the Brazilian army has no immediate need to purchase the most sophisticated tanks and armored equipment, thus losing leverage to pressure industrialized buyers to purchase Brazilian equipment. Overall, ENGESA's export prospects remain dim throughout the 1990s.

AVIBRAS' Exports

AVIBRAS is highly dependent on exports of defense material. Despite the broad range of products offered in the civilian line and to the domestic armed forces, 90% of AVIBRAS' revenues derive from foreign military sales. Emphasizing the importance of international marketing to the firm, AVIBRAS marketing director Pedro Vial simply says, "It is export or die."[38] The domestic military market is too limited to warrant the production of missiles and other armaments. Although the firm also produces civilian goods, the projects are large scale technology ventures with limited production runs. Like ENGESA and EMBRAER, AVIBRAS must look abroad to support economical production. Information from the firm on AVIBRAS' export performance is scarce.

CACEX totals, shown in figure 7.7, demonstrate the rapid take-off of the firm in the mid 1980s. In 1980, AVIBRAS exported only $4 million worth of defense equipment. This figure rose to $35 million in the following year and hit $80 million by 1982.[39] Exceeding 300 million dollars worth of sales in 1987 made AVIBRAS one of Brazil's top exporters of manufactured goods.

Strong export performance brings dividends in enhanced national security and hard currency earnings. Given limited defense needs, Brazil could be virtually self-sufficient in missile systems. As AVIBRAS claims to be capable of producing missiles in the class with the French EXOCET, it is largely able to supply the Brazilian forces with current armament needs. AVIBRAS has the potential to bring more hard currency into the country than either ENGESA or EMBRAER due to low import requirements. AVIBRAS does not have to contend with the costly engine markets and uses fewer imported components. Additionally, technology acquisition costs have been minimal. Thus, with low import to export ratios in both intermediate products and technology servicing, the foreign exchange dividend is greater.

The weakest aspect of the foreign marketing strategies of AVIBRAS is the limited number of trade partners. Ninety percent of the business of the firm is with the Middle East, and within that region, principally Iraq. The financial stability of the firm was seriously hampered by peace in the Iran-Iraq war. Like ENGESA, AVIBRAS' second largest trade partner is Libya. Libya has reportedly placed a multi-year order for the Astros II system and has also purchased smaller rockets.

While rapid export growth is an indicator of the acceptance of AVIBRAS products in international markets and a test of the competitive quality of the products, the concentration of trade with only two countries calls the strength of the products into question. If indeed the product is superior to its competitors in terms of cost and performance, why have more nations not purchased the missiles and rockets of AVIBRAS? Rather, is the success of the firm due to the fact that pariah states Iraq and Libya cannot find other suppliers? Or is the concentration in these two countries a result of war and military buildup

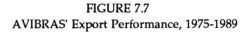

FIGURE 7.7
AVIBRAS' Export Performance, 1975-1989

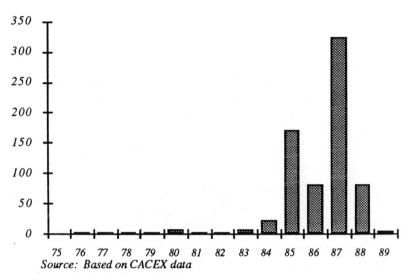

Source: Based on CACEX data

in the region? Whether AVIBRAS will be able to market its products more broadly in the nineties will help to resolve these questions.

Factors Determining Export Success

EMBRAER, ENGESA and AVIBRAS have indeed achieved significant results in international markets What were the critical factors contributing to such strong and rapid export penetration? The analysis of why the Brazilian armaments industry has been successful in international markets centers around two broad, complementary explanations. The first draws upon the earlier discussion of the role of the state in the industry, arguing that the public-private mix in the armaments sector was conducive to international marketing. By allowing firms to pursue foreign marketing without political restraint, the Brazilian government promoted the dynamic growth of the defense sector. This policy stands in contrast to other third world producers where nearly exclusive focus on the domestic market encouraged inefficiency.

FIGURE 7.8
AVIBRAS Exports, 1987

4.05% Undeclared

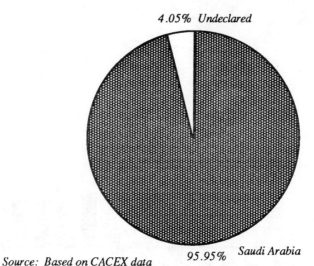

Source: *Based on CACEX data*   *95.95% Saudi Arabia*

But if the Brazilians did not offer reputable products at reasonable prices, foreign buyers would be scarce. Thus, a second explanation for successful Brazilian international marketing focuses on why Brazilian products are more competitive. The ensuing discussion of why Brazilian defense products were chosen over others draws upon Dahlman and Sercovitch's analysis of technology exports from semi-industrialized economies which argues the products are offered at a lower cost than the competitor's and that the good is more appropriate to the buyer's needs.[40]

Public-Private Mix

The Brazilian government's pragmatic approach to armaments exports created a policy environment conducive to international marketing success. Then Chief of EMFA, the Brazilian Joint Chiefs of Staff, Waldir de Vasconcelos, supported pragmatism in foreign military sales because of the benefits to the Brazilian military. As Vasconcelos argued, "Brasil is not in any condition to limit the sale of armaments."[41]   Given the limited size of the domestic market,

FIGURE 7.9
AVIBRAS Imports, 1987

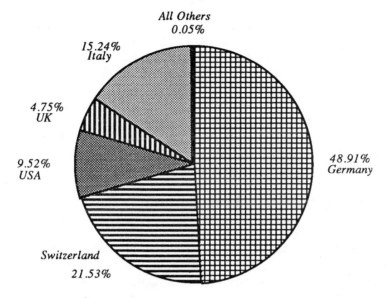

All Others
0.05%

15.24%
Italy

4.75%
UK

9.52%
USA

48.91%
Germany

Switzerland
21.53%

Source: Based on CACEX Data

defense firms had to export to lower production costs. Exports worked to achieve the strategic objective of autonomous procurement while enhancing the economic viability of the firms. Without exports, an economically viable domestic military industry would have been impossible due to economies of scale. As President Figueiredo said:

> The growing Brazilian Defense Industry must keep exports in sight because if it is to exist only on the internal market this will be the road of weakness.[42]

The economic rationale for defense exports prompted an almost purely commercial foreign military sales policy. While the United States and the Soviet Union employed arms sales as a political tool, Brazil followed the French lead of armaments sales as a commercial product nearly like any other. A strong selling point of Brazilian armaments is their purely commercial nature. They are sold without bias to any nation with the ability to pay. This policy was clearly emphasized by General Calderari, then president of IMBEL:

> The sale is purely commerce. All developed nations make this type of transaction and there is no problem for Brazil, in her enhanced independence, to also engage in this business.[43] We're looking to the Third World, and we'll sell to the right, the left and the center.[44]

The moral questions involved in being a "merchant of death" were addressed by the Brazilian military by drawing on the argument that buyers will find a seller and it might as well be Brazil. An Army Public Relations officer, General Rezende, emphasized: "It is an international fact that all countries that produce armaments also export them."[45] From the Brazilian perspective there was much to be gained, including scarce foreign exchange and economies of scale rendering the domestic supply viable and secure, and very little to be lost in engaging in arms trade.

To enhance economic gains and mitigate potential foreign policy problems, the Brazilian government is careful to emphasize the private, commercial nature of the transactions:

> Military sources always clarify that it is not the Brazilian government that is exporting, but the national industry, within normal commercial channels; that is, the armaments are exported just like any other product without the political ties of government to government deals.[46]

This benefits both the government and the enterprise. By distancing itself, the government hopes to avoid international disapproval of its clients, decreasing direct diplomatic accountability for sensitive transactions such as sales to pariah states or nations engaged in war. This non-interventionist position is an asset to the firm, enhancing the credibility of the guarantee of purely commercial transactions. For example, the ENGESA catalog pronouncement that "ENGESA as a true ally neither creates dependence nor imposes commitments," is an enticement to purchase arms without political compromise. Customers purchasing through ENGESA are billed only for the economic value of the goods and not charged with political ploys for foreign policy leverage. Army General José Albuquerque, as the chief of the department of defense equipment, defended this position of "pragmatic" exports of arms, observing that the country with too many scruples in this area of commerce loses excellent opportunities to make money.[47]

The careful distance maintained between state and firm is not to be mistaken for no state participation. Indeed, the Brazilian government monitors all armament sales. The National Program for the Export of Military Material, PNEMEM was instituted in 1976 to provide the policy framework for military sales. As a monitoring program, its purpose is to establish that the products are not needed by the Armed Forces and that the sale would not harm Brazilian foreign policy.[48] However, PNEMEM, has also been described as a broad-ranging vehicle for the promotion of defense exports.[49] Beyond monitoring of defense exports, governmental organizations were charged with creating conditions favorable to the military export drive. Support included the use of diplomatic channels to create export opportunities as well as preferential financing and assistance in technology transfer.

Four institutions are involved in the export of armaments: the Secretariet of Strategic Affairs, SAE;[50] the Department of State, Itamarati; the Export-Import authority, CACEX; and the relevant arm of the military, the Army, the Navy or the Air Force through EMFA, the Joint Chiefs of Staff.[51] To clear a foreign military sale, the firm files for an export license from CACEX; the export agency directs the request to the SAE. At the same time, Itamarati is consulted. It appraises potential changes in the regional strategic balance, assesses negative foreign policy repercussions and considers the political regime in the country to determine whether the sale might create undue animosity. Above all, it is concerned with the stability of the importing regime to ensure future payments. If a government appears near collapse, Brazil does not want to be vulnerable to a succeeding administration for payment.[52] When SAE receives clearance from both EMFA and Itamarati, CACEX issues an export license. The time for approval can be as short as fifteen days and, despite involving four institutions, is very secret and guarded.[53]

The Brazilian government is a cooperative and supportive supervisor of armaments trade. It places key diplomatic officials in countries noted for armaments purchases. For example, two retired chiefs of EMFA were sent to the embassy in Baghdad to facilitate marketing of armaments. Military sources involved explain:

> For this post, with current significant negotiations in armaments we can only send a General to Iraq as he can make all the contacts that he wants without the limitations of an employee of Itamarati that couldn't, for example, make direct contacts with the PLO.[54] It is not unusual for Army generals to accompany the president of ENGESA on trips to potential

clients. The Armed Forces, for example, have attempted to bring pressure upon the Saudi Arabian purchase of Osório tanks.[55]

Four nations are officially restricted from receiving Brazilian armaments: Israel, the Soviet Union, Cuba and Taiwan.[56] Brazil is neutral in the Central American conflict and therefore vetoed the sale of ENGESA combat cars to Honduras and El Salvador.[57] Nicaraguan Defense Minister Bernardino Larios' trip to Brasília in December 1978 in search of armaments was not fruitful.[58] Although Brazil maintains friendly relations with Nicaragua, it preferred not to alienate the United States. It is possible, nevertheless, that Brazilian armaments have been shipped to Nicaragua through third parties. When a Libyan plane carrying armaments to Nicaragua was discovered in Brazil, the Brazilians refused to allow international representatives to inspect the cargo. The speculation was that the armaments aboard the aircraft were of Brazilian origin, a confirmation that the Brazilians clearly did not want to reach Washington. The only exception to non-intervention in Central America was a military favor to the U.S.: the sale of Tucano trainer/fighter aircraft to Honduras.[59] Originally secret, when the transaction was discovered it was argued the trainer's primary purpose was not battle. If the Hondurans chose to use the Tucano for conflict missions, there was nothing Brazil could do.

The second informal embargo on foreign military sales was on Iranian transactions. To avoid offending the Iraqis, who accounted for between 20% and 30% of Brazilian sales of armaments,[60] the industry refrained from active marketing in Iran. Nonetheless, Brazilian armaments found their way to both sides of the Iran-Iraq war. Some Brazilian tanks were captured and supposedly third party re-exports of Brazilian arms regularly reached Iranian forces.[61] Ships chartered to Iran, usually flying foreign flags, reportedly left São Paulo on a regular basis carrying Brazilian military equipment destined for Tehran. Iraq was not able to openly confront Brazil on sales to Iran because it would not be unusual for captured Iraqi equipment to be found in the Iranian battle order. However, Iraq may have taken silent compensation as ships bound for Iran have disappeared, victims of sting operations.[62]

On occasions the Brazilian government violated its distance equation to employ armaments as a foreign policy tool. Such was the case with sales to Suriname. After the Chief of the Suriname High Army Command Captain Graanoogost visited Brazil in June 1983, it was announced that Suriname would acquire $4 million in war material from the Brazilians.[63] This sale was politically motivated, possibly at the urging of the United States. Chief of Staff General Vasconcelos announced in 1984:

> Military exchange between Brazil and Suriname has begun with negotiations on supplying provisions to Suriname and this exchange will be intensified in 1984.[64]

The reason, he stipulated, was to decrease Cuban influence. What distinguished this sale from others was that the terms were not negotiated by the firms but the government. The delegation to Suriname, headed by General Secretary of the National Security Council who is responsible for enforcing the national export policy, PNEMEN, was a high level diplomatic initiative. Rumors of U.S. urging are given added credibility by the fact that the Brazilians are not threatened by Cuba; concurrently discussions were in progress on joint U.S. military industrial cooperation.

A test of the tenacity of the Brazilian arms export policy was at the onset of the Iran-Iraq war. By 1980 ENGESA had contracted to place 2,000 armored cars in Iraq, making it the country's major supplier.[65] At the outbreak of war, Brazil was under diplomatic pressure to stop shipments. Despite the international taboo against arms sales to nations in conflict, the Brazilians felt that since they were impartial in their sales, the transaction was fair. A spokesperson for the Palácio do Planalto, Carlos A'tila, argued that

> the sale of Brazilian armaments to countries in conflict does not create any type of constraint for her foreign policy as these sales are not made preferentially to any country but to whatever country is interested in Brazilian products.[66]

Moreover, Brazil argued that the contract was signed before the outbreak of war, and ENGESA was obliged to deliver according to terms.[67] The Brazilians worried about current and future losses if deliveries were abrogated. Not only was immediate income at stake, but Brazil's credibility as an unbiased, guaranteed source of arms also was on line. They honored the contract.

Brazil derived other benefits from supplying Iraq. The war was a splendid opportunity to battle test ENGESA products, bringing new sales.[68] *Comércio e Mercados* wrote:

In the Middle East confrontation, we must take maximum advantage of our neutral position to negotiate stronger terms of trade than our current deficits indicate.[69]

As Brazilian tanks outperformed both Eastern and Western vehicles in rugged desert conditions, they gained a reputation for strength and reliability. Thus the Iran-Iraq war was a profitable advertising campaign for ENGESA vehicles. The war also created a new source of demand. As equipment was destroyed or captured, new armaments were ordered to replace them, augmenting ENGESA's sales to the region. Finally, the war pushed Brazil to develop relationships with other clients to ensure continuity in oil shipments. With war threatening the half of its petroleum imports from Iraq,[70] the country cultivated new trade partners. Trade agreements were signed with Nigeria and Angola; ENGESA then placed 30 tanks in Angola and signed to deliver 90 million cruzeiros worth of armaments to Nigeria.[71]

These examples of politically motivated on foreign military sales are the exception rather than the rule. Restrictions were imposed for pragmatic reasons, upon deciding that the sale would damage Brazilian foreign policy. Sales are not withheld as a sanction to pressure for a change in client behavior nor as a reward for international loyalty. Indeed those restrictions imposed revolve not around Brazil's relationship with the potential client, but the strong disapproval registered by a third party. Thus, the rationale to sell weapons on a commercial basis without political obligation defines the Brazilian arms sales policy.

It is important to note that while ENGESA and EMBRAER demonstrate two contrasting patterns of ownership, private and public, both are highly successful exporters The policy environment facilitated export efforts independent of ownership status. Although EMBRAER had more formal connections to the military and the government, ENGESA was able to take advantage of formal and informal networks of export promotion. Both firms were favored by the state's permission of commercial sales as well as the fiscal incentives to export. They were given substantial state support but allowed maneuverability in international marketing.

EMBRAER stands in contrast to typical state owned enterprises in its export orientation. Jones specifies the reasons which inhibit state enterprise exports.[72] Primary on his list is that public enterprise control systems may inhibit exports. In contrast, the bureaucratic system for export of EMBRAER's goods is fast and efficient, allowing for entrepreneurial activity in international markets. Second, Jones cites the lack of competitive experience which fosters little pressure for cost consciousness, quality control and task adaptation.[73] In contrast, the formal and informal objectives of EMBRAER have oriented the firm to the international market. Only through international marketing could the firm take advantage of scale economies to remain viable. In this sense, the directives of the state encouraged competitive behavior. This international orientation was facilitated by a strong, highly motivated management with broad knowledge of international aviation practices. This is different from most public enterprises where, as Jones points out, "there is little motivation or ability to negotiate, adjust, monitor and meet tight export contracts."[74]

These characteristics of state promotion, competitive experience and motivation have permitted EMBRAER to act "as if" private, pursuing entrepreneurial activity in international markets. We see a similar blend of state support and independence in ENGESA and EMBRAER—a policy mix determined not by the degree of state ownership in the firm, but by pragmatic requirements of export success: state promotion which encourages, rather than stifles the ability to create new marketing opportunities abroad. Indeed, Jones argues that public enterprises should behave just like private firms in international markets.[75] Thus, we may conclude that a primary reason EMBRAER is one of few public enterprises which demonstrates export success is because it is emulating the behavior of a private enterprise in international marketing.

In summary, allowing maximum independence in marketing while quietly supporting the activities of exporters has brought economic and political dividends to defense producers and the state in Brazil. The next section considers additional sources of comparative advantage beyond the state-firm relationship.

Sources of Comparative Advantage

While the foregoing explanation of the apolitical aspects of arms sales is important in determining international sales, it is not sufficient to explain the strong export performance of the Brazilian armaments industry. Attention must also be paid to the product. Dahlman and Sercovitch specify four sources of competitive advantage for technology exports from semi-industrialized countries:

- A cost advantage in providing basically the same type of process, or service, that could be supplied by developed countries, the advantage most likely being based primarily (but not exclusively) on lower labor costs. Exports based on this advantage can be expected to go to both developed and developing countries.

- An advantage based on supplying an adapted or older process, product of a technical service that is more appropriate to the needs of the purchaser, because of characteristics such as smaller scale, greater ease of operation, better knowledge of similar local environments, or better match between product attributes and local needs. Exports based on this advantage—which is rooted in experience in developing country conditions—may be expected to go to other developing countries.

- A head start in experience which may be reflected in lower cost or greater appropriateness, is usually the result of country-specific conditions--such as the availability of natural resources or government promotion—whereby an acquired advantage in experience follows from a natural advantage. Exports based on this advantage may go to both developed and developing countries.

- An advantage based on having developed a major technological breakthrough. Exports based on this advantage may also go to either developed or developing countries.[76]

The following discussion applies these criteria to Brazilian defense exports. Specifically, it is argued that lower labor cost, the adoption of a technology specifically suited to Third World needs and the development of simple, yet unique, technologies have contributed to the export of Brazilian armaments.

Brazilian defense products are priced lower than international competitors. An Urutu amphibious vehicle, for example, is 40% less expensive than the British Saracen tank;[77] at $225,000 it is also cheaper than the M-113.[78] In the aircraft sector, EMBRAER benefits from offering clients long term payment schedules at preferential rates.[79] This low-cost financing offered through the Brazilian government reduces monthly payments on EMBRAER planes below those of Beech and Fairchild Metroliner.[80]

Sarathy and Rao argue the lower cost of Brazilian equipment is primarily due to government financing. Three other sources of cost-competitiveness must also be considered: subsidies of technology, the basic level of technology employed in the products, and lower wages. The high cost of technology is repeatedly called upon as an explanation for expensive American weaponry. With technological cooperation between Brazilian firms and state institutions, these costs are significantly reduced. Moreover, as Brazilian tanks are simple they are less expensive to produce. The firms employ intermediate technologies explored and largely abandoned by international producers. Costly electronics, standard in sophisticated tanks, were minimal in ENGESA 's export successes such as the Urutu and the Cascavel. Said Paulo Meira, Director of Sales for GM of Brazil,

> ENGESA is only reproducing what has already been done. The small research and development cost doesn't carry the weight of frontier technology.[81]

Thus, high research and development costs, the bane of defense contractors, were limited to perfecting simple but unique systems. This, however, changes as the firms attempted to offer more sophisticated products. With respect to labor costs, results are ambiguous. Clearly wages for skilled workers in Brazil are less than in industrialized countries, but wage differentials in Brazil, India, Argentina or Mexico hardly explain significant differences in export performance.[82]

In addition to a cost advantage, the second criterion suggested by Dahlman and Sercovitch is the development of a product better suited to the needs of the purchaser than offerings by competitors. Indeed, of the four sources of competitive advantage discussed in their article, the suitability of Brazilian defense products for Third World applications best explains the success of its foreign military sales. The simplicity of Brazilian equipment, ease of operations, maintenance and durability under adverse Third World conditions made Brazilian armaments a popular choice among less industrialized countries.

The Brazilian tank was designed for the country's Armed Forces to fulfill internal, defensive missions. Brazil has few external enemies and no immediate threats to national security from outside its borders. The country is not an aggressor, and has no need of offensive weaponry.

The Armed Forces' requirement was a tool to control domestic unrest also capable of defensive functions should conflict arise. It needed a tank which worked in the Amazon jungle, the marshes of the interior or the ranch land of the Rio Grande do Sul. It wanted a vehicle affordable to purchase and maintain. ENGESA's Urutu and Cascavel models met these specifications. It needed an airplane that could land on unpaved airstrips; the Bandeirante brought access to the Brazilian interior.

Simplicity of design in ENGESA tanks is accompanied by simplicity of operation. ENGESA products can be easily operated and maintained by soldiers in the field without extensive training. When the country first began exporting armored cars the Brazilian newspaper *Jornal da Tarde* highlighted this:

> The Urutu as well as the Cascavel can be driven by any person that knows how to drive a truck. This has helped the commercial success of the Urutu and Cascavel among the nations of Africa and Latin America which have reduced military budgets and cannot afford the luxury of spending much money training special drivers for new types of tanks.[83]

The *Jornal do Brasil* echoed this opinion several years later:

> It is enough for a technician to know how to drive an automobile in order to be able to manage a light tank of the firm perfectly.[84] Ease of operation is an asset in countries where the average soldier has low literacy and little engineering.

As arms analyst Pereira de Andrade suggested, "Imagine an uneducated soldier who has never seen a car trying to operate a complicated driven tank!"[85] In contrast, ENGESA vehicles are widely useful for all personnel.

These defense products were also demanded by other developing countries with limited resources for military procurement and tough terrain. While industrialized nations perceive the arms race in terms of ever increasing sophistication, developing nations are concerned with internal unrest or aggression from other Third World states with similarly limited capabilities. As NATO and Warsaw pact countries set the technological pace for weapons systems beyond the needs and budgets of developing nations, the standard, inexpensive Brazilian tank met with a strong, receptive market.

Brazilian defense equipment thus tapped new, underexplored market for armaments. In this respect, in the earlier stages Brazilian exports of armaments did not supplant industrialized nations but attended to a

different market. Said U.S. military aide Brig. General Dudley
Wiegand

> Brazilian arms sales to Latin America do not imply the substitution of a
> market until now dominated by Americans because the two countries
> have different objectives. In light of being more expensive and more
> sophisticated, American armaments are destined to the European
> scenario, and are different from those offered by Brazilian armaments,
> generally restricted to the Third World.[86]

That Brazilian armaments attended to an untapped market
indicates an international division of labor in the global military
production structure. Due to the rapid advance of military technology,
gaps within the production capabilities of newly industrializing
nations have been left in the international armaments market. With
the attention of the industrialized nations on frontier technologies,
markets are opened for countries such as Brazil. These new participants
in armaments sales then gain power and prestige over non-producing
nations, institutionalizing a new international pecking order. However,
this decreases reliance upon traditional suppliers and traditional
world powers, altering the global balance of power. Of course as Brazil
attempted to compete in industrial country markets, the power balance
switched back.

The resource argument for defense production, Dahlman and
Sercovitch's third criteria, may be applied in an inverted fashion. A
key motivator behind the Brazilian defense industry's export drive
was the *scarcity* of a critical resource: oil. Armaments exports comprise
a key component in the attempt to ease the oil burden, stimulate
industrial manufacturing, earn foreign exchange, balance international
trade and meet interest payments on the country's staggering
international debt.[87] As *Strategy Week* stated:

> With Brazil taking an economic downturn following the successive hikes
> in oil prices since 1973, the country must now also concentrate on selling
> its military equipment overseas as a way of ensuring the continued
> stability of the arms industry since the domestic market is considered too
> small and unsteady. More importantly, the export of arms has materially
> impacted on Brazil's balance of payments at a time of escalating costs on
> imported goods and raw materials, particularly oil.[88]

Armaments are well suited to this task. Over the last decade the
Middle East and African oil producing nations have logged a real

annual increase of 12% in military purchases.[89] The region accounts for 42% of international arms trade and in 1982 received 51% of all arms transferred to developing countries.[90] Thus, in light of massive expenditures on armaments, the Middle East, currently providing Brazil with 90% of oil imports, is perceived a natural trade partner.[91] One army general emphasized:

> Brazil could attain excellent results in her commercial balance by means of exporting material for war use for countries that have strong purchasing power, such as the Arabs.[92]

In addition to strong demand, other qualities make weapons exports to the Middle East to offset oil an especially lucrative venture. First is the quantity: the potential for selling other products to Middle Eastern nations in sufficient quantities to balance the oil burden is limited by the small market for other manufactured products in the region.[93] Second, armaments have a short product life span. This high replacement rate of armaments is important against the continuing need to import oil. Since the market is not easily saturated, arms present a strategic long term factor in Brazil's trade profile. Third, and perhaps most significant, many Middle Eastern and North African nations find armaments difficult to purchase under restrictive policies from the East and West. By virtue of these restrictions, Brazil inherited a market position in the region by default.

Barter terms and increased trade in other goods are characteristic of arms for oil exchanges.[94] Many oil exporters, although resource rich, are dollar short and eager to write countertrade contracts. Thus, most agreements with the Iraqis and the Libyans are concluded on barter terms:

> Normally, when negotiating arms sales with oil producing countries, Brazil utilizes the system of trading the merchandise to better the commercial balance, a strategy already adopted in the exchange of tanks with Iraq, Libya and Qatar.[95]

Itamarati, the Brazilian State Department, reports the Brazilian oil company Petrobras actively negotiates offsets of armaments for oil.[96] For example, Braspetro, a subsidiary of Petrobras, discovered oil in south Iraq at Majnoun; compensation for the crude was offset by the delivery of 200 ENGESA tanks.[97] The sale of 400 cars to Libya in March 1977 included a concession for Petrobras to drill oil in the North African country.[98] Deals of this type, and straight barter contracts such as the Libyan US$500 million dollar trade of armored vehicles and trucks for oil in 1979, helped alleviate Brazil's balance of problems.

Arms trade with Middle Eastern and Northern African nations has been accompanied by increased exchange of other goods. In the case of Israel, Klieman reports that "trade has followed not the flag but, symbolically, the Uzi machine gun, with contacts extending in the course of time to nonmilitary commerce."[99] Likewise Brazil has signed countertrade agreements with Chile, Nigeria and France. Although not officially announced as such, the US$ 50 million sale of 41 Xingu trainers to France in exchange for the purchases of the French Mirage would fall into this category. French participation in the Brazilian helicopter industry sweetened the deal.[100] Linked, for example, to the 1977 Libyan purchase was Khadafi's contract to construct a sugar refinery.[101] A $250 million purchase of armored cars in 1981 by Iraq was combined with a total trade package worth over $2 billion over five years, encompassing goods as diverse as chicken, dried beef, paper, iron, Volkswagens and a small steel refinery.[102] In the financial sector, an Iraqi-Brazilian bank in Rio de Janeiro was set up to to facilitate bilateral trade and insurance [103] as part of an exchange signed the preceding year.[104] As an ENGESA administrator said:

> The most significant advantage of sales of armaments is to open the road for non-defense sales. Today we sell chickens in some countries because there first existed the sale of a high quality amphibious tank. No one can imagine how important it is to demonstrate the military capacity of a country in foreign circles. It is as if it were a calling card that proved efficiency in all other areas.[105]

Whitaker, president of ENGESA, corroborated:

> The most important aspect is not the value of the goods ENGESA exports, but the political influence that the defense material brings in tow, making possible the sales of other materials and products, especially food and supplies.[106] In an interview with the São Paulo newspaper, the *Folha*, Whittaker Ribeiro gave the case of Iraq, where Brazil constructed a railway and sold cars "all done under the mantle of the arms industry." Furthermore, he salutes the efforts of Itamarati, the

Brazilian State Department, for opening new embassies and beginning
to follow up on leads for product sales.

Indeed ENGESA is credited with opening up markets to other industrial
exports:

> The principal buyers of Brazilian armaments are developing countries.
> The power of decision making as to what armaments are bought by these
> countries is held by the same persons who later make other decisions
> with respect to imports of other products and services. If the military
> equipment satisfies the customer after it has been used, it opens the door
> for other products and services. This is how it was in the Middle East
> where the first national firm was ENGESA. Later, large Brazilian
> engineering firms arrived as did quantities of other manufactured
> articles.[107]

For the Brazilians, the positive effects of armaments exports have
outweighed slight negative political repercussions. Without arms
trade, Brazil would be in a tighter bind with the IMF.[108]

Although the U.S. disapproves of the Middle East sales, outright
criticism has been minimal as the foreign exchange is helping the
country meet it debt obligations. Even the fallout from the grounded
Libyan jets carrying armaments to Nicaragua was slight, all parties
cognizant that after appearances it would be business as usual.[109] Thus,
Brazilian pragmatism has allowed it to tap a profitable market,
providing opportunities to augment the sales of all Brazilian goods to
the region.

Dahlman and Sercovitch argue the fourth advantage, technological
breakthroughs, is rarely encountered as a source of competitive
advantage in developing countries. A high degree of technological
competence is required to move beyond replicating a product or process.
Nevertheless, an example of a successful technological breakthrough
cited in the article is the turboprop technology in the EMBRAER
Bandeirante. In addition to aircraft technology, the boomerang
suspension system in ENGESA tanks and the AVIBRAS Astros II multiple
launcher should be included. These technologies are products of
Brazilian research and development in private and public institutes.
They are distinctly Brazilian as development was commissioned in
response to domestic conditions and the rights to the technology are
held without multinational participation. That Brazilian defense

producers have been able to achieve this level of technological sophistication is testimony to the maturity of the industry.

The Brazilians have registered successful international sales due to the favorable armaments export policy of the Brazilian government in conjunction the competitive advantage of low prices, appropriate products and technological breakthroughs. In conclusion we can see that by allowing firms maximum maneuverability in international markets to sell to all interested purchasers, Brazil has promoted exports of defense products, which have in turn opened the way for the export of a variety of goods. Promoting arms exports, a policy consistent with Brazil's outward orientation, brought foreign exchange as well as broadened other trade opportunities. We noted that both EMBRAER, AVIBRAS and ENGEXCO, the trading company representing ENGESA and IMBEL, behaved similarly despite different ownership patterns. Thus, it is suggested that the government policy with respect to armaments exports is consistent across the sector, based not upon formal state affiliation, but upon the conviction that arms exports bring political and economic dividends for Brazil. Indeed, such pragmatism has paid off as demonstrated by the strong performance of each of the firms in international markets. However, as we will see in the next chapter, the successful chemistry that defined export achievements began to come apart in the late eighties.

Notes

1. Renato Dagnino, "A Indústria de Armamentos Brasileira: Uma Tentativa de Avaliação," Doctoral Thesis, Institute of Economics, UNICAMP, Campinas, São Paulo, Brazil, August 1989.

2. This can be calculated from "Values of Exports of Major Weapon Systems," Table 7A.2, *SIPRI Yearbook* 1990.

3. L. P. Jones and L. H. Wortzel, "Public Enterprise and Manufactured Exports in Less-developed Countries," Public Enterprises in Less-Developed Countries, L. Jones, ed. (New York: Cambridge University Press, 1972), p. 228.

4. See Table 7.2 below and *Informações*.

5. *Interavia* 7, 1981.

6. It logged US$70 million in exports of US$142.8 million total sales in 1979. while in 1980 registered US$84.1 million exports of US$171.3 million total sales. *Strategic Latin American Affairs*, March 6, 1980.

7. "EMBRAER vende 12 aviões para a França e amplia mercado com os Estados Unidos," *Jornal do Brasil*, January 14, 1982.

8. Unfortunately, under the new government of President Fernando Collor, the Economics Minister Zélia Cardoso Melo temporarily (and perhaps

permanently) suspended the operations of the statistical department which provides this data. Hence the full year's data could not be obtained.

9.   Ibid.

10.   "EMBRAER vende 12 aviões para a França e amplia mercado com os Estados Unidos," *Jornal do Brasil,* January 14, 1982.

11.   *The New York Times,* October 4, 1982, p.4; *The Guardian* October 4, 1982; and *The Washington Post,* October 7, 1982, p. 42.

12.   "EMBRAER e Líbia retomam venda de US$190 milhões," *Jornal do Brasil,* June 23, 1983; "EMBRAER Sells 25 Xingu Planes to Libya," Foreign Broadcast Information Service 6 (FBIS), February 18, 1983, p. D1; "EMBRAER Negotiates Aircraft Sale to Libya," *Gazeta Mercantil,* January 6, 1983, pp. 1, 3.

13.   "The Secret of Defense," African Defense, February 1981.

14.   *EMBRAER News,* Press Release 066, September 2, 1990.

15.   Interview with EMBRAER CEO Jõao da Cunha, São José dos Campos, March 11, 1991.

16.   *EMBRAER News,* Press Release 059, September 2, 1990.

17.   Ibid.

18.   "O successo das Armas Brasileiras produz resultados em Paris," *Estado de São Paulo,* January 21, 1983.

19.   *EMBRAER News* V, No. 33, March-April 1985.

20.   Mr. Turner, Fairchild Hiller, at Strategy '85 Convention, Washington, D.C., June 1985.

21.   *EMBRAER News* V, No. 33, March-April 1985.

22.   P. Verzariu, *Countertrade, Barter and Offsets* (New York: McGraw Hill, 1985), p. 45.

23.   *EMBRAER News* Press Release No. 059/90 September 2, 1990.

24.   Mario B. de M. Vinagre, EMBRAER Press Officer, lecture "EMBRAER: A Brazilian Aerospace Success Story," at the Smithsonian Air and Space Museum, Washington, DC October 12, 1989.

25.   Helena Tuomi and Raimo Vayrynen, Transnational Corporations, Armaments and Development (New York: St. Martins, 1982), p. 85.

26.   "Brazil's Import Duty Intentions Watched," *Aviation Week and Space Technology,* February 19, 1979.

27.   This discounts third party retransfers of equipment such as may have occurred in the cases of Iran and Nicaragua.

28.   "Defense: Neves worries military buyers," *Latin American Weekly Report,* February 22, 1985, p. 10.

29.   "Brazilian Defense Directory," *Defense and Foreign Affairs,* April 1985, p. 16.

30.   *Wall Street Journal,* March 19, 1981.

31.   *Financial Times,* October 14, 1980.

32.   "Brazilian Arms Shipment for Iraq," *Summary of World Broadcasts,* British Broadcasting Corporation, January 2, 1985, Part 4, p. a1.

33.   *Defense & Foreign Affairs,* February 1985, p. 1.

34.   R. Marshall, "Southern Superpower," *Defense & Foreign Affairs,* April 1985, p. 11.

35. Ibid.
36. R. Godoy, "A Líbia, um grande cliente," *Estado de São Paulo,* June 11, 1980.
37. Marshall, "Southern Superpower."
38. "Indústria de armas será maior exportadora do Brasil em 85," *Jornal do Brasil,* November 1, 1982.
39. "Brasil terá maior fábrica de foguete do mundo em 83," *Jornal do Brasil,* April 25, 1982.
40. C. J. Dahlman and F. C. Sercovich, "Technology Exports from SICs," *Journal of Development Economics* Vol. 16, (1984), pp. 63-99.
41. "Armamentos, comércio cada vez mais rendoso," *Estado de São Paulo,* June 12, 1983.
42. "Figueiredo apoia a política de exportação de material bélico," *O Globo,* March 2, 1979.
43. "Calderari justifica a venda de armas para o Exterior," *Estado de São Paulo,* August 10, 1979, p. 5.
44. *Newsweek,* November 9, 1981, p. 34.
45. "Armas e equipamentos bélicos renderam em 81 mais de US$1b," *Folha de São Paulo,* August 4, 1982.
46. "Armamentos, comércio cada vez mais rendoso."
47. "Geral defende venda 'pragmática' de armas," *Estado de São Paulo,* June 3, 1984
48. "Exportação de material bélico receberá mais incentivos fiscais," *Jornal do Brasil,* December 3, 1979.
49. Renato Peixoto Dagnino, "A Indústria de Armamentos Brasileira: Uma Tentativa" de Avaliação.
50. SAE was formerly the National Security Council, CSN
51. "Venezuelano vem ver armamentos," *Jornal do Brasil,* March 17, 1980.
52. "Exportação de material belico receberá mais incentivos fiscais."
53. "Pais pode vender US$2.2b em armas," *O Globo,* May 1, 1983, p. 46.
54. "Vendas de armas serão aumentadas," *Estado de São Paulo,* November 30, 1979, p. 6.
55. R. Godoy, "Saudita, canal permanente," *Estado de São Paulo,* October 12-10, 1986 and interview with Col. Duque, U.S. Consulate, São Paulo, July 1989.
56. Ibid.
57. "Estatizar comércio exterior poderá ser o próximo passo," *Estado de São Paulo,* January 6, 1980.
58. "Nicarágua-Brazil: Arms Deal Sought," *Strategic Latin American Affairs,* February 20, 1979.
59. "Military Planes May Be Sold to Honduras," FBIS , 6, May 4, 1985, p. D2.
60. "País pode vender US$2.2b em armas."
61. *Defense and Foreign Affairs Daily,* Vol. XIII, No. 150, August 7, 1981.
62. "A Importância das Armas," *Jornal Brasilese,* April 22, 1983.

63. "Suriname leva peças de campanha," *Estado de São Paulo*, June 3, 1983.
64. *Daily Report on Latin America*, FBIS, LAM 84 002, January 4, 1984, Vol. VI, No. 02.
65. *Strategy Week*, May 19-25, 1980.
66. "Venturini: é normal a venda de armamentos," *Estado de São Paulo*, October 28, 1982.
67. *Strategy Week*, October 6-12, 1980.
68. *The Wall Street Journal*, March 19, 1981.
69. "As guerras também abrem mercados," *Comércio e Mercados*, August 1982.
70. *Strategy Week*, October 6-12, 1980.
71. "O Brasil vende para a Nigéria," Isto é, April 22, 1981; and *Strategy Week*, May 19-25, 1980.
72. L. Jones, *Public Enterprises in Less Developed Countries*, (New York: Cambridge University Press, 1982), p. 229.
73. Jones, *Public Enterprises in Less Developed Countries*.
74. Ibid.
75. Ibid.
76. Dahlman and Sercovich, "Technology Exports from SICs," p. 80.
77. "O Brasil começa um novo negócio: exportação de tanque," *Jornal da Tarde*, April 1, 1974.
78. "Standard Arms Price Index," *Defense and Foreign Affairs*, April 1985, p. 27.
79. Nagaraja Rao and Jack Philip Ruina, "Disarmament and Development: The Case of Relatively Advanced Developing Countries," working Paper, Center for Policy Alternatives, MIT, Cambridge, Mass.
80. R. Sarathy, "High Technology Exports from Newly Industrializing Countries: The Brazilian Commuter Aircraft Industry," *California Management Review*, Vol. XXVII, No. 2, Winter 1985. See table 6, p. 72.
81. Interview on October 24, 1983 at General Motors of Brasil, São Paulo.
82. It is difficult to specify relative wages in developing countries. The International Labor Office does not even publish statistics for Brazil.
83. "O Brasil começa um novo negócio: exportação de tanque."
84. "Indústria Bélica Negocia com os EU e a China," *Jornal do Brasil*, August 3, 1980.
85. *Wall Street Journal*, March 19, 1981.
86. "Adido dos EUA elogia armamento," *Jornal do Brasil*, November 11,
87. Oil exploration was not successful. See the *Wall Street Journal*, October 11, 1984, p. 37, column 6.
88. *Strategy Week*, October 6-12, 1980.
89. W. Leontief and F. Duchin, *Military Spending* (N.J.: Oxford University Press, 1983), p. 31.
90. A. Klieman, *Israel's Global Reach* (VA.: Pergammon-Brassey's International Defense Publishers, 1985).
91. *Strategy Week*.

92. "Oficial sugere a troca de armamentos por petróleo," *Estado de São Paulo,* July 11, 1979.

93. *Latin American Political Report,* March 4, 1977.

94. Barter has become popular in international armaments markets. See Stephanie G. Neuman, "Coproduction, Barter, and Countertrade: Offsets in the International Arms Market," *Orbis,* Spring 1985, pp. 183-209. Also published in the U.S. Arms Control and Disarmament Agencies' *World Military Expenditures and Arms Transfers, 1985.* For a general discussion of barter, see P. Versariu, *Countertrade, Barter, Offsets,* (New York: McGraw Hill, 1985).

95. "A ENGESA negocia com os Sauditas," *Gazeta Mercantil,* July 3, 1980; "EMBRAER e ENGESA vendem aos Árabes," *Gazeta Mercantil,* February 18, 1983; "Iraque pode comprar carros bélicos do Brasil e pagar US$500m em oleo," *Jornal do Brasil,* January 27, 1979.

96. Reported by João Augusto de Medicis, of Itamarati, "EMBRAER e ENGESA vendem aos árabes," *Gazeta Mercantil,* February 18, 1983.

97. *MEED,* June 30, 1978.

98. *Christian Science Monitor,* March 9, 1977, p. 1.

99. Klieman, *Israel's Global Reach.*

100. "A Compra do Bimotor Xingu pela França," *Jornal da Tarde,* February 6,1980.

101. "Armas do Brasil podem ser usadas no OM," *Jornal do Brasil,* July 28, 1978; *Latin American Political Report,* March 4, 1977.

102. "ENGESA venderá ao Iraque US$250 mh em armas; contratos vão a US$700mh," *Jornal da Brasil,* November 17, 1981.

103. "Brazilian Visit Turns Up Trumps," *MEED,* December 11, 1981.

104. *Summary of World Broadcasts,* April 11, 1980.

105. *Diário Popular,* May 30, 1982.

106. "Em nova fase relações com EUA," *Estado de São Paulo,* June 8, 1983.

107. "Indústria de armamento está firme no exterior," *Jornal do Brasil,* September 10, 1982.

108. "A importância das armas," *Jornal Brasilese,* April 22, 1983.

109. Ibid.

8

The Brazilian Defense
Industry in Crisis

Introduction

The success that Brazil experienced in international armaments markets in the early 1980s became severely strained by the end of the decade. Beginning in late 1987, signs of financial strain appeared: layoffs, losses, the buildup of inventory. Although industry sales were reportedly US$1 billion in 1986 and predicted to soar to US$2 billion in the following year, 1987's performance was a disappointing US$ 500 million.[1] ENGESA, the armored vehicle producer and AVIBRAS, the missile producer, are particularly hard pressed. Financing almost all of its activities with third party funds, ENGESA had one of the highest national losses in 1987, 31% of sales.[2] By January of 1989 both AVIBRAS and ENGESA had halved their work forces from 1988 levels.[3] AVIBRAS went from the largest exporter in Brazil in 1987 to the firm with the eighth largest losses and sixth largest debt in 1989.[4] By January 1990 AVIBRAS requested legal protection from its creditors to allow for reorganization;[5] ENGESA followed suit in March.[6]

Although also facing difficulty, the record of EMBRAER, the aircraft producer should be distinguished from the dismal performance of ENGESA and AVIBRAS. EMBRAER continued to show a healthy growth of receipts of 38.3%[7] and ranked forty-fifth in order of national sales.[8] Ahead of EMBRAER were the giant Brazilian oil firm PETROBRAS, multinationals such as Shell, Mercedes Benz, Ford, and Nestle and state owned utilities such as the phone companies of Rio de Janeiro and São Paulo. But despite the best sales record in the defense sector, EMBRAER also shows strain. Although sales were high, EMBRAER posted losses that placed it as the 7,779th firm in the nation in terms of profitability.[9] It, too, suffered layoffs. Why has an industry widely seen as successful in the first half of the 1980s experienced such difficulties?

The profundity of this crisis was caused by the coalescence of a range of trends negatively affecting nearly every aspect of the firms' operations. Weak international sales certainly contributed to the crisis. After strong exports in the first part of 1987, particularly to the Middle East, markets became saturated and new orders dried up. The winding down of the Iran-Iraq war led the decline in demand. Sales to the United States by EMBRAER declined due to fears of a retaliatory tax on imports which could be imposed retroactively against Brazilian products. At the same time there was increased competition in both industrial and Third World markets. The Arab countries were bombarded by marketing of other Third World arms producers such as China, India, Pakistan, N. Korea.[10] The United States and the Soviet Union have increasingly replaced grants of obsolete weapons with foreign military sales, while Western European nations continued arms exports to support domestic industries.

But the crisis was not simply one of slow markets. The firms in the Brazilian defense industry were especially vulnerable to international market shocks because they were in a period of technological transition. While the success of the Brazilian defense sector had been predicated upon the selection of an intermediate technology that was simple to use and maintain under adverse conditions, the firms were attempting to push their technological frontiers further into the market for advanced weaponry. Such technological change involved increasing investments and imports as well as enhanced research and development efforts.

Unfortunately for the industry, the macroeconomy and political climate in Brazil did not favor such ambitious plans. With inflation hovering at 1,000 percent, government coffers emptied and political energies consumed by the democratic transition, the firms did not receive the timely support critical to technological change. Furthermore, some contend that the destabilizing macroeconomy was the primary cause of the industry's profound crisis.[11] Thus, rather than support the industry as had historically been the case, the Brazilian government inadvertently worked against it.

This chapter analyzes the contemporary crisis of the Brazilian defense industry. It characterizes its causes as endemic to the defense economy. That is, the Brazilian defense industry is passing through cycles similar to those of defense sectors in industrial countries where technological change is accomplished over long lag times during which the macroeconomic fundamentals are likely to shift. The Brazilian industry, at an earlier stage of development than industries in more industrialized countries, is that much more vulnerable to adverse conditions.

However, despite the crisis of the industry when the Brazilian economy as a whole is under considerable stress, it is argued that the partnership of the firm and the state will weather these difficult times. The rationale for the defense industry in Brazil as based in security and development has long historical roots and considerable support among military elites. Although out of office, the military continues to wield power. In the eyes of these elites the crisis of the industry holds within it the promise of growth in Brazil: technology. The defense industry, although costly, will, according to the elites, act as a technological locomotive pulling the economy into a position competitive with global industrial powers. It is an investment Brazilian elites are likely to make.

Causes of the Crisis

International Markets

Brazilian armaments were successfully marketed to a particular international niche designed to meet economic and military conditions in Third World nations. But in 1987 spending by the Third World on armaments fell 9.1%[12] Debt burdened and dollar starved Africa and Latin America were not able to afford ambitious rearmaments programs. Feeling the impact of lower oil prices, orders from the Middle East region declined drastically.[13] The export success of ENGESA and AVIBRAS relied primarily on this narrow market within the Middle East. As can be seen in figure 8.1, the decline in Brazilian foreign military sales closely parallels the contraction of the Middle East arms market. As a percentage of government expenditures, Iran's defense expenditures fell from 45.3% in 1984 to 15.8% in 1987; Saudi Arabia declined from 37.5% to 35.8% in the same period. Although no aggregate figures are given for Iraq, its spending per capita declined from US$929 to 880.[14] Not only was Iraq's spending declining, but so was its ability to pay. By May 1989 Iraq was reported to owe more than US$100 million to AVIBRAS. These late payments compounded AVIBRAS' difficulty.[15]

It is interesting to contemplate whether the depression in the arms trade with the Third World is a permanent or temporary

FIGURE 8.1

Brazilian Arms Exports v. Middle East Arms Imports

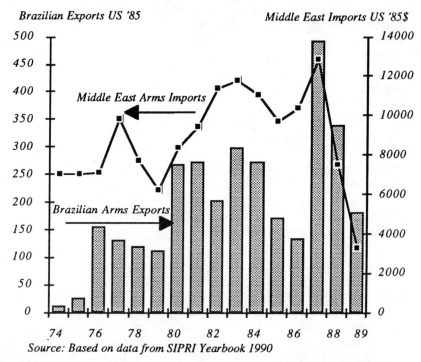

Brazilian Exports US '85   *Middle East Imports US '85$*

Source: Based on data from SIPRI Yearbook 1990

Note: the different scales on the two vertical axes; Brazilian weapons do not
come close to meeting the import demands of the Middle East.

phenomenon.[16] Three trends suggest that sellers can expect weak
markets throughout the decade. First, as a group, developing countries
burdened with debt find it difficult to support arms payments. Nations
have been forced to implement economic austerity plans severely
limiting central government expenditures. In the context of democratic
transitions, in many countries the political economy is not as conducive
to ambitious armament programs. Liberal arms purchases are a luxury
of the past which competing interest groups, facing declining shares of
national income, are unwilling to support. Secondly, oil prices have not
recovered to the highs of the 1970s which sustained the Middle East
weapons trade. Finally, even if economic conditions shifted and debt or
relatively weak oil prices did not constrain purchases, it is not clear
that countries would renew procurement programs with vigor. Warming
relations between the Soviet Union and the United States may be

mirrored in decelerating regional arms races which fueled earlier purchases. As the benefits of cooperation instead of confrontation become evident, the demand for weaponry is likely to remain slow.

In addition to smaller military budgets, on the supply side there is a fundamental shift toward greater sales competition. In 1988 U. S. weapon sales to the Third World increased by 66%. The Middle East was its largest market, receiving two-thirds of all weapons delivered.[17] The U.S. can be expected to promote sales of weaponry as a means of counterbalancing the industrial impact of tighter domestic defense budgets. The Soviet Union has also become more active in international sales as a means of earning much needed hard currencies. In 1987 Soviet sales represented nearly half of the value of weapons transfers to developing countries.[18] Because Soviet systems are not as sophisticated as those in the West, the Soviet Union is increasingly likely to be in direct sales competition with Brazil.[19] China has also become a player in the international market as it has begun to modernize its arsenals. Now the fourth largest weapons dealer in the world, it has provided Iran with 15% of its arms since 1980.[20] These larger players join a host of smaller but significant arms exporters such as France, Britain, Italy and Spain as crowded contenders in a shrinking market. Not to be forgotten are the range of Third World countries which have embarked on autonomous production programs and are looking to sell abroad to sustain production.

With increased rivalry in the face of declining demand, it is not surprising that Brazilian arms sales have been less robust. Furthermore, it is likely that tighter, more competitive markets will be a permanent feature of international arms sales. The international defense industry is confronting the paradox of defense production in the modern era. Each country, as a condition of sovereignty, wants to maintain indigenous weapons production. But because of the high investment of physical and human capital, technologically advanced systems must be produced on a large scale to recover research and development costs. Exports, then, become the answer to support production. However, it is a fallacy of composition to assume that a strategy of export promotion which worked for one country will work for all defense producers. Markets simply become saturated, and domestic economies must absorb the costs of producing at less than the minimum efficient scale.

Nevertheless, it is interesting to note that AVIBRAS President João Verdi Carvalho Leite did not believe that the overriding causes of the crisis were found in the contracting and competitive international market. Rather, he contends that the defense firms have had several years to prepare for the slowing of Middle East markets, and that the primary difficulties stem from the Brazilian government's destabilizing economic policies during the critical time.[21] This is in contrast to ENGESA, which maintains that the principle reason for its weak performance had to do with the declining volume of sales in the Middle East.[22] The AVIBRAS position is clearly the more optimistic one for the long run future of the Brazilian defense industry: rational economic policies would produce the conditions for success. On the other hand, the ENGESA argument, while not discounting the disruptive role of government, places a much higher priority on exogenous forces of demand.

Reason, it seems, lies between these two positions. Weak Middle East sales negatively affected the defense firms' performance, and this trend is likely to continue. But this demand side factor must be seen in the broader context of such supply concerns as technological choice and Brazilian economic conditions. The position of the firms surely would have been less fragile had sales been stronger and the chaotic business environment not pressured these vulnerable firms further.

EMBRAER's position is again different from that of ENGESA and AVIBRAS. It faced different demand conditions, and also has a greater likelihood of long run success. In addition to the slowdown in the Middle East markets, EMBRAER had to contend with problems in its primary civilian market, the United States. Due to disagreements over a broad range of products, the United States was threatening to impose a 100% surtax on selected Brazilian goods; the tax would be applied retroactively. With this measure looming, U.S. airlines held off on planned purchases of Brazilian planes. In the seven month period from November 1987 to June 1988 not a plane was sold in the United States for fear of the stiff tariff penalty. The economical Brasília, a favorite of North American commuter lines, would have jumped in price from approximately US$6 million to US$12 million.[23] At the end of 1987 EMBRAER had five Brasilias sitting in its yard, representing a US$50 million loss for the firm.[24] To displace the risk of the tariff, EMBRAER held US$32 million in credit in United States banks as a guarantee to assume the burden of the tariff should it be levied. However, this constrained the firm's cash flow and did not stem the losses in sales.[25] Furthermore, EMBRAER found its position in international financial markets strained as foreign banks began to restrict new lending.[26] Although the tax ultimately was not levied, weak sales in the civilian line and financial uncertainty compromised the firm's overall performance.

As damaging as it was in the short term, EMBRAER's difficulty with the United States does not threaten the future viability of the firm. This decline in demand in EMBRAER's civilian line was due to a temporary trade dispute rather than a secular decline in purchases. Moreover, with the resumption of normal relations, the civilian U.S. market broadens EMBRAER's sales beyond weaponry to the Third World. This injects needed stability into EMBRAER's future profitability.

Both the slowdown in the Middle East and the temporary protectionist measures that EMBRAER faced in the United States made it, like AVIBRAS and ENGESA, more susceptible to destabilizing macroeconomic policy at a time of technological transition. While any industry must expect to contend with changes in demand, the Brazilian defense firms, having grown quickly under favorable demand conditions, were not well structured to absorb short run losses. ENGESA, as noted, is heavily indebted, as is EMBRAER and AVIBRAS. From 1982 through 1989 all three firms appear on the list of the most indebted firms in the material transport sector published by the business journal *Gazeta Mercantil*.[27] As we will now see, this weak position of the firm was derived in good part from the technological gamble the firms began during the earlier period of ample demand.

The Technological Leap

An important ingredient of success in the Brazilian armaments industry was the ability to supply an international market niche for relatively simple, inexpensive, and easy to operate machinery. Having mastered those technological systems, the momentum was toward projects of greater sophistication. This demand for another class of weapons systems in part emanated from the Brazilian Armed Forces, who have long held as a goal the nationalization of their equipment. But the Brazilian Armed Forces, given limited procurement demands, could not economically sustain production of more complicated and expensive weaponry. Thus, the primary impetus for more advanced systems came from international markets. It was perceived that the same clients in the Middle East that had purchased Tucano trainer aircraft and Cascavel armored cars would be interested in an economical strike fighter or main battle tank. With successful sales networks and a solid reputation for value at a reasonable price, the firms expected to expand easily. But, as was just shown, by the time the projects advanced from the drawing board to commercialization, conditions had changed in international markets. This is not uncommon in defense production. Since weapons systems take from five to fifteen years to move from research to deployment, it is not surprising that economic conditions and military needs would have changed.[28]

For ENGESA the technological leap to the Osório tank necessitated plant expansion and increased imports. Specifically, it needed greater access to parts and electronic subsystems. When explaining its losses in the first term of 1988, it included the fact that it had to purchase FNV and that its subsidiary ENGETRÔNICA had not yet received imported equipment critical to Osório production.[29] ENGESA invested US$ 100 million in the Osório, without the payout of sales.[30] As ENGESA representatives noted in an interview in July of 1989, the firm expanded technologically on many fronts, having overestimated the size of international markets.[31] But when the Osório prototypes were ready for commercialization, the principle target market, the Middle East, had contracted. And because of the fiscal crisis of the Brazilian State discussed below, the government structurally was not prepared to support the technological transition of the firm.

EMBRAER, for its part, embarked on the AMX strike fighter program. The AMX, a subsonic jet, was a new class of aviation technology for the Brazilians. To master new production processes they signed a coproduction agreement with the Italian firms Aermachi and Aeritalia with whom they had completed earlier work on the Xavante. EMBRAER is allegedly having difficulty in its coproduction arrangements with the Italians, involving misunderstandings of the contractual obligations of the parties. Costs are out of control, reportedly reaching US$17 million which puts it in the same financial group as the US F-16. Why not, according to an attache in the United States consulate, buy a F-16?[32] Indeed in creating a plane that is technologically in the same market as a proven system, new suppliers are at a competitive disadvantage. Given the riskiness of new systems, purchasers prefer established products. But this choice is often a moot point as the countries which have purchased EMBRAER's successful Tucano trainer such as Honduras, Venezuela, Peru, Paraguay and Argentina, are unlikely to have the funds to purchase either F-16s or AMXs.[33]

AVIBRAS spent $800 million developing the missile SS-300 but then had no Army orders.[34] A similar case is that of the anti-ship Barracuda missile, which AVIBRAS announced as a project ordered by the Brazilian Navy. But Navy Minister Admiral Henrique Saboia said that the Navy is not interested in the Barracuda missile. AVIBRAS, like EMBRAER and ENGESA, has tried to acquire technology through international coproduction agreements. AVIBRAS has entered into a coproduction agreement with China for satellite systems.

However, AVIBRAS reports that China will not transfer any technology because of the pressure it has felt from the United States to withhold even civilian technologies with applications for ballistic missile systems. AVIBRAS president Verdi recently noted that this program is dead.[35]

All three programs—the AMX, the Osório and the SS-300—represent substantial technological leaps in production technologies and gambles in international markets. All three systems require increases in imported components and the incorporation of more sophisticated subsystems. The Osório is even promoted as an amalgam of the most advanced subsystems. However, given the intensity of the investments necessary to develop these products, the lack of sales in weak international markets has severely compromised the future of the Brazilian defense firms.

Mary Kaldor, in *The Baroque Arsenal*,[36] argues this drive to produce ever more sophisticated weapons systems is part of the internal dynamic of defense production. The upward spiral of technological change creates less marketable products. That is to say, as Third World producers of armaments systems graduate up the ladder of sophistication, the number of buyers of such costly systems falls precipitously. But as technological sophistication progresses, the scale at which production is cost efficient becomes increasingly larger. This is the paradox of defense production for Third World countries. As products become more sophisticated, export markets do not support a large number of purchases. But scale requirements increase because production is cost efficient only at large quantities. This conflict between the shrinking number of potential buyers and the increasing quantity of production for efficiency is likely to result in a drain of resources of states which, for political-military reasons, maintain domestic defense industries.

Wulf (1987) notes that we might expect this increasing opportunity cost of defense production as technological systems evolve, and product cycles characterized by short production runs at less than the critical value of efficient production tend to dominate. Defense investments come to have fewer connections with the civilian sector. He says:

> In other words military and civil technology tends to diverge; capacities installed for meeting the demand of arms production might not result in the expected backward linkages or if these backward linkages are established it might be a costly and uneconomic investment.[37]

Thus, as the scale requirements become larger, the potential size of the international market begins to shrink and domestically the industry has fewer direct linkages with the broader industrial structure. Hirschman's notion of "semi-naive exhaustion" in explaining the failure of import substitution industrialization might be instructive here.[38] Essentially, the argument runs that as one moves backward up the industrial chain, economies of scale dominate. More sophisticated products must be produced at a larger scale because of the gains from specialization and division of labor. However, the market cannot absorb the quantity of products manufactured at that scale, and the import substitution process becomes exhausted.

While Brazilian defense production was closely tied to the automotive sector, scale economies could be derived from like processes and bulk purchases. Suppliers were able to meet the firm's needs at a reasonable cost. As systems became more sophisticated, costs, including those for research and development, increased markedly and domestic sourcing became less common. Imports of technologically advanced subsystems with specifically military applications were necessary. But, at the same time, the factor critical to the success of the Brazilian defense industry, its export orientation, was not longer a rich source of sales. This is consistent with Hirschman's contention that market size and export possibilities are critical complementary variables.

Macroeconomic Factors

In addition to the increasing difficulties Brazilian defense producers confronted with declining international markets and increasing costs, a variety of poor macroeconomic factors constrained profitability in the late 1980s. Heavy taxation, exchange rate distortions, and inflationary pressures made the continued performance of any firm almost unbelievable. Given the fragility due to slow markets and technological transition, they were particularly burdensome to the defense industry.

The State of São Paulo, in levying its ICM, a state tax, added 17% to the purchase price of aircraft for Brazilians after August of 1988. Although this is not a tax particular to the aviation industry, it is certainly a cost to the firm. With the hefty tax making purchase economically unprofitable, some Brazilian firms were reportedly importing planes through EMBRAER's Argentine partner Chincul because the bilateral trade agreement between Argentina and Brazil allowed for tax free entry.[39] As financial difficulties for the firm mounted, EMBRAER convinced the State to suspend the tax.[40] But sluggish sales had come just at the point where EMBRAER needed liquid capital to support the production of the new high technology strike fighter, the AMX. To soften the impact of short run losses on the AMX program, EMBRAER requested US$4.7 million from the National Development Fund, the FND.

The exchange rate policy of Brazil was prejudiced against export earnings. All exports from Brazil are licensed by the Bank of Brazil. When an exporter receives hard currency such as dollars for sales this is invoiced, and the exchange into the Brazilian currency is made by the Bank of Brazil at the official exchange rate. However, in the late 1980s there was a large discrepancy between what the Central bank would pay out on the dollar of exports versus what firms could receive in the black market. For example, Brazilian managers argue that balance sheet losses would become profits had the conversion into Brazilian currency been at the more favorable black market rate.[41] In explaining its problems, AVIBRAS notes that in 1987 it sold US$322 million, but with the official exchange rate at 35% under the real value, lost US$100 million of this. To compensate for these losses, they had to borrow. Thus their debt increased five times in real terms.[42]

Contracts for armaments sales are written in dollars. When the arms exporters are finally paid in Brazilian currency, the value of the domestic currency has deteriorated substantially. But in the meantime, the firms have had to honor their commitments to their suppliers, paid in Brazilian currency. This crunch between paying for supplies and being paid for sales squeezes profitability.[43] ENGESA president José Luiz Whitaker Ribeiro places a large part of the blame for reduced sales as a result of government policy. He charges:

> The government has not defined the rules of the game. There is no stable exchange policy, and this creates an atmosphere of insecurity for exporters. We have produced a lot and sold a lot, but had great losses.[44]

The Brazilian defense producers, like other Brazilian firms,[45] have also had to contend with the microeconomic repercussions of Brazil's external debt stance. For example, in 1987 when the Brazilian government suspended payments on its US$113 billion external debt, EMBRAER had to work frantically with its bankers to keep open its short term lines of credit.[46] Creating a double bind, private banks don't want to deal with military producers because goods cannot be sold freely in liquidation.[47] Thus military firms find it difficult to access commercial credit lines.

Resource Constraints: Labor Problems

EMBRAER, as a mixed state enterprise with state ownership, faces particularly difficult constraints with its labor force. Not able to readjust salaries above a governmentally set base, wages and salaries at EMBRAER were rapidly falling behind spiraling prices in the economy. In January 1988 line operatives initiated "Operation Turtle" a work slowdown aimed at forcing the government to relax the salary constraint.[48] Within weeks the slowdown escalated into a full-blown strike for higher wages.[49]

Technical personnel such as engineers accelerated an already problematic trend in the professional labor force at the firm: using EMBRAER as a training center before entering private industry. With the cap limiting salaries to 38% lower than private industry, graduates from the aeronautical training center ITA work at EMBRAER for short durations at the beginning of their careers. They later capitalize on the skills acquired and transfer to the private sector.[50] Thus high inflation and fixed salaries weakened EMBRAER's pool of human capital.

While creating problems for labor force stability, the cap on salaries has the positive effect of holding down costs for the firm. When the Federal Government permitted EMBRAER to adjust wages in May of 1988, in the following weeks the firm had to let more than 200 workers go.[51] By the beginning of 1989 their work force shrank from a high of 10,700 to 10,100.[52]

In summary, international and domestic conditions threaten the economic viability of the Brazilian defense industry. Conditions outside the control of the firm on both the demand side as well as the production front create a scenario which, unless there is a fundamental shift in the orientation of the firms, make it unlikely they will be able to survive without a great cost to Brazilian society. We now turn to consider approaches to improve the future viability of the Brazilian defense industry.

The Future of the Brazilian Defense Industry

The Implications of the Gulf Conflict
for Brazil's Defense Industry:

Rearmament after the Gulf may provide a reprieve from the Brazilian defense industry's crisis in the short run. In contrast to the markedly downward trend shown in Figure 8.1, Middle East countries are likely to return to ambitious armament programs--including the simpler systems offered by Brazil. Some find this assessment improbable, arguing that the Gulf conflict was a demonstration of advanced technology leaving little room for intermediate range systems offered by Brazil. For example, Brazilian political scientist and military analyst Rene Drefus said "Iraq's invasion of Kuwait completely changed the requirements of the countries in that region in terms of armaments. From now on, they are going to give preference to highly sophisticated weapons which Brazil does not and cannot make."[53] However, it appears more likely that as the Middle East rearms it will purchase more of all kinds of systems. While indeed sophisticated systems will be sought after, so too will trainer aircraft, multiple launch rockets and armored vehicles be in demand. Given the degree of insecurity in the Middle East, spending on advanced systems will come at the expense of spending on civilian goods, not fewer basic guns.

It should be noted that relatively small purchases would prompt recovery in the Brazilian industry. At the height of the Brazilian export boom, all foreign sales only amounted to $491 million, or 3.8% of all Middle East imports. With Brazil's strong ties to the Middle East, it would be surprising if some new business were not thrown its way.

There have already been indications of interest in Brazilian equipment. AVIBRAS was able to meet its financial obligations under Brazilian bankruptcy law because of a $69 million dollar shipment of Astros-II weapons to Saudi Arabia.[54] This equipment was originally produced for Iraq, but was withheld in 1989 when the country lagged in payments. The firm's attorney Nelson Marcondes Machado said "It was the money from that sale of weapons to Saudi Arabia which provided the firm with the funds for paying its debts. To pay the remainder of the debt, the firm will have to sign new contracts this year".[55] AVIBRAS is discussing $400m worth of rocket trailers and multiple warheads. AVIBRAS president João Verdi de Carvalho Leite is optimistic because he believes he has a superior product--reliable, with greater ability to fire without re-aiming, that was used successfully by both sides in the Gulf conflict. [56]

Negotiations also continue for EMBRAER and ENGESA in the Middle East. There may be some interest on the part of the Iranians in purchasing EMBRAER equipment.[57] The Iranians already fly Tucano trainers acquired through EMBRAER's production line in Egypt. The Estado de São Paulo reports a potential package deal for all defense firms which, if concluded, could reach 3 billion dollars. ENGESA is negotiating once again for the Osório, a $2.2 billion deal. Although this negotiation has dragged on for years, it has come up again in response to an Israeli lobby's blocking the second shipment of American M1A2s to Saudi Arabia.[58] While the magnitude of the transaction is unlikely to reach into the billions, sales at this time would certainly give the Brazilian defense industry a lifeline to the future.

But an improved market in the Middle East can only bring temporary benefits to the Brazilian defense industry. Once again the market will become saturated at a new level of demand. Brazilians suppliers cannot count on an improved market for stable, long run growth. Other, more fundamental industrial changes must also take place.

There are also political difficulties stalling change. The economic evolution of the Brazilian defense industry will be constrained by the political repercussions of several unfortunate incidents during the Gulf crisis. Most important from an international policy standpoint was the activity of retired Brigadier General Hugo Piva, and his consulting company HOP, which was contracted by the government of Iraq to work on improving the accuracy of missile systems.

Piva's activities in the Middle East prompted much attention from the United States. Press reports described the activities of a number of firms still dealing with Iraq--all of which were denied by both the firms and the Brazilian foreign ministry. Foreign Minister Rezek noted in an interview with *ISTO É SENHOR* that Brazil was no longer selling armaments to Iraq when the Gulf crisis began.[59] The reason for the halt in arms sales was simple: Iraq was 18 months behind in payments to AVIBRAS, and the firm was unwilling and unable to extend further credit.[60] Rezek, however, was frustrated by the fact that he felt that the United States looked upon the Piva activity as representative of the Government of Brazil—while the government was strictly upholding the UN sanctions against Iraq, and threatening punishment for any who violated them.[61] The political attention garnered through the Piva exploits, however, will constrain what has always been a Brazilian asset in arms sales: the ability to place products in countries irrespective of political repercussions.

The Emerging Shape of the Brazilian Defense Industry

Given its profound industrial crisis and the implications of the Gulf War, does the Brazilian armaments industry have a future? Several factors indicate that we can expect the Brazilian defense industry to survive, albeit in a different form. Domestically, there are strong political and strategic reasons to maintain a defense industry in Brazil. The defense sector allows Brazil to project itself as a regional and international power. Much has been made of the sector in the international press, and the myth of its size and capabilities raises concerns for those with vested interests in controlling the spread of weapons technologies. Western powers pay more attention to Brazil because of its indigenous production and export capabilities than they would in the absence of the sector. While this has political and economic costs, its also provides Brazil a bargaining chip in international strategic circles.

Although limited by the domestic fiscal crisis, the Brazilian state appears willing to support the defense sector. Elites perceive that the defense industry brings technological benefits to Brazil. Indeed 18.2% of the $2.2 billion 1991 science and technology budget recently approved by the Brazilian Congress is dedicated to research within the military ministries.[62] Additional appropriations of up to ten percent of the total may be passed for research projects being carried out by various ministries.

The health of the defense industry has attracted the attention of the Collor administration. The Secretariat for Strategic Affairs (SAE) is preparing a plan for the defense sector with the input of the Brazilian Defense Manufacturers Association ABIMDE.[63] That SAE Secretary Leone Ramos and not the Minister of the Army is responsible for negotiations over the resolution of ENGESA'S bankruptcy underscores the direct hand the Collor government wields in defense industrial policy. Leone was also involved in negotiations with the Saudis for the purchase of the Osório; President Collor reportedly intervened" on behalf of the Brazilian product "as well.[64] It should, however, be emphasized that the Collor government support for the defense industry is far more nuanced than in previous administrations. This administration appreciates the international constraints on armaments exports. It appears willing to bargain compliance with export regimes such as the MTCR (Missile Technology Control Regime) for technology transfer in nonmilitary areas.

But intervention has a different character than in the past. The administration is interested in maintaining a healthy sector, but not at the expense of sacrificing domestic goals and international disapprobation. The question of resolving ENGESA's looming bankruptcy is a case in point. Given its strategic importance, the State has interest in the renewed health of the firm. While it wants to head off final insolvency, the goal is to do so without nationalization, financial assistance from the government, or complete foreign control.[65] The resolution of this problem is likely to assume a mixed approach: shared ownership and control between a European group, a Brazilian group and IMBEL, the Army munitions firm.[66]

Beyond the political rationale to support the Brazilian defense sector, there are indications that the industry itself has a more realistic vision of its capabilities and limitations. To survive the crisis created by unfavorable international market conditions at a time of technological vulnerability and weaker state support, the Brazilian firms have begun to pursue new strategies. Primary among these strategies has been an amplification of their civilian lines. EMBRAER, in an attempt to ride out the poor market conditions, has moved into producing parts for other international aircraft concerns. For example, it was negotiating a composites production agreement with British Airways and signed a contract to work on the MacDonnell Douglas MD-11 for a sum of US$200 million.[67] EMBRAER will build 200 sets of carbon composite outboard flaps for the wings of the MD-11 with an option of 100 more if needed.[68] This contract would augment sales in the technologically advanced arena of composites, allowing EMBRAER greater production experience. EMBRAER also entered into a coproduction agreement with Argentina to produce the nineteen-seat CBA-123, a commuter plane designed to fill a market niche in Latin America.

The amplification of civilian lines has thus far been a successful strategy for EMBRAER. A recent report by the firm notes that revenues jumped 34% in 1989, such that the firm finished the year with net profits of US$89 million as opposed to US$35 million losses in 1988. In 1989 it delivered fifty-five of the popular *Brasilias* to regional airlines; the order book stands at 291 orders and 135 options worldwide, with roughly 73% of its market in the United States.[69] Explaining its poor 1988 performance as a function of the threat of retaliation discussed above, EMBRAER also looks forward to strong markets for its new EMB-145 forty-five-seater and the CBA-123, in cooperation with Argentina. To meet this projected demand, the company announced that it plans to hire almost 700 employees for a work force total of 13,300. It is interesting to note that to finance expansion in the civilian market, EMBRAER arranged a debt for equity swap and issued shares on the public stock market for a total of US$ 185 million in capital.[70] With the debt for equity swap, short term debt of the Brazilian National Economic and Social Development Bank (BNDES) was swapped for US$100 million non-voting shares by Bank of America, Continental Bank, Bank of Tokyo, Credit Suisse, Banque Français du Commerce Exterieur and the Arab Bank Corporation.[71] This is an important signal of the renewed health of EMBRAER, showing its ability to borrow, as well as an indication that it must go to private markets for funding given the paucity of State funds.

Although ENGESA and AVIBRAS have not historically had the same strength in civilian production as EMBRAER, the crisis is prompting such changes in production line. AVIBRAS has started making antennas for the home television market.[72] Instead of tanks, ENGESA will focus on tractors, buses, trucks, and railroad cars.[73] In July 1989 AVIBRAS' strategy to overcome the constraints of the crisis was threefold: explore new markets, convert some production lines to civilian products, and consider production outside of Brazil. AVIBRAS would like to follow the lead of EMBRAER in gaining a presence in first world markets. If it were able to conquer a niche in North America, this would enable it to escape the instability of sales to Third World nations. AVIBRAS' participation in an annual weapons exhibit organized by the Association of the U.S. Army signals its eagerness to sell to Western industrial nations.[74] Examples of products they might offer for the Brazilian internal market include radars and trolleybuses. However, given the problems of the Brazilian economy it is unlikely that internal demand will be strong for the coming years. As the President of AVIBRAS noted with respect to the trolleybuses, AVIBRAS already produces and sells them, but the mayors of the purchasing cities have no money to pay for them.[75] Finally, in order to escape the plethora of regulations strangling producers in Brazil, the President of AVIBRAS noted that production outside of the country has been contemplated.

Industrialists and politicians appreciate the need for the internationalization of the defense industry. An autonomous national defense industry is nearly impossible even in industrialized countries. President Collor's openness toward foreign capital resulted in increasing the number of negotiations between domestic and foreign arms firms during 1990 for the purpose of forming joint ventures. In response to the difficult economic situation of the defense sector, the xenophobia of many military commanders was shelved. AVIBRAS president João Verdi de Carvalho Leite jokingly noted that he would even welcome a CIA-sponsored firm as a partner in missile production.[76] EMBRAER is looking to acquire risk partners, most likely international subsystems producers, willing to invest in development costs for the chance to share in the project's profits.[77] Development of EMB 145 is now a priority. The project calls for investment of $300 million; such international agreements would leave EMBRAER less vulnerable to failure. [78]

The smaller defense firms are also seeking international cooperation. One joint venture is D. F. Vasconcelos and the British firm Pilkington.

The British appear more persistent and interested than anyone else in the Brazilian arms industry. At the start of 1990 the British firm Royal Ordnance even signed a contract with FI Industry and Commerce to manufacture medium and large caliber ammunition. The deal fell through when the Navy announced it was taking over FI to straighten out irregularities in management.[79]

The United States has been less aggressive than the British in establishing associations with Brazilian defense firms. The rest of this chapter details why it is in the foreign policy interests of the United States and Brazil to expand cooperation. The argument proceeds by discussing the change in the foreign policy objectives of Brazil, characterizing US concerns in the area, and then showing why the risks associated with expanded cooperation are outweighed by the potential gains.

National Security and Foreign Policy Interests of Brazil

The security interests of Brazil would be served by expanded cooperation with the United States. Changes in the Brazilian definition of the means for securing its national security make possible a new relationship with the United States. As described in chapter 4, Brazilian national security has traditionally been defined by the binomium *Segurança e Desenvolvimento,* or security and development.

Castello Branco further emphasized the technical basis of war, such that industrial strength was a prerequisite to defense. This security policy was fundamentally nationalistic, and placed responsibility in the hands of the state to implement policies for growth. Drawing upon the earlier work of strategist Góes Monteiro, it placed economic development at the heart of the greatness of the homeland.

Whereas under the military government the focus of Brazilian security policy was on providing the internal stability as a precondition for domestic growth, Brazilian foreign policy and its security policy component is now outward looking. Central to security policy is the acquisition of technology. Before the final cabinet meeting of 1990 President Collor noted that "to become a modern, first world nation, Brazil must catch up with technological progress".[80] Secretary for Strategic Affairs Leone Ramos echoes this sentiment in saying that "the bomb is unnecessary because in the 21st century, technology will be the chief means of asserting national power... A country will be classified as developed or underdeveloped on the basis of whether it absorbs technology or controls it."[81] This emphasis on technology is not contradictory to the past military policy of emphasizing the economic bases of security; however, achieving this new goal requires a different strategy. Brazil has learned that it will never catch up in isolation from the industrialized nations. It, therefore, must open further to the international system to acquire technology. But the terms of acquisition from industrial countries demand assurances and responsible international behavior.

Foreign Minister Francisco Rezek contends that the "Third World minded" foreign policy has been abandoned because "its rhetoric has proved to be ineffective." The Collor plan on foreign policy is to sit at the table with the First World countries to work and "to participate in the center of international decision-making."[82] There are indications of Brazilian willingness to make concessions in order to receive technology. To prepare the way for bilateral talks with the United States on technology transfer, Brazil, in conjunction with Argentina, announced their intention to bring the Tlatelolco non-proliferation treaty into force. President Collor's action of filling the Cachimbo hole for nuclear testing was a dramatic statement about his nation's new commitment to greater transparency and accountability in military programs. Foreign Minister Rezek has shown a certain willingness to change course—a careful openness to pressure from the United States. When asked whether US pressure would affect the Brazilian nuclear submarine program Rezek, after first defending the consistency of the program with the argument for the peaceful use of nuclear energy, said that

If the US Government—whose thorough understanding of Brazilian projects is important for the development of our technology—"has a quarrel" with the building of a nuclear-powered submarine, we will have to negotiate and perhaps give up the project....depending on the cost-benefit relationship. We must analyze, however, whether to insist on building the submarine against the will of a country that can transfer high technology to us at reasonable prices. ...I believe that we will benefit more from other aspects of high technology. I wonder whether a specific method of moving a submarine justifies the renunciation of other types of technological assistance that we hope to receive in the short term. [83]

Of course it is not surprising that the Minister of the Navy, to whom acquisition of submarine technology is critical, publicly disagreed with the Rezek position the following day. What is important is that the Collor Administration has been willing to take the military on, to establish the position that certain military programs might have to be sacrificed in order to achieve the greater policy goal of technology transfer.

If the costs of an indigenous defense industry are to be minimized for Brazilian society, consideration must be given to a new vision of national defense. Building upon the Brazilian military's long held conception that true national security is possible only with stable economic development, a multi-dimensional defense policy for the 1990s should be examined. As Jessica Tuchman Matthews argues in "Redefining Security," this concept must be broadly specified to include environmental and demographic challenges confronting global society.[84] Careful consideration should be given to how state research and development centers as well as defense firms can be restructured to respond to this comprehensive definition of defense. For example, should the political will exist, there are clearly civilian applications of ENGESA's trucks and tractors to sound agricultural strategies. A systematic study of the possibilities for partial conversion from defense to civilian production is in order. The potential benefits of strengthening the financial and sales performance of the firms, while permitting the defense production and research and development capabilities to be maintained are a compelling reason for further investigation.

There are benefits to the United States to supporting a multidimensional security policy in Brazil. Within the crisis of the Brazilian defense industry there may be a missed foreign policy opportunity for the United States. With U.S. interests currently focused on the opening of Eastern Europe, the United States has given scant attention to democratic transitions in the Southern Cone. However, enhanced cooperation with Brazil, including agreements in the area of military production, could improve bilateral relations as well as help stabilize the Brazilian conventional defense economy by increasing demand for its goods and enhancing access to technology. Although efforts to these ends were unsuccessfully begun under the Reagan Administration, conditions have changed. Brazil has since suffered a prolonged period of economic instability. With consolidation in Western Europe, the gains from enhanced integration on the American continents are apparent. Of course, the United States must approach the export of any militarily sensitive material with caution. However, the cooperation need not take place within the military arms of the defense firms. Rather, cooperation might better be focused in the civilian arena since this type of production limits re-export difficulties.

An example of this type of cooperation might be how the technology for the EMBRAER contract with MacDonnell Douglas MD-11 (discussed above) was acquired from the Sikorsky aircraft unit of United Technologies Corporation for the use of carbon fibers in making composite materials. This knowledge was of primary benefit to the production of EMB's thirty passenger Brasilia commuter aircraft.[85] Rather than rely on the state to supplement efforts in technological acquisition, the firm was able to acquire needed production information commercially. There have also been initiatives in the military field. In April 1988 Aeronautics Minister Brigadier Octavio Julio Moreira Lima received an invitation from the U.S. General Dynamics for EMBRAER to participate in a project to manufacture F-16 Fighting Falcon fighter planes in Brazil. The F-16, currently used by the U.S. Air Force, will be undertaken in two stages: initially, EMBRAER will manufacture for General Dynamics composite material for the wings and fuselage as well as avionics for the plane; at that point technology for the F-16 manufacture will begin to be transferred.[86] This type of agreement allows Brazilian firms access to needed technology to enhance domestic capabilities, but does so in a way that minimizes costs to the firm and Brazilian government subsidies to the industry.

What Will the Brazilian Arms Sales Policy Look Like in the Future?

The political fallout surrounding the Gulf crisis made it clear to the Brazilians that in order to receive the technology necessary for national security, controls must be imposed on the export of armaments. As Foreign Minister Rezek noted, "Brazil today is simply convinced that it is essential to act with extreme prudence and make certain analyses relating to the political future before getting involved in that kind of trade."

The government of Brazil is preparing a new policy for the conventional arms materiel sector. According to the foreign minister, "the most sensitive area" relates to exports and involves not only the sale of military materiel but the performance of services abroad. He said the latter aspect had become manifest recently with the activities carried out in Iraq by HOP consultants, the company owned by retired Brigadier General Hugo Piva. He quickly defended Piva's actions, but stated a willingness to change. "The company's situation was perfectly legal; it was work done by private enterprise," Rezek maintained. "In other words, the government had nothing whatever to do with it, but we can improve our performance in this area."[87]

Despite the desire to be perceived as accountable to first world nations, Rezek has not come out squarely for strict controls of conventional weapons exports. In response to a reporter's query as to whether Brazil would sell weapons to potentially bellicose nations, including Iran, Rezek did not rule out this possibility, saying:

> We have not ruled it out, but neither is it on our agenda. Moreover, any prospective deal with Iran would take a little longer, would require some reflection. Although from the point of view of the Brazilian Government, Iran has turned over a new leaf since that period. The Iranians are sensible; they know what Brazil is and what it stands for, and this must have influenced the Iranian decision to immediately offer us all the petroleum we need.[88]

In response to the question will the government allow exports of weapons to Iran, Rezek answered,

> Yes, but within a new perspective. We hope to establish three main guidelines for exports of national weapons. First, that the weapons we export be defensive, not offensive. There seems to be a very small difference here, but the military know how to differentiate between them very well. Second that we will be completely convinced that those weapons will not be enough for the purchasing country to begin a war. Third, that the export of weapons will not figure as the main trade item with any country. You will see that if weapons are included on our list of exports to Iran, they will appear in a very small scale.[89]

According to foreign minister Rezek, the Government of Brazil "recommends" that businessmen consult diplomatic channels whenever a trade deal involves other countries.[90] This is an important rhetorical shift in the government "hands off" policy of arms exports. It is not clear, however, that it will be enforceable in practice.

Brazil is hedging on its conventional arms export policy. Brazilian goals of sitting at the table with the industrial powers demand that the country behave like a first world power. It is clear what this means in terms of the nuclear industry. But apart from MTCR guidelines, there is no conventional armaments export regime. With no formal international standards for conduct it is unlikely that that Brazilians will change their pattern of arms exports.

If the United States would like Brazil to modify its weapons sales policy it must give incentives to do so. The US must provide Brazil the rationale to identify its security interests with those of the United States. Three programmatic means for doing so come to mind. First, because it is difficult to control the behavior of the defense firms legislatively, market incentives ought to be used. That is to say, if

Brazilian defense firms had a vested economic interest in the United States market, the calculus of exports to undesirable nations versus loosing the U.S. market would be a risky one. The Brazilian defense industry offers products of potential interest to the U.S. Armed Forces because of the particular market niche that they fill. Weight should be given the the foreign policy considerations of such a purchase. Joint ventures with U.S. firms should be encouraged.

Another area with joint gains for both countries would be the purchase of Brazilian equipment for use in the drug war in Latin America. While offshore procurement is problematic, the dividends are clear. Simple to use and designed for jungle environments, Brazilian equipment is ideal for riverine and costal patrol operations. Once again, the purchase of the equipment would give the Brazilian firms the carrot to identify its interests with those of the United States for fear of loosing a significant market.

Finally, an area complementary to the defense industry that should be considered is an exploration of a hemispheric energy policy. One of the driving forces behind Brazil's export of armaments is the need to counterbalance oil imports. Forty percent of the nation's oil is imported; before the Gulf crisis, 30% of these imports had come from Iraq.[91] Because of these magnitudes, Brazilian foreign policy will always be driven by oil diplomacy. Given the instability and the changing alliances in the Middle East, the politics of oil will surely demand that the Brazilians sell arms to someone the United States does not like. The best way to avoid that is to relieve some of the underlying pressure for sales through a hemispheric energy policy.

In sum, if the United States is to achieve its security interests of decreasing proliferation of weapons systems, creating incentives for the Brazilians to share U.S. security concerns is a policy with clear payoffs. The Bush visit to Brazil in the fall of 1990 began the momentum toward such policies; the return Collor visit to the United States the following June may continue it. This is not a costly endeavor--but rather one which demands political will and an understanding of the potential interests to both parties.

Conclusion

If the Brazilian defense industry is to survive the crisis that plagued it in the late 1990s, both the firms and the Brazilian state will need to reorient themselves to new conditions in the domestic and international markets. Cyclical instability is a feature of the international defense economy that is best met with a strategy that flexibly adapts to changing patterns of supply and demand. The momentum toward technological advance must be tempered by the linkages to the civilian sector and the ability to market goods internationally. Constrained by the fiscal crisis of the Brazilian state, official support must look to measures that work with and not against the market. Consideration should be given to the benefits of supporting a broader vision of national security and the investigation of enhanced Inter-American relations.

EMBRAER appears to have a created a successful recipe for weathering the downturn in the industry: amplification of the civilian line, creation of financial mechanisms through private sources, and technological acquisition via coproduction agreements. It has taken advantage of a variety of international agreements, including ones with the United States. AVIBRAS and ENGESA, to the extent that it is possible, might wisely follow suit. If they do not, it is likely that the costs will be high for the Brazilian economy. Given the strong commitment to the central role of military production in technology acquisition, it is unlikely that any government will be able to resist substantial subsidization of the defense industry. Yet, because the direction of technological change has moved to advanced, "baroque" systems, the "technological trickle-down" to civilian applications will be a costly drip.

Notes

1.   "Indústria de Armamentos Acusa Queda de Vendas em 87," *Folha de São Paulo,* December 27, 1987, p. A-5.

2.   Dante Matarazzo, "ENGESA—Altos Prejuízos" Caderno de Empresas, *Estado de São Paulo,* October 20, 1987.

3.   AVIBRAS went from 4600 to 2500 workers; ENGESA from 2600 to 1400. "AVIBRAS demitiu 1900 so em Janeiro," *O Globo,* February 7, 1989.

4.   Márcio Chaer, "Indústria bélica vive pior crise em 10 anos," *Jornal Do Brasil,* January 15, 1990.

5.   More specifically, AVIBRAS entered into receivership, along the lines of a United States Chapter 11 code, which allows the firm protection from creditors during reorganization. Fax communication with AVIBRAS, April 10, 1989.

6.   "ENGESA pede concordata preventiva," *O Globo,* March 22, 1990, p.17.

7.   Balanço Anual 1989 *Gazeta Mercantil,* Vol. XIII, No. 13, p. 302. The average for the sector "transport material" was a positive growth of 6.6%.

8.   Quem é Quem na Economia Brasileira 1989, Visão, Vol. XXXVIII, No. 36A.

9.   Ibid.

10.   Roberto Lopes, "CSN prevê estagnação na venda de armas," *Folha de São Paulo*, July 7, 1988.
11.   Interview with the president of AVIBRAS, João Verdi Carvalho Leite, *São José dos Campos*, Brasil, July 1989.
12.   Peter Grier, "Arms Spending Slows Worldwide," *The Christian Science Monitor*, August 10, 1989, p. 8.
13.   "ENGESA sofreu perda em 87 de Cz$2.5 b," *Jornal do Brasil*, April 22, 1988.
14.   Robert Bailey, "Defense in the Middle East," Defense Special Report, *Middle East Economic Digest* 32, December 6, 1988, pp. 21-33.
15.   "AVIBRAS demite 382," *Estado de São Paulo*, May 24, 1989.
16.   Aaron Karp discusses this question in "Trade in Conventional Weapons," in the Stockholm International Peace Research Institute, *SIPRI Yearbook 1988 World Armaments and Disarmament* (Oxford: Oxford University Press, 1988).
17.   Robert Pear, "U.S. Weapon Sales to Third World Increase by 66%," *The New York Times*, August 1, 1989, p. A1.
18.   "Third World States Spending Less on Arms in Recent Years," *The Christian Science Monitor*, May 16, 1988. The article reports on Library of Congress researcher Richard Grimmet's study of weapons for the world.
19.   Karp, "The Trade in Conventional Weapons."
20.   "Third World States Spending Less on Arms in Recent Years."
21.   Interview with João Verdi Carvalho Leite.
22.   Interview with Eng. José Carlos Pereira Carvalho, director of EXGEXCO, (exporting arm of ENGESA), Barueri, São Paulo, Brasil, July 1989; and "ENGESA sofreu perda em 87 de Cz$2.5 b."
23.   "EMB teme perder até US$5m," *Estado de São Paulo*, June 16, 1988.
24.   "Sale of Materiel Industries Decline in 1987," Foreign Broadcast Information Services, FBIS-LAT-87-250, December 30, 1987, originally in *Folha de São Paulo*, December 7, 1987, p. A-5.
25.   "EMB teme perder até US$5m."
26.   *Estado de São Paulo*, "EMBRAER faz 19 anos" August 19, 1988.
27.   Balanço Anual, annual editions from 1982-1989, Nos. 6-13, published by Gazeta Mercantil.
28.   Jacques S. Gansler, *Affording Defense* (Cambridge, Mass.: The MIT Press, 1989). Gansler reports on a U.S. Congressional Research Service study that found that it used to take five to seven years to acquire a weapons system; today it takes twelve to fifteen.
29.   "ENGESA teve prejuízo de Cz$1.25 bi no 1o trim," *O Globo*, June 12, 1988.
30.   "ENGESA sofreu perda em 87 de Cr$2.5b."
31.   Interview with Eng. José Carlos Pereira Carvalho.
32.   Interview, U.S. Consulate, Rio de Janeiro, Brazil, July 5, 1989.
33.   Roberto Lopes,"CSN prevê estagnação na venda de armas," *Folha de São Paulo*, July 7, 1988.
34.   "Indústria de Armamentos Acusa Queda de Vendas em 87."

35.   Conversation with AVIBRAS president João Verdi Carvalho Leite, Montevideo, Uruguay, March 17, 1991.

36.   Mary Kaldor, *The Baroque Arsenal* (New York: Hill and Wang, 1981).

37.   Herbert Wulf, "Arms Production in the Third World," in Christian Schmidt, ed., *The Economics of Military Expenditures* (New York: St. Martins, 1987), p. 374. See also pp. 104-134.

38.   A. O. Hirschman, "The Political Economy of Import Substitution Industrialization in Latin America," *The Quarterly Journal of Economics* , Vol. LXXXII, No. 1, February 1968. It should be noted that Hirschman does not find the exhaustion theory exploration convincing for all cases of import substitution industrialization.

39.   "EMBRAER não conseque vender e vai ao Confaz contra ICM," *Estado de São Paulo*, February 23, 1988.

40.   "Avião: ICM é suspenso," *Estado de São Paulo*, March 29, 1988.

41.   Interviews at defense firms, São José dos Campos, Brazil, Summer 1989.

42.   "Crise abala Indústria de Armamentos," *O Globo*, February 7, 1989.

43.   "Crise financeira causa atraso de salários na AVIBRAS," *Fohla de São Paulo*, January 8, 1989.

44.   "Sales of Materiel Industries Decline in 1987."

45.   See "Firms in Brazil Struggle to Keep Credit Lines Open and Avoid Input Shortages," *Business Latin America*, March 2, 1987, p. 65.

46.   "EMBRAER leva susto com moratória mas não altera planos," *Folha de São Paulo*, March 20, 1987.

47.   "ENGESA faz ofensiva para obter $US 65 mi do BNDES," *Folha de São Paulo*, June 16, 1988.

48.   "Operação Tartaruga," *Estado de São Paulo*, January 23, 1988.

49.   "Trabalhadores da EMBRAER iniciam greve," *Folha de São Paulo*, February 3, 1988.

50.   "EMBRAER teme fuga de técnicos," *Estado de São Paulo*, April 19, 1989.

51.   "EMBRAER dá aumento, mas demite mais 58," *Estado de São Paulo*, May 12, 1988; "EMB demite mais 74," *Estado de São Paulo*, May 13, 1988; "Mais 79 demissões na EMBRAER," *Estado de São Paulo*, May 17, 1988.

52.   "AVIBRAS demitiu 1,900 so em Janeiro," *O Globo*, February 7, 1989.

53.   FBIS-LAT-90-203 October 19, 1990, first appearing in the *Gazeta Mercantil*, September 20, 1990, p.6

54.   FBIS-LAT-90-233 December 4, 1990, first appearing on Brazilian television *Rede Globo*, October 30, 1990

55.   FBIS-LAT-91-040 February 28, 1991, first appearing in *Folha de São Paulo* January 6, 1991 p. A9. This payment represents 40% of the total due by January 1992 to get out of receivership. When the firm filed for the Brazilian equivalent of Chapter 11, its liabilities were calculated at $450m. In addition to principal, the firm is paying interest at the rate of 12 percent a year. Most of

AVIBRAS' debt is owed to financial insitutions, with the balance divided among 400 creditors.

56. Conversation with AVIBRAS president João Verdi Carvalho Leite, Montevideo, Uruguay, March 17, 1991.

57. FBIS-LAT-91-048 March 12, 1991 first published in *Estado de São Paulo* (Roberto Godoy) October 24, 1990, p.9. Also see FBIS-LAT-90-199 October 15, 1990, first appearing in *Estado de São Paulo* August 30, 1990 p.5. Mention is made in the article about Iranian interest in the AMX strike fighter. EMBRAER CEO João da Cunha, however, vehemently denied in an March 11, 1991 interview any interest expressed to EMBRAER by Iran for the purchase of the AMX.

58. FBIS-LAT-90-214 November 5, 1990, first appearing in *Estado de São Paulo*, November 1, 1990 p. 14

59. FBIS-LAT-90-233 December 4, 1990, first appearing in *ISTO É SENHOR*, November 14, 1990 p.4-6

60. Conversation with AVIBRAS president João Verdi Carvalho Leite, Montevideo, Uruguay, March 17, 1991.

61. FBIS-LAT-90-233 December 4, 1990, first appearing in ISTO É SENHOR, November 14, 1990, p. 4-6.

62. FBIS-LAT-91-026 February 7, 1991, first appearing in the *Gazeta Mercantil* January 3, 1991, p. 11. The dollar figures are the Secretariat for Strategic Subject, $46.9 m; the High Command of the Armed Forces, $47.3m, the Air Force, $171.8m; the Army $46.6m, and the Navy $95.8m. The Air Force was the only military force which was not increased over 1990. The Army, in contrast, had its budget for research increased almost threefold. Navy technology funds about doubled.

63. Interview with the director of ABIMDE, São Paulo, March 12, 1991.

64. FBIS-LAT-90-176 September 11, 1990, first appearing in *Estado de São Paulo*, July 27, 1990 p. 3.

65. "The rebirth of Brazil's ENGESA," *International Defense Review*," May 1991, pp.500.

66. Ibid; the same information was also conveyed to the author in a conversaton with an Army official.

67. "EMBRAER não conseque vender aos EUA," *Estado de São Paulo*, June 8, 1988.

68. "Brazil Firm Wins MD-11," *American Metal Market*, Vol. 95, June 29, 1987, p. 5.

69. EMBRAER News, March 30, 1990, press release no. 02690.

70. Ibid.

71. EMBRAER News, January 4, 1990, press release no. 0016/90.

72. "Peace Unhealthy for Brazilian Arms Industry," *The New York Times*, February 25, 1990, p. 19.

73. Márcio Chaer, "Indústria bélica vive pior crise em 10 anos," *Jornal Do Brasil*, January 15, 1990.

74.   Interview with João Verdi Carvalho Leite. See also "AVIBRAS Denies Selling Weapons to Libya," FBIS-LAT-87-203, October 21, 1987, first published in *Estado de São Paulo*, October 15, 1987.

75.   Interview with João Verdi Carvalho Leite, July 25, 1990.

76.   Interview with AVIBRAS President João Verdi de Carvalho Leite, São José dos Campos, July 1990.

77.   Interview with EMBRAER CEO João da Cunha, São José dos Campos, March 11, 1991. Da Cunha has since resigned and been replaced by Osires Silva, who was the first president of EMBRAER.

78.   FBIS-LAT-91 February 1, 1991 first appearing in *O Estado de Sao Paulo*, January 29, 1991, Economy Section, p. 11.

79.   FBIS-LAT-91-040 February 28, 1991, first appearing in *Folha de São Paulo* January 6, 1991 p. A9.

80.   FBIS-LAT-90-247 December 24, 1990, first appearing on Brazilian television *Rede Globo*, Rio de Janeiro, December 21, 1990.

81.   *Jornal do Brasil*, December 18, 1990 p. 13.

82.   FBIS-LAT-91-034 February 20, 1991 first published in *Folha de São Paulo*, February 17, 1991 , p12.

83.   FBIS-LAT-91-045 March 7, 1991, first appearing in *O Estado de São Paulo*, March 3, 1991 p. 8.

84.   Jessica Tuchman Matthews, "Redefining Security," *Foreign Affairs*, Vol. 69, No. 2, Spring 1989, pp. 162–177.

85.   "EMBRAER Expands Capabilities to Use Composites," *Metalworking News*, Vol. 14, October 5, 1987, p. 36.

86.   Dalton Moreira, "Aeronautics Minister on Building F-16s," FBIS-LAT-88-065, April 5, 1988, p. 25, first appearing in *Folha de São Paulo*, April 3, 1988.

87.   FBIS-LAT-90-229 November 28, 1990 first appearing in *Gazeta Mercantil*, October 10, 1990 p.3.

88.   *Jornal do Brasil*, February 9, 1991 p. 7.

89.   FBIS-LAT-91-046 March 8, 1991 first appearing in *Folha de São Paulo*, March 1, 1991 Second Section p.8.

90.   FBIS-LAT-91-040 February 28, 1991; first appearing in *Folha de São Paulo*, February 23, 1991 second section, p. 3.

91.   FBIS-LAT-90-199 October 15, 1990 first appearing in *Estado de São Paulo*, August 30, 1990 p. 5.

Bibliography

Adler, Emanuel. 1986. "Ideological Guerillas and the Quest for Technological Autonomy in Brazil's Domestic Computer Industry." *International Organization*. 40:3.

Adler, Emanuel. 1987. *The Power of Ideology: The Quest for Technological Autonomy in Argentina and Brazil*. Berkeley, Los Angeles and London: University of California Press, 1987.

African Defense. 1980. "Sales to Gabon." October.

——. 1980. "Sales to Madagascar." October.

——. 1981. "Aircraft and Industry: Brazil." January, p. 3.

——. 1981. "The Secret of Defense." February.

Air International. April 1978, October 1977, November 1977, May 1982.

Air Pictorial. 1976. Allivard, Maurice. "Embraer Bandeirante." June.

——. December 1977, May 1982.

Air Quarterly. December 1980, July 1980, April 1981.

Albano do Amarante, Coronel José Carlos. 1985. "A Capacitação Tecnológica de Empresa Nacional no Desenvolvimento de Sistemas de Armas." *Defesa Nacional* 718, March/April.

——. 1989. "O Papel do Setor de C&T do Exército na Interação Universidade-Empresa." Paper presented in the Universidade-Empresa (University-Firm Seminar), COPPE-UFRJ: Rio de Janeiro. June 5-8.

Albrecht, Ulrich. 1977. "Technology and Militarization of Third World Countries in Theoretical Perspective." *Bulletin of Peace Proposals* 9.2.

——. 1986. "The Federal Republic of Germany and Italy: New Strategies of Mid-sized Weapons Exporters?" *Journal of International Affairs* 40: 140.

Albrecht, Ulrich, D. Ernst, P. Lock, and H. Wulf. 1975. "Militarization, Arms Transfer and Arms Production in Peripheral Countries." *Journal of Peace Research* 12.3.

Albrecht, Ulrich, D. Ernst, P. Lock, and H. Wulf. 1978. *A Short Research Guide on Arms and Armed Forces*. London: Croom Helm, pp. 49-61.

Armies and Weapons. 1978. Special Report. "ENGESA military production." 49, December.

Assessoria de Planejamento e Coordenação. 1981. "Indústrias em São José dos Campos." Curso de Pesquisa e Planejamento sócio-econômico.

Atlantic News. March 21.

Aviation Week and Space Technology. January 6, 1975; March 29, 1976; "Brazil's Import Duty Intentions Watched," February 19, 1979; March 31, 1980; June 21, 1982 p. 60; January 3, 1983.

——. North, David. "Embraer Develops New Aircraft," August 14, 1978; "Brazilian Air Taxi Expansion Expected, "September 11, 1978, pp. 83-86; also unnamed articles on June 27, 1977, June 11, 1978, July 10, 1978.

AVIBRAS Catalog.

AVIBRAS. 1989. Fax communication, April 10.

Ayres, Ron. 1983. "Arms Production as a Form of Import-Substituting Industrialization: The Turkish Case." *World Development* 11.9: 812-823.

Baer, Werner. 1989. *The Brazilian Economy: Growth and Development* Third Edition, New York: Praeger.

Baer, Werner, Issac Kerstenetsky, and Annibal Villela. 1973. "The Changing Role of the State in the Brazilian Economy." *World Development* 1.11: 23-24.

Baer, Werner; Richard Newfarmer and Thomas J. Trebat. 1976. "On State Capitalism in Brazil: Some New Ideas and Questions." *Inter-American Economic Affairs* 30.3: 69-91.

Bailey, Robert. 1988. "Defence in the Middle East." Defence Special Report. *Middle East Economic Digest* 32.6: 21-33.

Balassa, Bela. 1981. *The Newly Industrializing Countries in the World Economy.* New York: Pergammon Press.

Ball, Nicole. 1984. "Measuring Third World Security Expenditure: A Research Note." *World Development.*

————. 1986. "The Growth of Arms Production in the Third World." *National Forum* 66: 24-27.

Ball, Nicole and Milton Leitenberg. 1979. "Disarmament and Development: Their Relationship." *Bulletin of Peace Proposals* 10.3.

Ball, Nicole and Milton Leitenburg, (eds). 1983. *The Structure of the Defense Industry.* New York: St. Martin's Press.

Bandereira de Zueirz, Alberto. 1982. "O Valor das Despesas Militares." *Segurança e Desenvolvimento* 189.

Baranson, Jack. 1981. *North South Technology Transfer.* Mt. Airy, MD: Lomond Publications.

Barnaby, Frank. 1981. "World Arsenals in 1981." *Bulletin of Atomic Scientists.* August/September.

Barros, Alexandre. "The Brazilian Arms Industry: An Instrument of Foreign Policy." Article prepared for Arms Production in Developing Countries: An Analysis for Decision, Instituto Universitário de Pesquisas do Rio de Janeiro.

Benoit, Emile. 1973. *Defense and Economic Growth in Developing Countries.* MA: Lexington Books.

Bienen, Henry, ed. 1971. *The Military and Modernization.* New York: Aldine.

Bluestone, B., P. Jordan, and M. Sullivan. 1981. *Aircraft Insustry Dynamics.* MA: Auburn House Publishing Co.

Bolsa. 1982. "A Força do Brasil—Indústria Bélica." September.

Bonelli, Regis and Paulo Vierada Cunha. 1984. "Crescimento Econômico Padrão de Consumo e Distribuição de Renda no Brasil: Uma Abordagen Multinacional para o período 1970-75." *Pesquisa e Planejamento Econômico* II.3.

Bowles, Roger and David Whynes. 1979. *Macroeconomic Planning.* London: Allen & Unwin.

Branco, Castello. As quoted in Meira Mattos. 1979. *Brasil: Geopolítica e Destino.* Rio de Janeiro: Livraria José Olympio Editora.

Brasil Defesa. 1982. "A EMBRAER e o Mercado Militar." [Interview with Ozires Silva] 1.5: 17-18.

"Brasil na era espacial." Publication of the Ministério da Aeronáutica—Public Relations Center.

Brasil, Francisco. 1979. "Poder e poder Nacional." *Carta Mensais* April, pp. 15-25.

"Brazil Firm Wins MD-11." 1987. *American Metal Market* 95.29: 5.

Brazilian Army Ministry. 1975. "IMBEL." Publication of the Brazilian Army. (September).

Brazilian Defense Equipment 1983. Brasília: Fundação Visconde de Cabo Frio.

Brazilian Defense Equipment. 1987. Brasília: Fundação Visconde de Cabo Frio.

Brigagão, Clovis. 1981. "The Case of Brazil: Fortress or Paper Curtain?" *Impact of Science on Society* 31.1 (January/March).

———. "O Brasil e o Comércio Internacional de Armas: Uma Nova Modalidade Industrial?" (Working paper from the Pontifícia Universidade Católica do RJ, Instituto de Relações Internacionais.)

Bruneau, Thomas C. and Phillipe Faucher. 1981. *Authoritarian Capitalism: Brazil's Contemporary Economic and Political Development.* Colorado: Westview Press.

Brzoska, Michael. 1981. "The Reporting of Military Expenditures." *Journal of Peace Research* 18.3: 264.

Brzoska, Michael and Thomas Ohlson. 1987. "The Trade in Major Conventional Weapons." in *The SIPRI Yearbook 1986.* Stockholm: The Stockholm International Peace Research Institute.

Bulmer, Thomas V. 1982. *Input-Output Analysis in Developing Countries: Sources, Methods and Applications.* New York: Wiley.

Business Latin America. 1982. "Brazilian State Firms' 1982 Spending Plan." January 27.

———. 1987. "Firms in Brazil Struggle to Keep Credit Lines Open and Avoid Input Shortages." March 2, p. 65.

Business Week. "1978. "Brazil: A Major Contender in the Arms Business." July 31.

———. 1979. "The Hot Race to Sell Arms to the Arabs." March 12.

Bussacos, Rubens Jr. "Indústria Aeroespacial Brasileira." published by ESG, Departamento de Estudos, Curso Superior de Guerra, 1975.

Cahn, Anne Hessing. 1977. *Controlling Future Arms Trade.* New York: McGraw-Hill.

Campos de Araripe Macedo, Joelmir. 1973. "Ministério da Aeronáutica: Seu Papel " September 19, (conference given at ESG).

Carvalho, José Murilo. 1979. "A Política Científica e Tecnológica no Brasil." *Revista de Finanças Públicas* 39 (No. Especial), March.

Catrina, Christian. 1988. *Arms Transfers and Dependence.* New York: Taylor and Francis.

Centro de Tecnologia Aeronáutica (CTA). 1988. "O Esforço de Nacionalização da EMBRAER e do Ministério da Aeronáutica." Unpublished document.

Chenery, H., and P. Clark. 1959. *Interindustry Economics.* Wiley and Sons.
Christian Science Monitor. 1977. Goodsell, James Nelson. March 9.
————. 1977. Sieniawski, Michael. November 12.
————. 1988. "Third World States Spending Less on Arms in Recent Years."
   May 16.
————. 1989. Cellaney, Brahma. "India shoots for military self-sufficiency."
   March 21, p. 10.
————. 1989. Grier, Peter. "Arms Spending Slows Worldwide." August 10, p. 8.
Coelho, Edmundo Campos. 1976. *Em Busca da Identidade: O Exército e a
   Política na Sociedade Brasiliera.* Rio de Janeiro: Forense Universitária.
Coleman Sercovich, Francisco. *The Exchange and Absorption of Technology in
   Brazilian Industry,* in Bruneau.
Collier, David. *The New Authoritarianism in Latin America. 1979.* Princeton, N.
   J.: Princeton University Press.
Comércio e Mercados. 1981. "As Exportacões Brasileiras e a guerra do—
   Iraque." April, pp. 33-34.
————. 1982. "As guerras também abrem mercados." August.
Conjuntura Econômica. 1974. "A tecnologia indústrial da construção
   aeronáutica." 28.1: 91-93.
Convivium. 1979. "Origens Nacionais da Doutrina da ESG." Ano XVII, Vol. 22:
   514-518.
Correa, General Antonio Jorge. 1976. Ministro Chefe do EMFA, "A Influência
   da ESG no Pensamento Político e Estratégico das Elites Brasileiras."
   Inaugural lecture at ESG, reprinted in *Segurança e Desenvolvimento* No
   163.
Correio Brasiliense. 1975. "Decretado o fim da dependência em armamentos."
   July 15, p. 15.
————. 1981. "IMBEL é a lição de nacionalismo." August 20.
————. 1982. "Brasil em breve produzirá canhão italiano." April 16.
Correio do Povo. 1979. "Brasil tem que queimar etapas para atingir auto-
   suficiência bélica." January 11.
Dagnino, Renato Peixoto. 1983. "A Indústria de Armamentos No Brasil."
   Mimeo.
————. 1983. "Indústria de Armamentos: O Estado e a Tecnologia." *Revista
   Brasileira de Tecnologia* May/June, pp. 5-17.
————. 1989. "A Indústria de Armamentos Brasileira: Uma Tentativa de
   Avaliação." Doctoral thesis presented to the Institute of Economics,
   UNICAMP, Campinas, SP, Brasil, August.
Dahlman, Carl J. and Francis. C. Sercovich. 1984. "Technology Exports from
   SICs." *Journal of Development Economics* 16: 63-99.
Damiani, José Henrique de Sousa. 1983. "O EMB-110 Bandeirante e o Processo
   de Inovação Tecnológica," VII Simpósio Nacional de Pequisa em
   Administração de Ciência e Tecnologia, Promoção e Realização por
   FINEP/USP, São Paulo.

Defense and Foreign Affairs Weekly. March 14-20, 1982; November 15-21, 1982.

Defense and Foreign Affairs. 1980. "Brazil: Engesa in RDF Bid?" September.

———. 1980. "Brazil: Integrated AD systems," October.

———. 1980. December.

———. 1981. "Sales to Iraq." February.

———. 1982. "Brazil: New Arms to Libya." January 14.

———. 1982. "Brazil: Arms to Argentina, Algeria." April 28.

———. 1982. October.

———. 1983. January/February.

———. 1981. January/February.

———. 1985. "Brazilian Defense Directory." April, p. 16.

———. 1985. "China's Arms Industry Finds a World Market." June.

———. 1985. Marshall, R. "Southern Superpower." April, p. 11.

———. "Brazil: Success Beneath the Southern Cross." Vol. XIII, No. 4.

Defense Latin America. 1978. September.

Defense Review International. 1977. "Brasilians ready to start on missile production." Vol. V, No. 9, March 4.

Defesa Latina. 1983. "As Versões Militares do Brasília." Ano IV, No. 24, September/October.

———. 1983. "Míssil da Casa Para a Marinha Brasiliera." Ano IV, no. 24, September/October.

———. "O Fabuloso Projecto AMX." Ano IV, No. 23, July/ August 1983.

Deger, Saadat and Somnath Sen. 1983. "Military Expenditure Spin-off and Economic Growth." *Journal of Development Economics.*

———. 1985. "Technology Transfer and Arms Production in Developing Countries." *Industry and Development.* No.15.

Dervis, K., J. De Melo, and S. Robinson. 1982. *General Equilibirium Models for Development Policy.* New York: Cambridge University Press.

Diesing, Paul. 1971. *Patterns of Discovery in the Social Sciences.* New York: Aldine Publishing Company.

Diário Comércio e Indústria. 1980. "Conjuntura favorece expansão da indústria bélica nacional." September 6-8.

Diário Popular. 1982. "A Indústria Bélica Nacional na 'Guerra' das Exportações." May 30.

Dye, David R. and Carlos Eduardo de Souza. 1979. "A Perspective on the Brazilian State." *Latin American Research Review.* 14.1.

Eide, Asbjorn. 1977. "Arms Transfer and Third World Militarization." *Bulletin of Peace Proposals.* 8.2.

EMBRAER News. 1985. No. 33. March-April.

———. 1987. "Light Aircraft Subsidiary Neiva Reaches 2000 Aircraft Produced." Press Release No.058. November 16.

———. 1987. "EMBRAER is Partner in New Aerospace Business." Press Release No. 003/87. January 30.

———. 1988. Press Release No.039/88. September 4.

————. 1989. "EMBRAER and Chincul Sign Agreement for Light Aircraft Production and Marketing." Press Release No. 009/89. May 17.

————. 1990. Press Release 0016/90. January 4.

————. 1990. Press Release 059, September 2.

————. 1990. Press Release 066, September 2.

————. 1990. Press Release 02690. March 30.

Embraer Company Report, "General Information: Brazilian Aeronautical Industry, 1981."

EMBRAER, Fax communication. April 1990.

EMBRAER. Unpublished document on ENGETRôNICA.

Encinas, José. "The Declaration of Ayacucho." Annex #6, for 1980 UN Working Group Study on Disarmament and Development.

ENGESA catalog. 1988.

ENGESA Group. 1983. "ENGESA Military Products," Barueri, SP, Brasil.

Equipamento Militar. 1983. "Edição Aeronáutica," Ano 1, No. 2, August/September.

————. 1983. "Edição Naval." Ano 1, No.1, March/April.

————. 1983/84. "Edição do Exército," Ano 1, No. 3 December/January.

Erber, Fabio Stefano. 1979. "Política Científica e Tecnológica no Brasil: Uma Revisão da Literatura." in J. Sayad (ed.) *Resenhas da Economia Brasileira.* Editora Saraiva, Rio de Janeiro.

————. 1980. "Desenvolvimento Tecnológico e Intervenção do Estado: Um Confronto Entre a Experiência Brasiliera e a dos Paises Capitalistas Centrais." *Revista Administração Pública.* Rio de Janeiro, October/December, pp. 10-72.

Erickson, Kenneth Paul. "State Entrepreneurship, Energy Policy and the Political Order in Brazil." In Bruneau.

Ernst, Dieter. 1979. "International Transfer of Technology, Technological Dependence and Development Strategies." *Bulletin of Peace Proposals* 10.2.

Estado de São Paulo. 1967. "Armas descobrem a nossa indústria—Até 1964 o atraso; agora, o avanço." July 13.

————. 1971. "Exercito usará logo sua arma adaptada." May 23.

————. 1971. "Indústria amplia o re-equipamento militar." April 27.

————. 1972. "Brasil busca melhor preço de armas." November 12.

————. 1972. "Tecnologia é a meta em armas, dizem militares." March 24.

————. 1975. "Brasil atrai a indústria bélica." Feburary 25.

————. 1975. "Cessna gaucho promete 90% de nacionalização." September 9.

————. 1975. "Empresa bélica apoia indústria nacional." July 13.

————. 1975. "En junho chega um novo modelo." May 23.

————. 1975. "FAB quer montar seus pára-quedas." November 6.

————. 1975. "Geisel cria empresa para produzir matérial bélico." April 25, p. 17.

————. 1975. Holanda, Tarcisio. "Multinacionais querem fabricar armas no Brasil." August 24.

————. 1975. "Projeto do CTA prevê motor nacional de avião em breve—1." August 8.

————. 1976. "Brasil exportará armas para os EUA." February 27.

————. 1976. "Geisel pronunciamentos." March 2.

————. 1977. "Cresce produção bélica do Brasil." April 13.

————. 1977. de Souza Queiroz, Luiz Roberto. "Indústria bélica garante autosuficiência ao Brasil." March 6.

————. 1977. "O Brasil vai fabricar 400 tanques de guerra." January 18.

————. 1977. "Potyguara: não faltam fornecedores de armas." March 8.

————. 1978. "Calmon justifica mudança." April 14.

———— 1978. "Emb 111—um brasileiro na crise de Beagle." November 26.

———— 1978. "FAB assina contrato para novo avião de treinamento." December 7.

————. 1978. Heller, Frederico. "Capital estrangeiro e indústria bélica." March 1.

————. 1978. "Italianos participam de fábrica de armas." February 10.

————. 1978. "Submarinos terão baterias nacionalizada." October 19.

————. 1979. "Calderari justifica a venda de armas para o exterior." August 10.

————. 1979. Heller, Frederico. "Troca de armas por óleo." September 25.

————. 1979. "Isentos de IPI 74 produtos de uso das Forças Armadas." January 6.

————. 1979. "Oficial sugere a troca de armamentos por petróleo." August 11.

————. 1979. "Vendas de armas serão aumentadas." November 30, p. 6.

————. 1980. "Brasil vai fabricar tanque de 30 toneladas." March 16.

————. 1980. "China quer comprar armas do Brasil." February 24.

————. 1980. "Chinês admite que pode haver negócio." February 26.

————. 1980. "Estatizar comércio exterior poderá ser o próximo passo." January 6.

————. 1980. "Exportação de armas brasileiras." September 9.

————. 1980. "Finep apoia pesquisa de desenvolimento militar." December 7.

————. 1980. "Frota não é adequada, dizem os especialistas." September 9.

————. 1980. Godoy, Roberto. "Brasil lança nova arma: o míssel 'Piranha'." May 20.

————. 1980. "Italianos vão construir 12 corvetas." June 6.

————. 1980. "Meta é superar atraso." December 7.

————. 1980. "Missão vai à Argentina conduzir acordo espacial." July 9.

————. 1980. "Nacionalizar armas é meta da Marinha." July 5.

————. 1980. "Novo crédito para Fs As." August 15.

————. 1981. "AM-X servirá para defesa, diz Brigadeiro." October 8.

————. 1981. "Brasil amplia venda de armas." February 27.

————. 1981. "Brasil pode vender armas à Colômbia." September 27.

————. 1981. "Brasil poderá fabricar arma anti-aérea da OTAN." November 11.

————. 1981. "Brasil vende armas a 33 países." December 18.

————. 1981. "Exército define IMBEL: 'Rentável e eficiente.'" August 15.

————. 1981. "Exército divulga seu programa de gastos." January 15.

————. 1981. "Fiesp vai militar para reativar bens de capital." September 23.

————. 1981. Godoy, Roberto. "Brasil reage e defende mercado de armas." February 19.

————. 1981. "Nossas armas ameaçando o mercado russo." April 24, p. 12.

————. 1981. "Novo acordo do AM-X." October 7.

————. 1981. "O sucesso das armas brasilieras produz resultados em Paris." January 21.

————. 1982. "A Imbel reconhece falta na área bélica." September 16.

————. 1982. "A Marinha utilizará técnica alemã para fabricar submarino." July 1.

————. 1982. "Brasil distante das potências na venda de armas, diz Werner." June 11.

————. 1982. "Brasil e EUA renovam relacionamento militar." November 9.

————. 1982. "Brasil faz a revisão da estratégia militar." May 16.

————. 1982. "Brasil não deseja corrida às armas." May 19.

————. 1982. "Delfin anuncia que programa de defesa deve durar dez anos," May 20.

————. 1982. "Exército padroniza e torna mais potentes veículos de combate." May 28.

————. 1982. Godoy, Roberto. "O Brasil projeta novo míssel estratégico." May 26.

————. 1982. Godoy, Roberto. "OLP quer mísseis brasileiros." May 3.

————. 1982. "Indústria de arma tem isenção." June 26, p.6.

————. 1982. "Iraque compra bombas e foguetes." October 26.

————. 1982. "Marinha acha perigosa a dependência de armas." September 12.

————. 1982. "Marinha condena dependência." March 6.

————. 1982. "Marinha poderá vender corvetas para Exterior." December 12.

————. 1982. "Modernização é prioridade, diz industrial." May 19.

————. 1982. "Venturini: é normal a venda de armamentos." October 28.

————. 1982. "Palanque: Despesas militares." May 20.

————. 1982. "Penna: Desenvolver, sem armas." June 12.

————. 1983. "Em teste a primeira turbina a jato nacional." August 27.

————. 1983. "AM-X faz primeiro vôo em 1984." July 28.

————. 1983. "Armamentos, comércio cada vez mais rendoso." July 12.

————. 1983. "Armas renderão US $1.5 bilhão." July 8.

————. 1983. "Em nova fase relações com EUA." June 8.

————. 1983. "Em sigilo, Brasil e EUA discutem sobre a cooperação militar." June 16.

————. 1983. "Em teste a primeira turbina a jatos nacional." August 27.

————. 1983. "EMBRAER promete encomendas." September 6.

————. 1983. "EUA cedem tecnologia militar para o Brasil." August 31.

————. 1983. "Exército desenvolve técnica para fabricar mísseis teleguiados." July 12.

————. 1983. "FAB só recebe novos Mirage no início de 1984." July 9.

————. 1983. "FAB vai conter as despesas." June 1.

———. 1983. Godoy, Roberto. "Brasil assume venda de armas." May 8.

———. 1983. Godoy, Roberto. "Embraer vai vender ao Egito 120 aviões na maior transação." December 16.

———. 1983. "Marinha apoia arrendamento de base naval." June 1.

———. 1983. "Militares querem cessão de tecnologia dos EUA." June 19.

———. 1983. "Militares têm estratégia industrial de emergência." August 28.

———. 1983. "Para Délio a Emb. é "O Brasil que deu certo." July 30.

———. 1983. "São Paulo, sede da Imbel." August 15.

———. 1983. "Suriname leva peças de campanha." June 3.

———. 1983. Waldir de Goes, "Indústria bélica pode liberar exportações." September 25.

———. 1983. "Washington nega pressão para ter apoio do Brasil." June 18.

———. 1984. "General defende venda 'pragmática' de armas." June 3.

———. 1986. Godoy, Roberto. "Saudita, canal permanente." October 10-12.

———. 1987. Matarazzo, Dante. "ENGESA—Altos Prejuízos." Caderno de Empresas, October 20.

———. 1988. "Avião: ICM é suspenso." March 29.

———. 1988. "EMB demite mais 74." May 13.

———. 1988. "EMB teme perder até US$5m." June 16.

———. 1988. "EMBRAER dá aumento, mas demite mais 58." May 12.

———. 1988. "EMBRAER faz 19 anos." August 19.

———. 1988. "EMBRAER não conseque vender aos EUA." June 8.

———. 1988. "EMBRAER não conseque vender e vai ao Confaz contra ICM." February 23.

———. 1988. Godoy, Roberto. "Ecuador dá preferência a tanque da Argentina." May 26.

———. 1988. "Mais 79 demissões na EMBRAER." May 17.

———. 1988. "Operação Tartaruga. " January 23.

———. 1989. "AVIBRAS demite 382." May 24.

———. 1989. "EMBRAER se associa a Argentinos." May 13.

———. 1989. "EMBRAER teme fuga de técnicos." April 19.

———. 1989. "Governo corta verba e atrasa caça AMX." April 7.

———. 1989. "Militares argentinos testam um novo míssil." July 2, p. 8.

Exame. 1981. "Armas, o Novo Aliado da Balança Comercial." April 11.

———. 1981. "Guerra e paz nos planos da Engesa." November 4.

———. 1984. "O salto tecnológico da indústria nacional." November 28, p.85.

———. 1985. "As que mais gastam em pesquisa." October 2, p. 40.

Faini, Riccardo, Patricia Annex, and Lance Taylor. 1984. "Defense Spending, Economic Structure and Growth." *Economic Development and Cultural Change.* 32.3: April.

Fallows, James. 1981. "America's High Tech Weaponry." *The Atlantic Monthly.* May, pp. 21-33.

Faro, Irenio de. 1980. "Bandeirante para todas as bandeiras." *Comércio e Mercados.* August, pp. 33-36.

Fernandes, Praxy. 1979. *Control Systems for Public Enterprises in Developing Countries.* Ljubljana, Yugoslavia: International Center for Public Enterprise.

Fernandes, Praxy,(ed). 1981. *Seeking the Personality of the Public Enterprise.* Ljubljana, Yugoslavia: International Center for Public Enterprise.

Ferraez, Victorio W.R., president of GPMI, "Nacionalização de Nosso Equipamento Militar." (unpublished lecture.)

Financial Times. 1978. (London) "Brazil-Taiwan Rocket Deal." June 20.

———. 1979. (London) "Brazil turns away from the West." February 8.

———. 1980. (London) "Brazil in search of Iraq oil replacement." October 14.

———. 1980. (London) "ME War Threatens Brazil with Petro Rationing." September 30.

Flight. 1977. "Embraer Production Rising." January 27.

———. 1978. "Brazil to Build Aerospatiale Helicopters." February 25.

———. 1978. Fields, Hugh. "EMBRAER Emphasizes Exports." March 25.

———. 1980. "Brazil Plans Link with Italy and Argentina." March 29.

Folha de São Paulo. 1975. "Defesa Nacional, SA." July 15.

———. 1976. "FAB planeja uma aviação militar auto-suficiente." May 2.

———. 1976. "Material nacional terá prioridade na Marinha." July 5.

———. 1978. "Exército inglês compra equipamentos do Brasil." March 4.

———. 1980. "Armas para a China sairão sem problemas." February 26.

———. 1980. "Tucano um novo avião de treinamento brasileiro." January 3.

———. 1982. "Armas e equipamentos bélicos renderam em 87 mais de US $1 bi." August 4.

———. 1982. "As compras de material bélico sem restrições." May 15.

———. 1982. "Deputado propõe controle para venda de armas." June 5.

———. 1982. "Dom Paulo Evaristo é mau brasileiro, diz Coelho Neto." March 13.

———. 1982. "Exército nacional acelera re-equipamento." October 17.

———. 1982. "Governo investirá mais na área de armamentos." May 18.

———. 1982. "Novo presidente da Imbel apóia 'risco' pacifista." October 28.

———. 1982. "O Brasil tem programa próprio para satélites." May 9.

———. 1982. Picchia, Pedro del. "Dom Paulo reage a general e volta a condenar armas." March 14.

———. 1983. "Brasil e EUA farão armas em conjunto." July 8.

———. 1983. "Chefe militar discute compra de armas." May 31.

———. 1983. "Equipamento militar rendeu em 82 mais de US $100 milhões." February 6.

———. 1983. "Itamarati desconselha a compra do míssil Gabriel." April 19.

———. 1983. "O que a Líbia compra do Brasil?" April 23.

———. 1983. "País está exportando matéria—prima estratégica." June 10.

———. 1987. "EMBRAER investe US$350 mil em novos projetos até 1992." August 30.

———. 1987. "AVIBRAS afirma que criação da Órbita é inconstitucional." January 11.

————. 1987. "EMBRAER leva susto com moratória mas não altera planos." March 20.

————. 1987. "Indústria de Armamentos Acusa Queda de Vendas em 87." December 27, p. A-5.

————. 1987. "Investir em alta tecnologia é prioridade de empresa." March 20.

————. 1988. "ENGESA faz ofensiva para obter US$ 65 mi do BNDES." June 16.

————. 1988. Lopes, Roberto. "CSN prevê estagnação na venda de armas." July 7.

————. 1988. "Missão da Engesa está no Oriente Médio para vender tanques aos árabes." October 19.

————. 1988. "Orbita quer alta tecnologia para concorrer no exterior." January 29.

————. 1988. "Trabalhadores da EMBRAER iniciam greve." February 3.

————. 1989. "Cortes no Orçamento da União vão reduzir ritmo de projetos militares." January 3, p. A8.

————. 1989. "Crise financeira causa atraso de salarios na AVIBRAS." January 8.

————. 1989. "EMBRAER divide produção de aviões Piper com Argentina." May 20.

————. 1989. "Situação difícil no setor bélico facilita acordo." March 19.

Fonseca, Laura. *Jornal da Semana Inteira,* Brasília DF: Ano VIII, no. 339, week 22-28, p. 6.

Fonseca, Marcondes. 1983. "O Novo Sistema Astros—II." *Defesa Latina.* Ano IV, no. 24, September/October.

Foreign Broadcast Information Service (FBIS) Latin America (LAT) "Air Force Minister Favors Construction of AMX." August 7 1987, p. M 2.

————. "Development of Air to Air Missile Reported." January 13, 1988, p. 27, originally reported in *Estado de São Paulo.* January 7, 1988, p. 2.

————. "Aeronautics Minister on Building F-16s," FBIS-LAT-88-065. April 5, 1988, p. 25, originally reported in *Folha de São Paulo.* (Moreira, Dalton), April 3, 1988.

————. August 6, 1987, p. m1, originally reported in "State Development Fund to Finance AMX Plane." *Folha de São Paulo.* August 5 1987, p. 1.

————. "AVIBRAS Denies Selling Weapons to Libya." FBIS-LAT-87-203. October 21, 1987, originally reported in *Estado de São Paulo,* October 15, 1987.

————. "Brazilian Arms Shipment for Iraq." *Summary of World Broadcasts.* British Broadcasting Corporation, January 2, 1985, Part 4, p. a1.

————. "EMBRAER Sells 25 Xingu Planes to Libya." June 1983.

————. FBIS LAT-87-193. October 6, 1987, originally reported in *Estado de São Paulo.* September 29, 1987, p. 2.

————. FBIS-LAT-87-193. "Missile to be Built with British Aerospace." October 6, 1987, originally reported in *Estado de São Paulo.* September 29 , 1987.

————. FBIS-LAT-87-250. "Sale of Materiel Industries Decline in 1987." December 30, 1987, originally reported in *Folha de São Paulo*. December 7, 1987, p. A-5.

————. FBIS-LAT-88-002-5, "Tactical Missile Development Reported," January 1988, originally reported in *O Globo*, 3 January 1988, p. 7.

————. FBIS-LAT-90-176 September 11, 1990, originally reported in *Estado de São Paulo*, July 27, 1990, p. 3.

————. FBIS-LAT-90-199 October 15, 1990, originally reported in *Estado de São Paulo* August 30, 1990, p. 5.

————. FBIS-LAT-90-199 October 15, 1990, originally reported in *Estado de São Paulo* August 30, 1990, p.5.

————. FBIS-LAT-90-203 October 19, 1990, originally reported in the *Gazeta Mercantil* September 20, 1990, p.6.

————. FBIS-LAT-90-214 November 5, 1990, originally reported in *Estado de São Paulo* November 1, 1990, p. 14.

————. FBIS-LAT-90-229 November 28, 1990 originally reported in *Gazeta Mercantil* 10 October 10, 1990, p.3.

————. FBIS-LAT-90-233 December 4, 1990, originally reported in *ISTO É SENHOR* November 4, 1990, p.4-6.

————. FBIS-LAT-90-233 December 4, 1990, originally reported in *ISTO É SENHOR* November 14, 1990, p.4-6.

————. FBIS-LAT-90-233 December 4,1990, originally reported on Brazilian television *Rede Globo*, October 30, 1990.

————. FBIS-LAT-90-247 December 24, 1990, originally reported on Brazilian television *Rede Globo*, Rio de Janeiro, December 21, 1990.

————. FBIS-LAT-91 February 1, 1991 originally reported in *O Estado de Sao Paulo*, January 29, 1991, Economy Section, p. 11.

————. FBIS-LAT-91-026 February 7, 1991, originally reported in the *Gazeta Mercantil* January 3, 1991, p. 11.

————. FBIS-LAT-91-034 February 20, 1991, originally reported in *Folha de São Paulo* February 17, 1991, p12.

————. FBIS-LAT-91-040 February 28, 1991, originally reported in *Folha de São Paulo* February 23, 1991, second section, p3.

————. FBIS-LAT-91-040 February 28, 1991, originally reported in *Folha de São Paulo* January 6, 1991, p. A9

————. FBIS-LAT-91-040 February 28, 1991, originally reported in *Folha de São Paulo* January 6, 1991, p. A9.

————. FBIS-LAT-91-040 February 28, 1991, originally reported in *Folha de São Paulo* January 6, 1991, p. A9.

————. FBIS-LAT-91-045 March 7, 1991, originally reported in *O Estado de São Paulo* March 3, 1991, p. 8.

————. FBIS-LAT-91-045 March 7, 1991, originally reported in *O Estado de São Paulo* March 3, 1991, p. 8.

————. FBIS-LAT-91-046 March 8, 1991, originally reported in *Folha de São Paulo* March 1, 1991, Second Section, p.8.

————. FBIS-LAT-91-048 March 12, 1991 originally reported in *Estado de São Paulo* (Roberto Godoy) October 24,1990, p.9.

————. February 18, 1983, p. D1.

————. LAM 84 002. January 4, 1984, Vol. VI, No. 02.

————. "Military Planes May Be Sold to Honduras." May 4, 1985, p. D2.

Franco, Aldo B. 1973. "EMBRAER: Uma Loucura Nacional." *Banas*. May 21.

Frank, Andre. 1981. *Crisis in the Third World*. New York: Holmes and Meier Publishers, Inc.

Freeman, John and Raymond Duvall. 1981. "The State and Dependent Capitalism." *International Studies Quarterly* 25 (March): 99-118.

————. 1984. "International Economic Relations and the Entrepreneurial State." *Economic Development and Cultural Change* 32.2 (January).

Freeman, Chris. 1974. *The Economics of Industrial Innovation*. UK: Penguin.

Frost & Sullivan. 1981. *Defense Markets in Latin America*. New York: Frost & Sullivan, Inc..

Fyd, John Samuel. 1977. "More on the Military in Politics." *Latin America Research Review* 12.3.

Galbraith, John Kenneth. 1981. *The Economy of the Arms Race and After*. June/July.

Gansler, Jacques S. 1978. *The Diminishing Economic and Strategic Viability of the US*. PhD. dissertation, American University.

————. 1989. *Affording Defense*. Cambridge, MA: The MIT Press.

Gazeta Mercantil. 1977. "Empresas estrangeiras querem instalar 82 fábricas no Brasil." March 9.

————. 1977. "Os planos da Coester para a aviação." August 31.

————. 1980. "A Engesa negocia com os sauditas." July 3.

————. 1980. Sasse, Cintia. "Uma revisão na política." April 19.

————. 1980. "Satélite de interesse nacional." August 28.

————. 1982. do Rio, Pereira. "Cobra decide voltar ao mercado de sistemas militares." April 16.

————. 1983. "AVIBRAS tem encomendas que garantem três anos de operação." August 5.

————. 1983. de Medici, João Augusto. "EMBRAER e ENGESA vendem aos árabes," February 18.

————. 1983. "EMBRAER Negotiates Aircraft Sale to Libya." January 6, pp. 1, 3.

————. 1986. "A EMBRAER decide vender a Neiva, sua subsidiária de aviões leves." December 23.

Gazeta Mercantil. 1989. *Balanço Anual 1989*. XIII, No. 13, p. 302.

Geisenheyner, Stefan. 1978. "Brazilian Aerospace, A Power to Reckon With." *Armada International*. October.

Globe and Mail. 1981. Fraser, Kerry. "Canadians Share Aircraft's Success." October 5, p. 87.

O Globo. 1973. "Exército quer garantir a segurança nacional com tecnologia própria." April 18.

―――. 1974. "FAB desativa vários tipos de aviões para renovar equipamento." November 18.

―――. 1974. "FAB reduz o número de aviões que vai comprar." March 7.

―――. 1975. "Brasil exporta equipamentos militares para o Equador." May 4.

―――. 1975. "EMBRAER fabricará e venderá peças dos F-5 para a Northrop." October 10.

―――. 1975. "Indústria norte americana fabricará aviões no Brasil." April 15.

―――. 1976. "Aeronáutica quer tecnologia nacional." January 5.

―――. 1976. "Capital estrangeiro quer entrar no setor de material bélico." August 30.

―――. 1976. "Chefe do EMFA: Uma das metas da Imbel é exportar armamentos." July 12.

―――. 1976. "Convênio assentará comercialização de aviões de ICM." March 18.

―――. 1976. "Equipamento militar pode ser importado sem depósito prévio." February 27.

―――. 1976. "FAB vai dar prioridade à indústria brasileira." August 8.

―――. 1976. "Indústria aeronáutica terá plano para 20 anos." March 11.

―――. 1977. "Marinha aprova plano que reduz dependência externa." August 1.

―――. 1978. "Crise no setor de peças para aviões dura mais um ano e meio." May 13.

―――. 1978. "FAB pede financiamento para compra de avião nacional." February 27.

―――. 1978. "Fábrica de Canhões." April 19.

―――. 1978. "Firmas estrangeiras na indústria bélica só sem privilégios." July 3.

―――. 1979. "Figueiredo apóia a política de exportação de material bélico." March 2.

―――. 1980. "Aviões da Embraer são elogiados na Inglaterra." September 2.

―――. 1980. "Marinha de guerra contrata equipamento para submarino." April 24.

―――. 1980. "Nacionalização na aeronáutica já alcança 65%." July 15.

―――. 1981. "A Importância da Ciência e Tecnologia para a Economia Nacional." May 29.

―――. 1981. "Brasil desenvolve sistema de lançamento de satélites." July 20.

―――. 1981. "Brigadeiro fala na ESG sobre conquistas da EMBRAER." July 26.

―――. 1981. "CNI quer diálogo com militares." July 8.

―――. 1981. "EMBRAER parte para o AMX, um moderno avião de combate." October 26.

―――. 1981. "Empregados da Embraer continuam em greve." October 31.

―――. 1981. "FIESP prepara ampliação do grupo de Mobilização." April 14.

―――. 1981. "Helicóptero da Helibras fará operações off-shore." May 16.

―――. 1981. "Indústria pode fornecer 12 mil items para as Fs As." May 12.

―――. 1981. "Plano de Mobilização é estratégico, diz general." May 15.

————. 1981. "Vamos para o céu." April 15.

————. 1982. "Armamento não é saida para bens de capital." June 12.

————. 1982. "Brasil vai fabricar bomba com 400 grenadas." May 21.

————. 1982. "Delio quer FAB dez vezes mais forte mas com capital nacional." June 14.

————. 1982. "Eletrometal recebe prêmio por tecnologia estratégica." July 8.

————. 1982. "Em 6 anos País terá missil igual aos Exocet." October 24.

————. 1982. "EMBRAER fará 'Brasília'." July 4.

————. 1982. "ENGESA fatura Cr. $18bh." February 15.

————. 1982. "Inglaterra financia reaparelhamento da marinha brasileira." June 4.

————. 1982. "Kok acha difícil absorção de tecnologia de armamento."

————. 1982. "Marinha destaca avanço da tecnologia naval do Brasil." March.

————. 1982. "Protótipo do avião pronto." October 13.

————. 1982. "Uma administração nos moldes da empresa privada." October 28.

————. 1983. "Brasil quer tecnologia para fabricar `Exocet'." April 3.

————. 1983. "Circulação de armas pagará taxa em favor do Exército." May 2.

————. 1983. "Concluída fusão da Imbel e Engesa." July 12.

————. 1983. "EMBRAER tem 108 encomendas para o novo avião `Brasília'." July 25.

————. 1983. "FAB confirma interesse pela compra do Skyhawk." Ocober 19.

————. 1983. "Governo espera obter US $2 b com vendas de armamentos." February 7.

————. 1983. "Imbel: Calderari contesta Whitaker." September 1.

————. 1983. "Munição antimíssil vai ser fabricada no Brasil." September 19.

————. 1983. "País pode vender US $2.2 b em armas." May 1.

————. 1987. "Moreira Lima não confirma inclusão do AMX no PND." August 8, p. 18.

————. 1987. "Exército estuda projeto para se equipar com novos mísseis." June 21.

————. 1987. "Órbita anuncia vendas de US$ 3bi a mais em mísseis." August 17.

————. 1989. "AVIBRAS demitiu 1900 só em Janeiro." February 7.

————. 1989. "Crise abala Indústria de Armamentos." February 7.

————. 1989. "ENGESA teve prejuízo de Cz$1.25 bi no 1º trim." June 12.

Godwin, Paul H. B. 1983. *The Chinese Defense Establishment: Continuity and Change in the 1980s.* Boulder, CO: Westview Press.

Goldenberg, José. 1976. "O Bom Exemplo do Modelo Aeronáutico Brasileiro." *Dados e Idéias.* August/September.

Goodwin, R.M. 1949. "The Multiplier As Matrix." *The Economic Journal.* Volume LIX, London: Macmillan and Co.

Grupo Permanente de Mobilização Industrial da Federação das Industrias do Estado de São Paulo, 1970. São Paulo: Edição do Serviço de Publicações da Federação e Centro das Industrais.

Guardian, (London) 1979. "Arms Sales." May 25.

——. (London) 1982. "Guyana to buy Brazil's Planes." October 4.

Guedes, da Costa, Thomas. 1982. "Indústria de Material Bélico no Brasil." *Defesa Nacional.* no. 703, September/October.

Harkavy, Robert and Stephanie Neuman. 1980. *Arms Transfers in the Third World.* New York: Praeger.

Hayden, C.and J. Round. 1982. "Developments in Social Accounting Methods as Applied to the Analysis of Income Distribution and Employment." *World Development* 10.6: 451-465.

Head, Richard G. 1974. "The Weapons Acquisition Process." in *Comparative Defense Policy.* Horton, Rogerson & Walker, Baltimore: Johns Hopkins Press.

Helena, Silvia. 1977. "A Decolagem Segura de EMBRAER." *Dados e Ideas* October/November, pp. 13-21.

Hilton, Stanley. 1982. in "The Armed Forces and Industrialists in Modern Brazil: The Drive for Military Autonomy (1889-1954)." *Hispanic American Historical Review* 62.4: 629-673.

——. 1987. "The Brazilian Military: Changing Strategic Perceptions and the Question of Mission." *Armed Forces and Society 1987.* 13.3: 329-351.

Hirschman, Albert O. 1968. "The Political Economy of Import Substitution Industrialization in Latin America," *The Quarterly Journal of Economics* 82.1 (February).

——. 1981. *Essays in Trespassing: Economics to Politics and Beyond.* New York: Cambridge University Press.

Hodge, Warren. 1980. "Brazilian Arms Find Willing Buyers." *The New York Times.* .

Hudson, Rexford. 1983. "The Brazilian Way to Technological Independence: Foreign Joint Ventures and the Aircraft Industry." *Inter-American Economic Affairs* 37(Autumn): 23-43.

Huntington, Samuel P. 1968. *Political Order in Changing Societies.* New Haven, CT: Yale University Press.

Indústria e Desenvolvimento. 1976. "País Constroe a Indústria Aeroespacial com os Pés No Chão." Vol. IX, no. 6 (FIESP), June.

——. 1976. "Um Debate: Quem Deve Desenvolver a Tecnologia?" Vol. IX, No. 6, p. 9 (FIESP) July.

Inter-American Development Bank. 1988. *Economic and Social Progress in Latin America.* 1988 Report, Special Section: Science and Technology. Washington, D.C.: Inter-American Development Bank.

Interavia. 1975. "EMBRAER Production Up." May , p. 452.

Interconair. 1981. "SAAB Brazil/ Angola missile systems ND—SAM value ND delivery 1981." p. 15.

International Bulletin. 1977. Untitled Article. No. 3, March 28.

International Defense Review. 1980. "More Cascavel Procured." No. 4.

——. 1991. "The rebirth of Brazil's ENGESA." May, p. 500.

International Herald Tribune. 1977. "Brazil Develops Role as Exporter of Military Goods." July 13.

———. 1977. "Brazil is Making Major Drive towards Self-Sufficiency." December 29.

———. 1977. "Brazil May Sell Arms to Arabs." May 20.

———. 1982. "Arms Industry Rivals Chief Export Sectors." September 19.

———. 1982. "Aviation Success Story." supplement September.

———. 1982. Baer, Werner. "Export-Import Duality: Strength, Concentration." September 19.

———. 1988. Timmerman, Kenneth. "Home Grown Arms Industry is By-Product of Changing Alliances." June 29, p. 12.

Isto é Senhor. 1981. "Armas Made in Brasil." no. 35, February.

———. 1981. "O Brasil Vende Para a Nigéria Armas." April 22.

———. 1982. "Metralhadoras anticrise." June 9.

Janes Defense Review. 1982. Vol. 3 No. 4.

Janowitz, Morris. 1974. "Military Organization," in Horton, Rogerson & Warner, eds. *Comparative Defense Policy.* Baltimore: Johns Hopkins Press.

———. 1977. *Military Institutions and Coercion in the Developing Nations.* Chicago: University of Chicago Press.

Joint Economic Committee Staff Study. 1982. "Defense Buildup in the Economy." February.

Jolly, Richard. 1978. *Disarmament and World Development.* New York: Pergammon.

Jones, Leroy P., ed. 1982. *Public Enterprise in Less Developed Countries.* New York: Cambridge University Press.

Jones, Leroy P. and Ingo Vogelsang. 1983. *The Effects of Markets on Public Enterprise Conduct; and Vice Versa.* ICPE Monograph Series, No. 7, Ljubljana, Yugoslavia, The International Center for Public Enterprises in Developing Countries.

Jornal de Brasília. 1983. "A Importância das Armas." April 22.

———. 1983. "Material Bélico-nova alternativa industrial." April 1, p. 8.

Jornal da Tarde. 1967. "Brasil de Armas Novas." June 29.

———. 1971. "O Fim de nossas velhas armas de guerra." May 21.

———. 1972. "Um plano que permitia ao Brasil aumentar sua frota de veículos militares sem gastar muito, explica um dos seus diretores." July 10.

———. 1972. de Nigriso, Theobaldo. "A indústria a serviço da segurança nacional." July 22.

———. 1972. "O Brasil compra tanques no exterior para modernizar o Exército." May 17.

———. 1973. "Vende-se este tanque do guerra, tratar no Brasil." April 12.

———. 1974. "O Brasil começa um novo negócio: exportação de tanque." April 1.

———. 1975. "CTA planeja exportação de avião." May 20.

———. 1980. "A compra do bimotor Xingu pela França." June 2.

———. 1983. "As dez empresas que mais importaram." November 11.

———. 1983. "O vôo inaugural do revolucionário Brasília." July 29.

Jornal do Brasil. 1970. "Um re-equipamento que exige o melhor." October 5.

———. 1972. "Aeronáutica tem problemas financeiros e de pessoal." April 8.

———. 1972. "FAB contrata projetos no valor de cr $1100 mil na base aérea de Anápolis." January 8.

———. 1975. "Cava iniciará produção de aviões Cessna no Brasil." August 21.

———. 1975. "Chefe do EMFA afirma que cresce interesse de elites pela doutrina de segurança." August 15.

———. 1975. "Componentes têm novo mercado com a indústria aeronáutica." April 31.

———. 1975. "Indústria aeronáutica brasileira." November 28.

———. 1976. "Cooperação veio com a Revolução." September 6.

———. 1977. "As Armas da Denúncia." March 15.

———. 1977. "As Serpentes Blindadas." March 15.

———. 1977. "Brasil pode fabricar novo canhão." July 6.

———. 1977. "FAB compra 15 aviões da EMB." August 25.

———. 1977. "Ministro da Marinha expõe na ESG plano decenal de reaparelhamento da frota." July 12.

———. 1977. "Peritos contestam carência." October 23.

———. 1977. "Rossi, um exemplo de como vai a indústria de armas no Brasil." April 3.

———. 1978. Chimanitcl, Mario. "Armas do Brasil podem ser usadas no OM." July 28.

———. 1978. "Emb exportará 55 aviões Bandeirante durante 1979." December 11.

———. 1978. "ENGESA é quinta exportadora de veículos." September 9.

———. 1978. "Equipamento bélico é isento de ICM até 80." December 7.

———. 1978. "Nordeste ganha indústria bélica." February 1.

———. 1979. "Adido dos EUA elogia armamento." November 30.

———. 1979. Barros, Romualdo. "Brasil quer reduzir seu déficit no Oriente com armas." October 28.

———. 1979. "Brasil exporta este ano US $500 mh em armamento." May 25.

———. 1979. "Brasil produz tanques dentro de dois anos." May 9.

———. 1979. "Exportação de matérial bélico receberá mais incentivos fiscais." December 3.

———. 1979. "Iraque pode comprar carros bélicos do Brasil e pagar US $500 mh em óleo." January 27.

———. 1979. "São Paulo tinha hélice de Jequitiba o primeiro fabricado no Brasil." February 16.

———. 1980. "AVIBRAS." October 5.

———. 1980. "Brasil e Argentina poderão assinar acordo que prevê a fabricação de aviões." January 13.

———. 1980. "Brasil vai construir corvetas e submarinos com técnica italiana" June 11.

———. 1980. "Emb vende 51 Brasílias." July 14.

———. 1980. "EMBRAER quer avião militar." July 16.

———. 1980. "EMFA diz que gastou com armas em 79 apenas CR $3 bh." July 14.

———. 1980. "Graftigna admite a fabricação do avião argentino—brasileiro." March 4.

———. 1980. "Indústria bélica negocia com EUA e a China." August 3. 1st section.

———. 1980. "Venezuelano vem ver armamentos." March 17.

———. 1981. "EMBRAER entrega mais 5 Bandeirantes a empresas aéreas dos Estados Unidos," April 3.

———. 1981. "'Trading' de material bélico quer negociar venda de tecnologia." August 24.

———. 1981. AMX: Um vôo alto para a emb." November 8.

———. 1981. "Arsenal quer iniciar novo programa de US $1b." March 27.

———. 1981. "Brasil dobra este ano a exportação de armas." August 30.

———. 1981. "Brasil e Itália fazem novo caça-bombardeiro." October 7.

———. 1981. "Brasil testa Sonda IV, seu maior foguete, para 1982." July 20.

———. 1981. "Brigadeiro diz que Emb. fabricará avião supersônico." July 7.

———. 1981. "Caça AM-X feito por Brasil e Itália fica pronto daqui a 4 anos." October 8.

———. 1981. "Contratos vão a US $700mh." November 17.

———. 1981. "Emb começa testes do sucessor do Bandeirante." December 6.

———. 1981. "ENGESA Engenheiros Especializados SA." January 27.

———. 1981. "ENGESA não pagará IR por 3 anos." January 24.

———. 1981. "ENGESA negocia vendas de `muitos bilhões de dólares'." February 22.

———. 1981. "ENGESA pretende exportar US $250 mh este ano em armamentos e veículos." May 7.

———. 1981. "ENGESA venderá ao Iraque US$250 mh em armas; contratos vão a US$700mh." November 17.

———. 1981. "Engesa fará investimento em indústria de munições." January 28.

———. 1981. "Engesa vendera ão Iraque US $250 mh em armas." November 17.

———. 1981. "Este ano a exportação de armas." August 30.

———. 1981. "Exército aluga máquinas." January 27.

———. 1981. "Falta de urânio é o que atrasa submarino nuclear brasileiro." January 30.

———. 1981. "Ferranti deseja participar mais." May 20.

———. 1981. "Imbel criará companhia para operar no mercado externo de armamento." August 21.

———. 1981. "Indústria de aviões quer nacionalizar equipamentos." January 18.

———. 1981. "Luis Eulálio (presidente da FIESP) quer entrosamento de indústrias com militares." May 13.

———. 1981. "Marinha projeta submarino nuclear 100% brasileiro." June 27.

———. 1981. "Minasforte produzirá seus próprios blindados em 1982." December 23.

———. 1981. "Motortec já exporta serviços." January 18.

———. 1981. "Operários da Embraer mantêm greve." November 21.

———. 1981. "Portugal quer acordo com Emb." July 21.

———. 1981. "Programa espacial deve custar $5 mh." March 4.

———. 1981. "Vigorelli diversifica sua produção com armas leves." December 6.

———. 1982. "Emb exalta êxitos do Bandeirante no dia 23 ao entregar o 400th avião." April 15.

Jornal do Brasil. 1982. "Almirante diz que Brasil pode fazer bomba atômica." July 10.

———. 1982. "Aumento dos preços prejudicou a Imbel." March 10.

———. 1982. "Aviões Brasileiros." May 3.

———. 1982. Azevedo, Zenaide. "Guerra das Falklands leva o Brasil a rever sua defesa." May 9.

———. 1982. "Brasil defende seus interesses bilaterais." May 9.

———. 1982. "Buenos Aires quer blindados do Brasil." April 8.

———. 1982. Carneiro, Luiz Orlando. "China quer ajuda do Brasil para ter exército moderno." March 25.

———. 1982. "CNBB debaterá indústria bélica e pedirá pela paz." February 13.

———. 1982. "Comandante da ESG quer prioridade para educação." April 22.

———. 1982. Costa, Thomas Guedes da. "Uma dependência relativa." January 3.

———. 1982. da Rocha Filho. "Indústria bélica produz míssil." May 9.

———. 1982. da Rocha Filho. "Pentágono se interessa por chapas blindadas que Eletrometal criou." May 24.

———. 1982. de Rocha Filho, Milton F. "Brasil terá maior fábrica de foguetes do mundo em 1983." April 25.

———. 1982. "Emb vende 12 aviões para a França e amplia mercado com os EUA." January 14.

———. 1982. "EMBRAER vende 12 aviões para a França e amplia mercado com os Estados Unidos." January 14.

———. 1982. "Embramec revela falta de tecnologia bélica." June 10.

———. 1982. "FAB começa receber da Emb ainda este ano o avião de ataque Tucano." May 5.

———. 1982. "Galveas não sabe nada sobre rearmamento." May 21.

———. 1982. "General declara que Brasil não quer entrar em corrida armamentista." May 24.

———. 1982. "Guerra (das Falklands) aproxima militares." May 23.

———. 1982. "Guiana quer comprar armamentos no Brasil." October 2.

———. 1982. "Indústria de armamento está firme no exterior." September 10.

———. 1982. "Indústria já pode se mobilizar para as Fs As." July 7.

———. 1982. "Julian Chancel defende o reaparelhamento." May 13.

———. 1982. "Marinha construirá submarino com tecnologia alemã." June 10.

————. 1982. "Marinha vai aplicar US $1b para obter 80% de nacionalização." March 19.

————. 1982. "Material bélico." October 29.

————. 1982. "Metalúrgico pára greve." May 21.

————. 1982. "Militar confirma venda de avião brasileiro à-B.A." April 24.

————. 1982. Moreira, Aristeu. "Greve da Emb afeta a produção bélica do país." May 17.

————. 1982. "Nova Etapa." editorial, May 17.

————. 1982. "Nova tecnologia e opção da Taurus." September 10.

————. 1982. Oliveira, Antonio Augusto. "Indústria de armas será maior exportadora do Brasil em 85." November 1.

————. 1982. "Operários da Embraer param." May 18.

————. 1982. "Programa de expansão da Helibrás recebeu a aprovação do CDI." April 15.

————. 1982. "Reaparelhamento naval exige US $15 bilhões." May 6.

————. 1982. "Sinal de Alarme." editorial, May 5.

————. 1982. "Telebrás oferece ao EMFA para um centro bélico." June 17.

————. 1982. "TO's importa estações de recepção que Brasil produz." May 17.

————. 1982. "Walter Pires indica Whitaker presidente da Imbel." October 22.

————. 1983 "Fabricante de arma." May 15.

————. 1983. "Amplimatic faz tecnologia do Inpe satélite meteorológico." no date.

————. 1983. "AVIBRAS pode construir míssil anti-aéreo" July 4.

————. 1983. "Brasil é sexto exportador mundial de matérial bélico." September 2.

————. 1983. "Délio poderá ajudar indústria aeronáutica a importar componentes." September 18.

————. 1983. "Emb já enviou 2 aviões Emb 111 à Marinha Argentina." April 12.

————. 1983. "Emb pretende exportar US $100 mh este ano." June 27.

————. 1983. "EMBRAER e Líbia retomam venda de $190 milhões." June 23.

————. 1983. "EMBRAER toma precauções contra greve." July 25.

————. 1983. "ENGESA vai comprar FNV em 30 dias." September 25.

————. 1983. "Estaleiro exporta 'software'." January 21.

————. 1983. "FAB recebe 8 Tucanos no dia 29." September 23.

————. 1983. Ferreira, Augusto Mario. "Berdardini lança dois novos blindados." September, 11.

————. 1983. Filho, Rocha. "Equipamento militar pode ser saída para indústria nacional." Spetember 6.

————. 1983. "Greve da Embrear não saiu da prancheta." July 26.

————. 1983. "Imbel tem crédito suplementar." July 3.

————. 1983. "Imbel terá nova fábrica de pólvora." February 13.

————. 1983. "Nigéria quer US $2 b em armamentos." November 16.

————. 1983. "Protótipo de tanque de combate da ENGESA custa CR$ 27 bilhões," July 11, p. 13.

————. 1983. Resende, Pedro Paulo. "A importância das armas." April 22.

————. 1983. "Taurus fará blindagem." June 25.

————. 1983. "Tecnasa exporta equipamento aéreo." no date.

————. 1984. "Indústria opera mesmo que sua fábrica seja totalmente destruída ou ocupada." June 13.

————. 1987. "Fundo de Desenvolvimento não vai financiar O AMX." September. 24.

————. 1987. "Fundo social é usado para pagar projeto do caça AMX." August 8.

————. 1987. "Privatização só com sociedade." August 8.

————. 1988. Dorrêa, Maurício. "Indústria bélica da Argentina preocupa militares brasileiros." September 26.

————. 1988. "ENGESA sofreu perda em 87 de Cz$2.5 b." April 22.

————. 1990. Chaer, Márcio. "Indústria bélica vive pior crise em 10 anos." January 15.

————. 1990. December 18, p. 13.

————. 1991. February 9, p. 7.

————. no date given."Tecnologia nacional é usada nos Jumbo 747."

Jornal de Brasília. 1982. Bonfim, Otávio. "Acordo Militar." November 28.

————. 1982. "Governo define política para metais estratégicos." May 30.

————. 1983. "Brasil e EUA debatem indústria bélica." August 21.

Kaldor, Mary. 1980. *The Role of Military Technology in Industrial Development.* UN Working Group on Development and Disarmament.

————. 1981. *The Baroque Arsenal.* New York: Hill and Wang.

Kaldor, Mary and Asbjorn Eide, eds. 1979. *The World Military Order.* New York: Praeger.

Karp, Aaron. 1988. "Trade in Conventional Weapons." In *SIPRI Yearbook 1988 World Armaments and Disarmament.* Oxford: Oxford University Press.

Katz, Michael. 1986. *The Implications of Third World Military Industrialization.* Lexington, MA: Lexington Books.

————. 1984. "Understanding Arms Production in Developing Countries." *Arms Production in Developing Countries.* Lexington, MA: Lexington Books.

Keegan, John. 1979. *World Armies.* New York: Facts on File.

Kennedy, Gavin. 1974. *The Military in the Third World.* New York: Scribner's Sons.

————. 1983. *Defense Economics.* New York: St. Martin's Press.

Klare, Michael T. 1983. "The Unnoticed Arms Trade: Exports of Conventional Arms-making Technology." *International Security* 8.2 (Fall): 68-90.

Klieman, Aaron. 1985. *Israel's Global Reach.* Washington, D.C.: Pergammon-Brassey's International Defense Publishers.

Lassaga, Guillermo. 1986. "Fabricaciones Militares: crescimiento o desaparación?" *Realidade Economica* 6 (January): 77-81.

Latin America. 1972. "Brazil: Naval Power." November 3.

Latin American Daily Telegraph. 1980. "Iraqis Using Arms from Brazil." October 14.

Latin American Political Review. 1977. "Brazil: Arms to Libya." 11.9: 66.

Latin American Economic Review. 1978. "Brazil Boosts Local Aircraft Prodution." August 8, 1975, Vol. VI, No. 24, June 23.

———. 1982. "EMBRAER has High Hopes for New Turboprop." Brazil (London) July 3, p. 14.

Latin American Regional Reports. 1985. "ENGESA Cannon." April 26, p. 8.

Latin American Weekly Review November 9, 1979, April 4, 1980, June 20, 1980, November 7, 1980, January 23, 1981, August 14, 1981, September 17, 1981, December 23, 1981, January 19, 1982, Nov. 30, 1979.

Leontief, Wassily. 1977. *Essays in Economics Vol. II.* New York M. E. Sharpe.

———. 1977. *The Future of the World Economy.* New York: Oxford University Press.

Leontief, Wassily and Faye Duchin. 1983. *Military Spending.* Princeton, N. J.: Oxford University Press.

Lim, David. 1982. "Another Look at Growth and Defense in Less Developed Countries." *Economic Development and Cultural Change.* December.

Lock, P. and H. Wulf. 1977. *Register of Arms Production in Developing Countries.* Hamburg: Study Group on Armament and Underdevelopment, March.

Lock, Peter. 1977. "The Economic Consequenses of Military Technology Transfer." *Bulletin of Peace Proposals.* 8.2.

Looney, Robert E. and P.C. Frederiksen. 1986. "Profiles of Current Latin American Arms Producers." *International Organization* 40.3 (Summer).

Los Angeles Times. 1977. David Belnap. July 12.

Loveman and Davies, (eds). 1978. *The Politics of Antipolitics.* Lincoln, NB: The University of Nebraska Press.

Luz, Vincente, et al. 1983. "Aplicação de Método de Ordenação Prioridades no Planejamento de P & D do Exército." VII Simpósio Nacional de Pesquisa em Administração de Ciência e Tecnologia, Finep, São Paulo.

Macedo, Araripe. 1975. "Força Aérea determina a segurança." *Diário de Notícias.* August 31.

Macedo, Ubiratan de. 1979. "Origens Nacionais da Doutrina da ESG." *Convivium.* 17.

Mack, Andrew. 1981. "Militarism or Development: The Possibility for Survival." Prepared for the Labor Economists Conference in Canberra Australia, November.

Mallman, Wolfgang. 1979. "Arms Transfers to the Third World." *Bulletin of Peace Proposals.*

Mamalakis, Markos. 1986-87. "Introduction: Interamerican Economic Relations, The New Development View." *Journal of Interamerican Studies and World Affairs* 27.4 (Winter): 1–8.

Manwaring, Max G. 1981. "Brazilian Military Power." in Wayne Selcher, *Brazil in the International System.* Boulder, CO: Westview.

Matthews, Jessica Tuchman. 1989. "Redefining Security." *Foreign Affairs* 69.2 (Spring): 162–177.

McCann, Frank D., Jr. 1973. *The Brazilian-American Alliance, 1937-1945.* Princeton.
———. 1979. "Origins of the New Professionalism of the Brazilian Military." *Journal of Interamerican Studies and World Affairs.* 21.4 (November).
———. 1980. "A Influência Estrangeira no Exército Brasileiro, 1905-1945." *A Revolução de 30.* Seminário realizado pelo Centro Pesquisa e Documentacão de História Contemporânea do Brasil (CPDOC) da Fundação Getulio Vargas, Rio de Janeiro, September, Brasília: Editora Universidade de Brasília, 1983.
———. 1980. "The Brazilian Army and the Problem of Mission 1939-1964." *Journal of Latin American Studies* 12.1: 107-126.
———. 1982. "The Brazilian Army and Arms Supply." Paper presented at the LASA meeting in Washington DC, March 3-7.
———. 1984. "The Formative Period of Twentieth Century Brazilian Army Thought, 1900-1922." *Hispanic American Historical Review* 64 .4 : 762.
MEED. 1981. "Iraq: Military equipment deal signed with Brazil." June 30, 1978; "Brazilian Visits Turns Up Trumps." December 11.
Meira Mattos, General Carlos de. 1979. *Brasil: Geopolítica e Destino.* Rio de Janeiro: Livraria José Olympio Editora.
Merlo, Dr. José Walter. 1983. "Ciência e Tecnologia na Expressão Militar do Poder Nacional." Palestra Na Escola Superior de Guerra, Rio de Janeiro, September 12, (unpublished paper.)
Metalworking News. 1987. "EMBRAER Expands Capabilities to Use Composites." 14.5: 36.
Miami Herald. March 7, 1978, May 24.
Middle East Report. 1987. Bahbah, Bishara A. "Israel's Private Arms Network," February 17, pp. 9-10.
———. 1987. Ryan, Sheila. "U.S. Military Contractors in Israel." January-February, pp. 17-22.
———. 1987. Stork, Joe. "Arms Industries of the Middle East." vol. 17, pl. 15, Jan-Feb
Milenky, Edward S. 1980. "Arms Production and National Security in Argentina." *Journal of Interamerican Studies and World Affairs* 22.3 (August): 273.
Military Technology. "Brazil: Facts and Figures on National Defense." February/March 1980, Vol. V Issue 24, June/July 1981, Vol. VI Issue 4, May 1982, Vol. VII Issue 2, 1983.
Ministério do Planejamento e Coordenação Geral. *Anuário Estatístico do Brasil.* Fundação IBGE. Vol. 32.
Moodie, Michael. 1979. *Sovereignty, Security and Arms.* Washington: Georgetown Center for International Security Studies.
———. 1980. "Defense Industries in the Third World." In Harkavy and Newman, eds. *Arms Transfers in the Third World.* New York: Praeger.

Moreira, Lino. 1983. "The Choice of Technology of Multinational Corporations in Brazil and its Implications for Employment." PhD. dissertation, University of Notre Dame, March.

Murilo de Carvalho, José. 1979. "A Política Científica e Tecnológica no Brasil." *Revista de Finanças Publicas.* March.

Nabe, Oumar. 1983. "Military Expenditures and Industrialization in Africa." *Journal of Economic Issues,* June.

National Defense. 1982. Williams, John Hoyt. "Brazil: Giant of the Southern Hemisphere." October 1982, pp. 40-57; November 1982, pp. 16-20.

Neuman, Stephanie C. 1984. "International Stratification and Third World Military Industries." *International Organization* 38.1 (Winter).

―――. 1985. "Coproduction, Barter, and Countertrade: Offsets in the International Arms Market." *Orbis.* Spring, pp. 183-209.

New York Times. 1976. "Brasil's Output of Light Planes Stirs Fight." November 23.

―――. 1981. Melman, Seymour. July 26.

―――. 1989. Pear, Robert. "U.S. Weapon Sales to Third World Increase by 66%." August 1, p. A1.

―――. 1990. "Peace Unhealthy for Brazilian Arms Industry." February 25, p. 19.

Nolan, Janne. 1986. *Military Industry in Taiwan and Korea.* New York: St. Martins.

Notícias Econômicas. No. 292, Semana de 8 a 14 April 1973, pp. 483-486.

Oberg, Jan. 1975. "AT with the Third World as an Aspect of Imperialism." *Journal of Peace Research* 12.3.

―――. 1975. "Third World Armament: Domestic Production in Israel, South Africa, Brazil, Argentina and India." *Instant Research on Peace and Violence* 5.4.

Ohlson, Thomas. 1982. "Third World Arms Exporters—A New Facet of the Global Arms Race." *Bulletin of Peace Proposals* 13.3.

Oliveira, Antonio Cunha de. 1986. "Desenvolvimento de Sistema de Armas: Absorção de Tecnologia Específica." *Defesa Nacional.* September-October.

Olvey, Lee, James Golden and Robert Kelly. 1984. *The Economics of National Security.* Wayne, N. J.: Avery Publishing.

Pacetti, Tércio. 1978. "Tecnologia de ponta: uma proposta de longo prazo." *Dados e Ideas.* February/March.

Pack, Howard and Larry Westphal. 1986. "Industrial Strategy and Technological Change." *Journal of Development Economics* 22: 87-128.

Padín, Jorge Félix Neuñez. 1980. "Argentina expande exportações." *Segurança e Defesa* 21:30.

Palma, Gabriel. 1978. "Dependency: A Formal Theory of Underdevelopment or a Methodology for the Analysis of Concrete Situations of Development." *World Development* 6.7/8 (August).

PBDCT II 1975-80. Presidência da República. Fundação IBGE.

PBDCT III 1980. Presidência da República. Secretaria de Planejamento. CNPq.

Pereira de Andrade, Roberto and Antônio Ermete Piochi. 1982. *História da Construção Aeronáutica no Brasil.* São Paulo: Aquarius Editora Ltd..

Pereira, José Pelucio. "Ciência e Tecnologia dos países em Desenvolvimento: a experiência do Brasil." *Instituto de Economia Industrial.* Universidade Federal do Rio de Janeiro, Texto com discussão no. 20, (unpublished paper.)

Pereira, Roberto and José de Souza Fernandes. 1983. *Veículos Militares Brasileiros.* São Paulo: Aquarius Editora e Distribuidora de Livros Ltda.

Pereira, Roberto. 1979. "A Nuclep e nossos tanques." *Diário e Indústria.* February 21.

Pereira, Vera Madrid Cândido. 1976. "Reflexões Sobre Estado Ciência e Tecnologia No Brasil." Working paper, Codetec—Companhia de Desenvolvimento Tecnológico CGC November.

Perry, William. 1978. "Military Policy & Conventional Capabilities of an Emerging Power." *Military Review.* October 24.

Pierre, Andrew. 1982. *The Global Politics of Arms Sales.* Princeton NJ: Princeton University Press.

Pirró e Longo, Waldir. 1978. "Tecnologia e Transferência de Tecnologia." *Defesa Nacional* 576 (March/April).

O Plano Básico do Desenvolvimento Científico e Tecnológico. (PBDCT) I 1973-74. Presidência da República. Fundação IBGE.

Planejamento e Desenvolvimento. 1979. "EMBRAER a Indústria Aeronáutica do Brasil Já Tem o Reconhecimento Internacional." 6.68 (January): 46-53.

Pyatt, Graham and Jeffery Round. 1977. "Social Accounting Matrices for Development Planning." *The Review of Income and Wealth.* Series 23, No. 4, December.

Quem é Quem Na Economia Brasileira 1989, Visão. XXXVIII, No. 36A.

Ra'anan, Uri, Robert Pfaltzgraft, and Geoffry Kemp. 1978. *AT's to the Third World: The Military Buildup in Less Industrial Countries.* Boulder, CO: Westview.

Ramamurti, Ravi. 1982. "EMBRAER." Harvard Business School Case Study #0-383-090.

———. 1983. "High Technology Exports by SOEs in LDCs: A Brazilian Case Study." Presented at the Conference on Latin American Public Enterprises, IESA, Caracas, Venezuela, Nov. 10-13.

Ramos de Castro, Sebastião José. 1982. "Rearmamento e Tecnologia." *Defesa Nacional* 703 (September/October).

Rao, Nagaraja and Jack Philip Ruina. 1980. "Disarmament and Development: The Case of Relatively Advanced Developing Countries." Cambridge, Massachusetts: Center for Policy Alternatives, MIT, August.

Regeher, Ernie. 1980. *The Utilization of Resources and the Impact on Canadian Industrialization and Defense Procurement.* Report prepared for the UN group of governmental experts on the relationship between disarmament and development, May 15.

Reid, Gavin C. 1987. *Theories of Industrial Organization.* New York: Basil Blackwell.

Reis, Friede. 1983. "O papel do Brasil numa nova realidade de poder global." *Aviação em Revista.* Ano XLVI, no. 509/510, March/April.

Relatório Reservado. 1980. "Brasil e Itália fazem acordo de US $3.5 bh." September, p. 3.

Revista Aeronáutica. 1983. "Entrevista com José Carlos de Barros Neiva." Summer.

Revista de Economia e Negócios. 1972. "A indústria também tem o que mostrar na Expo." July 1.

Riddell, Thomas. 1985. "Concentration and Inefficiency in the Defense Sector." *Journal of Economic Issues* 19 (June): 451-461.

Ripper, Engenheiro José Ellis. 1979. "A EMBRAER e o CTA." *Segurança e Desenvolvimento* 28.174: 44-50.

Robinson, Joan. 1979. *Aspects of Development and Underdevelopment.* UK: Cambridge University Press.

Roett, Riordan. *Brazilian Foreign Policy: Options in the 1980's.* In Bruneau.

Rosenberg, Nathan. 1971. *The Economies of Techonological Change.* UK: Penguin.

Rosenblatt, Giden. 1978. *The Canadian Economy and Disarmament.* Toronto: McCleland and Steward Ltd.

Russett, Bruce. 1970. *What Price Vigilance? The Burdens of National Defense.* New Haven and London: Yale University Press, 1970.

Saraiva, José Drumond. 1989. "Brasil no Século XXI: Ciência e Tecnologia como Variável Estratégica no Pensamento Brasileiro." Unpublished working paper, Rio de Janeiro, July.

Sarathy, R. 1985. "High Technology Exports from Newly Industrializing Countries: The Brazilian Commuter Aircraft Industry." *California Management Review* 27.2 (Winter).

Sassone, Peter and William Schaffer. 1978. *Cost Benefit Analysis.* London: Academic Press Inc.

Saulniers, Alfred. 1985. "Public Enterprises in Latin America: Their Origins and Importance." *International Review of Administrative Sciences* 4: 329-349.

Scherer, F. M. 1981. *Industrial Market Structure and Economic Performance.* Boston: Houghton Mifflin.

Schmidt, Christian (ed). 1987. *The Economics of Military Expenditures.* New York: St. Martins.

Schneider, Ronald M. 1971. *The Political System of Brazil: Emergence of a `modernizing' authortarian regime, 1964-70.* New York.

———. 1976. *Brazil: Foreign Policy of a Future World Power.* CO: Westview.

Schultz, Charles. 1982. "Do more dollars means better defense?" *Challenge.* January/February.

Secretaria de Planejamento da Presidência de República. "Política Fiscal: Execução em 1980 e Diretrizes para 1981." Ministério da Fazenda.

Segurança e Defesa. 1988. "O Chefe do Centro Tecnológico do Exército." No. 20: 26.

Shields, Gail. 1982. "The Economic Impact of the MX Missile." *Science for the People.* September/October, pp. 6-11.

Silva, Ozires. 1980. "Pesquisa, de Tecnologia e Desenvolvimento Nacional." Conferência Proferida na Faculdade de Tibirica, texto no. 1.

———. 1982. "Manufacturing Aircraft in Brazil—Some Fair Trade Issues." Presentation at the Aviation/Space Writers Association Conference, Fort Lauderdale, May 4.

———. 1982. "O Vôo da EMBRAER." *Revista Brasileira de Tecnologia.* 13 (January/March): 20-30.

Simon, Julian L. 1978. *Basic Research Methods in Social Science.* New York: Random House.

Sivard, Ruth L. *World Military and Social Expenditures.* Washington, DC: World Priorities, annual editions.

Skidmore, Thomas. 1967. *Politics in Brazil.* London: Oxford University Press.

Smith, Adam. *The Wealth of Nations.* Book V.

Smith, David and Ron Smith. 1980. *Military Expenditures Resources and Development.* Burbeck College, University of London.

Souza Mello, Márcio de. 1968. "O Ministério da Aeronáutica e Seu Papel Institucional." Conferência proferida na ESG em 1 Agosto.

———. 1971. "A Aeronáutica no Esforço de Desenvolvimento." 143.

Stepan, Alfred. 1971. *The Military in Brazil.* Princeton, NJ: Princeton University Press.

———. 1988. *Rethinking Military Politics.* Princeton, N.J.: Princeton University Press.

Stewart, Francis and J. James, eds. 1982. *The Economics of New Technology in Developing Countries.* Boulder, CO: Westview Press, 1982.

Stockholm International Peace Research Institute Yearbooks. New York: Crane, Russok, and Co. Annual publication.

Strategic Latin American Affairs. 1979. "Nicarágua-Brazil: Arms Deal Sought." February 20.

Strategic Latin American Affairs. May 10, 1979, June 14, 1979, August 2, 1979, December 20, 1979, March 6, 1980, March 13, 1980, June 26, 1980.

Strategy Week. 1980. "Brazil Stake in Iran-Iraq War." September 29-October 5.

———. 1980. "Brazil's Defense Industry Impacts on ME." May 19-25.

———. 1980. "Brazil: Arms Exports Up." November 10-16.

———. 1980. "Brazil: AS to Iraq Control." October 6-12, 1980.

Summary of World Broadcasts. 1980. "Brazil and Arms Deals with Iraq and Libya." April 11.

Tavares de Oliveira, Carlos. 1982. "As Guerras Também Abrem Mercados," *Comércio e Mercados.* August.

Tavares, José. 1983. "A Indústria Bélica Brasileira." Camara dos Deputados. June 7.

Taylor, Lance, Edmar Bacha, and Frank Lysy. 1980. *Models of Growth and Distribution for Brazil.* New York: Oxford University Press.

Tecnologia e Defesa. 1983. "Aeroeletrônica." 5 (July).

———. 1983. "Astros." 5 (July).

———. 1983. "Bernardini, Cofres e Carros de Combate." 3 (May): 48.

———. 1983. "Biselli." 3 (May): 6.

———. 1983. "Brasil Defense Industry Survey." Edição Especial (May).

———. 1983. "Brasília: O Vôo Inaugural." 6.

———. 1983. "D.F. Vasconcellos." 3 (May): 42.

———. 1983. "Joseph Soucek." 5 (July).

———. 1983. "Le Bourget '83." 4 (June).

———. 1983. "Modelos Avibras." (June).

———. 1983. "Novatração." 3 (May): 13.

———. 1983. "O Longo Vôo do Tucano." 4 (June).

———. 1983. Olive, Renaldo. "As Metralhadoras IMBEL." 4 (June).

———. 1983. "Os Jipes Gurgel." 3 (May): 23.

———. 1983. "Os Programas do AMRJ." 7.

———. 1983. "Os Tucanos da Fumaça." 7.

———. 1983. "Os Venenosos Tanques Engesa." 3.

———. 1983. Souza, Fernandes de. "A Artilharia no Brasil." 5 (July).

———. 1983. Souza, Fernandes de. "Os Tanques do Brasil." 1 (March).

———. 1983. Souza, Fernandes de. "Um Veterano Reforçado." 7.

———. "Tecnasa: Especialistas em Eletrônica." p. 58.

Terhol, Peter. 1982. "Foreign Exchange Costs of the Indian Military, 1950-1972." *Journal of Peace Research* 19.3.

The Disarmament and Development Group, United Nations. 1984. United Nations Working Papers

The Military Balance. (1982) IISS London.

Time. 1989. Ross Munro. "The Awakening of An Asian Power." April 3, p. 34.

Tollefson, Scott D. 1991. *Brazilian Arms Transfers, Ballistic Missiles, and Foreign Policy: The Search for Autonomy.* Phd Dissertation, The Johns Hopkins University.

Totten, James B. 1981. "A política militar dos Estados Unidos e as relações militares entre o Brasil a os Estado Unidos." Brazilian Superior War College publication, September 28.

Trebat, Thomas. 1981. "Public Enterprises in Brazil and Mexico: A Comparison of Origins and Performance." In Bruneau, Thomas and P. Faucher. *Authoritarian Capitalism: Brazil's Contemporary Economic and Poitical Development.* Boulder, CO, Westview Press.

———. 1983. *Brazil's State Owned Enterprises: A Case Study of the State as Entrepreneur.* New York: Cambridge University Press.

Tribuna da Imprensa. 1982. "Exército quer maior participação na economia: O Regime não é capitalista." August 9.

———. 1983. Fernandes, Helio. "A ENGESA (falida) quer Engolir a IMBEL (Prosperíssima)." May 14, p. 4.

Tuomi, Helena and Raimo Vayrynen. 1982. *Transnational Corporations, Armaments and Development.* New York: St. Martins Press.

Turner, Rik. 1980. "Arms Manufacturers: a strong force in world markets." *Financial Times Survey.* (London) November 14.

United Technologies. "Principais Operações da United Technologies (UTC) no Brasil." Company handout, United Technologies.

US Deptartment of State. 1982. *Conventional Arms Transfers in the Third World 1972-1981.* Special Report No. 102, August.

Vargas, Augusto. 1981. "Relaciones Hemisfericas e Indústria Militar en América Latina." *Las Acacias,* July 2 & 3.

VEJA. 1970. "A Mundança Nova." May 20.

————. 1979. "Uma Nova Trincheira." October 17.

————. 1982. "Uma Boa Estrela." October 27, p. 37.

————. 1986. "O Estilo do Piloto." May 21, p. 24.

Viegas, João Alexandre. 1979. "Algo Além dos Aviões No Campo da Aeronáutica." *Dados e Ideas.* (April/May).

Vigris, Theobaldo de. 1973. "A Industrialização: A Segurança Nacional e o 'Grupo Permanente de Mobilização Industrial de FIESP'." *Segurança e Desenvolvimento.* 152: 53.

Vinagre, Mario B. de M., EMBRAER Press Officer. 1989. "EMBRAER: A Brazilian Aerospace Success Story." Lecture at the Smithsonian Air and Space Museum, Washington, DC October 12.

Visão. 1983. "Mudando de Área." January 31, p. 25.

Wall Street Journal. 1981. Gentil, Eduardo. "Brazil's Venture on Supersonic Plane Illustrates Growing Role in AT." March 19, p. 31.

————. 1984. October 11, p. 37, column 6.

Wallerstein, Michael. 1980. "The Collapse of Democracy in Brazil: Its Economic Detriments." *Latin American Political Review* 15.3.

Wanderley, EMBRAER Engineer. Presentation on November 11, 1983 in the Institute of Engineering, University of São Paulo.

Wanderley, Messias da Costa. 1982. "O Processo Contemporâneo de Industrialização." masters thesis, Dept. de Geografia, Faculdade de Filosofia, Universidade de São Paulo, SP.

Washington Post. 1978. Rohter, Larry. "Europeans Seek Arms Deals in Brazil." May 8, p. 21.

————. 1980. Gorney, Cynthia. untitled article. October 27, p. 9A.

————. 1990. Rivlin, Alice M. "New World, New Dangers." (editorial) April 10, p. A23.

Whynes, David. 1979. *The Economics of Third World Military Expenditures.* TX: University of Austin Press.

Wilber, Charles K. and Robert Harrison. 1978. "The Methodological Basis of Institutional Economics: Pattern Model, Storytelling and Holism." *Journal of Economic Issues.* 12.1 (March).

Wionczek, Miguel. 1984. "The Emergence of Military Industries in the South: Longer Term Implications." *Industry and Develoment.* 124.

Wolpin, Miles. 1979. "Military Dependency Versus Development in the Third World." *Bulletin of Peace Proposals.* 10.3.

World Bank Country Study. 1983. "Brazil: Industrial Policies and Manufactured Exports." Washington, D.C.: World Bank Publications.

Wulf, Herbert. 1984. "The Economic Impact of the Arms Sector in Developing Countries." *Development and Peace*. 5: 114-125.

———. 1987. "Arms Production in the Third World." in Christian Schmidt, ed. *The Economics of Military Expenditures*. New York: St. Martins.

Wulf, Herbert; M. Brzoska, P. Lock, R. Peters, and M. Reichel. 1980. "Transnational Transfer of AP Technology." IFSH Study Group on Armament and Underdevelopment. The 1980 United Nations Study on Disarmaments and Development.

Zayorski, Paul W. 1988. "Civil-Military Relations in Argentina." *Armed Forces and Society*. 14.3 (Spring)

Interviews

Almeida, Roberto. Director Technology and Marketing. ABC Sistemas Electronicos, São José dos Campos. July 25, 1990.

Amarante, Col. José Carlos Albano. CTEX. Rio de Janeiro. July 14, 1990.

Barros, Alexandre. Professor and Consultant. Rio de Janeiro. July 24, 1987.

Bassett, Lt. Colonel Loyal G. [USAF]. Office of the Secretary of Defense, Country Director, Latin American Region. July 24, 1985

Bechara, Nicola Nicola. Assistant Director, ENGESA. 1989.

Bidart, Dr. Luiz Carlos. IMBEL (Indústria de Material Bélico do Brasil). São Paulo. July 26, 1990.

Brennan, Kevin. Commercial Counselor, US Embassy, Brasília. July 30, 1990.

Brigagão, Clovis. Author. Rio de Janeiro. Numerous conversations between 1983 and 1991.

Cassanova, Raul. Director of ABIMDE (Brazilian Association of Defense Manufacturers). São Paulo. March 12, 1991.

Cavagnari Filho, Col. Geraldo Lesbat. Director of the Strategic Studies Group, UNICAMP. Campinas. July 7, 1989.

Costa, Fernando M. B. da. SFB Indústria, Rio de Janeiro. August 2, 1990.

Costa, Tomas Guedes de. Brasília. 1983.

Cunha, João da. EMBRAER CEO São José dos Campos. March 11, 1991.

Dagnino, Renato. Professor. UNICAMP. Campinas. Numerous conversations between 1983 and 1991.

Damiani, José Henrique de Souza. IFI, CTA, São José dos Campos. October 1983.

Dunlop, Ronaldo Edgar. Division of Commercial Promotion, Itamarati, Brasília. July 1989.

Duque, Col. George. Interview U.S. Consulate, São Paulo. July 1989.

Eliezer, Armando. ENGESA engineer. November 1983.

Godoy, Roberto. Estado de São Paulo. Various conversations: 1983, 1989.

Goes, Waldir de. Professor and Consultant. Brasília. July 1987.

Gray, Colonel Sam and Marie Sanchez Carlos. US Embassy, Brasília. August 12, 1987.

Hippolito, Vera and Dr. Norberto Chadad. DF Vasconcelos. São Paulo. July 20, 1990.

Hughes, L. Col. Donald. US Defense Attaché, US Consulate, Rio de Janeiro. August 4, 1987.

Leite, Engineer João Verdi Carvalho. President AVIBRAS. São José dos Campos. July 1989, July 25, 1990 and March 17, 1991.

Mattos, Fernando C. CBC (Companhia Brasileira de Cartuchos), São Paulo. July 26, 1990.

McAlexander, Captain Elroy. Naval Attaché, US Embassy, Brasília, July 1989 and July 27, 1990.

Meira Mattos, General Carlos, (retired). Rio de Janeiro. November 3, 1983.

Meira, Paulo. Director of Sales. General Motors do Brasil, São Paulo. July 6, 1987 and October 24, 1983.

Miller, Col. Paul, Assistant Military Attache, American Consulate. Rio de Janeiro. October 27, 1983.

Moura, Arthur Santos. Construtora Mendes Junior, Rio de Janeiro. July 9, 1987.

Nicolini, Carlos Alberto. Elebra São Paulo. July 23, 1990.

Paiva dos Santos, Col. Gerd. EMFA. Brasília. July 30, 1990.

Paula, Rubens de. Vice chief of the Department of Industrial Mobilization. FIESP in São Paulo. October 21, 1983.

Pereira Carvalho, Eng. José Carlos. Director of EXGEXCO. Barueri, São Paulo, Brasil. July 1989.

Pereira, Antônio Carlos. Editor, Política e Estratégia, Washington, D.C. May 1991.

Proença Jr., Domicio. Federal University of Rio de Janeiro. COPPE. Rio de Janeiro. Numerous conversations between 1987 and 1991.

Sallum, Fernando Said. Division of Commercial Promotion, Itamarati. Brasília. July 31, 1991.

Tobias, Barbara. Science Attaché. US Embassy, Brasília. July 13, 1989.

Tollefson, Scott. Professor, Naval Post Graduate School, Monterey, CA. Numerous conversations between 1984 and 1991.

Vieira Alves, Engineer Paulo. Chief, Industrial Division. CTA. São José dos Campos. July 19, 1989.

Vinagre, Mario B. M. Press Officer, EMBRAER, São José dos Campos. Numerous conversations between 1983 and 1991.

Index